Twice Migrants

TWICE MIGRANTS
East African Sikh settlers in Britain

PARMINDER BHACHU

Tavistock Publications · London and New York

First published in 1985 by
Tavistock Publications Ltd
11 New Fetter Lane, London EC4P 4EE

Published in the USA by
Tavistock Publications
in association with Methuen, Inc.
29 West 35th Street, New York NY 10001

© 1985 Parminder Bhachu

Photoset by Nene Phototypesetters Ltd,
Northampton
Printed in Great Britain by Richard Clay
(The Chaucer Press) Ltd, Bungay, Suffolk

British Library Cataloguing in Publication
Data

Bhachu, Parminder
Twice migrants: East African Sikh
settlers in Britain.
1. Sikhs – Great Britain
2. Sikhs – Africa, East
3. Great Britain – Emigration and
immigration
I. Title
305.6'946   DA125.S57

ISBN 0–422–78910–0
ISBN 0–422–78920–8 Pbk

Library of Congress Cataloging in
Publication Data

Bhachu, Parminder.
Twice migrants.

(Social science paperbacks; 311)
Bibliography: p.
Includes index.
1. Sikhs – Great Britain.
2. Great Britain – Foreign
population.
I. Title.   II. Series.

DA125.S57B43   1985
305.6'946'041   85–17280

ISBN 0–422–78910–0
ISBN 0–422–78920–8 (pbk.)

Dedicated to my mother

Contents

Acknowledgements

This book is a product of research undertaken from 1976 to 1980, fieldwork for which was conducted between 1977 and 1978 in London, updated during 1981–83.

I am grateful to the former Social Science Research Council and the present Economic and Social Research Council for financial assistance in the form of a grant to do the research. My special thanks go to my supervisor, Professor Adrian Mayer, who gave me all possible assistance during fieldwork and in writing the PhD thesis which forms the basis of this book. I am also grateful to Dr Verity Saifullah Khan for discussing with me some of the themes of the work in its earlier stages.

To my colleagues and friends, Dr John Solomos, Dr Sacha Josephides, and Shaista Farruki at the Centre for Research in Ethnic Relations, Warwick University, my thanks for encouraging me to complete the book during some difficult times. My gratitude to Rose Goodwin at the Centre, for typing a sometimes unreadable manuscript despite other pressures on her time; she has been a real gem and endlessly patient with me. My thanks also to Sam Hundal for helping with the typing, and to the Centre for allowing me the use of its facilities. My thanks to Debbie Spring for not letting me panic; she has always been patient and encouraging.

Finally, as a social anthropologist whose research has dealt with her own community, my major debt is to the very many East African and also non-East African Sikhs in Britain who helped me with the research and who cannot all be mentioned by name. They include old grandmothers who showed enormous tolerance for my endless questions. The people I have most to thank are all those Sikhs living in Southall and the surrounding areas on whose lives I perhaps intruded;

they were always kind and helpful. I hope this book will be of value to them and especially the young Sikhs who were always interested in my research.

Parminder Bhachu
Centre for Research in Ethnic Relations, Warwick University
January 1985

Glossary

Akand Path Non-stop reading of the *Guru Granth Sahib*, the Sikh holy book or sacred text, normally within forty-eight hours.

Bahu Term of address for clerks and administrators.

Barat Groom's marriage party.

Bhaiband Brotherhood.

Biradari Refers both to a brotherhood and also to a caste group and a patriline.

Bistra Bedding set, which consists of bedsheets, pillow cases, and a quilt.

Charkha Spinning wheel.

Chura A set of bangles, normally in odd numbers, 11, 21, 31, etc., given to the bride by the MB a few days before the wedding at the *chura* ceremony.

Daaj Dowry.

Daan Charitable gifts of money, and objects of food, for which no return is expected.

Darzi Tailor.

Dayna-Layna Gift exchanges (literally, giving and taking).

Dharmashastras Traditional legal treaties.

Dornay Two large headscarves worn together.

Dupatta Long headscarf.

Ghar-jamai A son-in-law who lives with his wife's natal group or parents.

Giani or **Granthi** Sikh priest.

Got Exogamous clan or sub-caste group.

Guli-Karas Derogatory term, used especially by Jat Sikhs to refer to Ramgarhia Sikhs.

Gurdwara Temple.

Guru Granth Sahib   The Sikh Holy Book.

Gur-riti   Compulsory rituals which take place in the presence of the *Guru Granth Sahib* within the temple. These are ordained rituals, as opposed to the optional ceremonies which do not involve a religious specialist or similar personnel.

Halki   Light or not eminent; also refers to a 'common' family background and low-caste status.

Halwai   Professional caterer or chef.

Jhillas   Regions of the Punjab, such as Doaba, Malwa, and Majha.

Kadesar   A woman who is from outside one's caste or community.

Kagra   Long loose skirt which fits a number of sizes.

Kameez   Tunic.

Kanyadaan   The gift of a maiden or virgin, the purest of gifts, for which no return is expected because its presentation is extremely meritorious for the giver, especially in the North Indian context.

Kara   Steel bangle, one of the five Sikh symbols. Steel represents Sikh egalitarianism, but at weddings in the UK, a gold *kara* has begun to be presented.

Khandan   Extended kinship group, but also the nuclear family, referring to its ancestry.

Kirtan   Religious singing.

Ladoos   Sweets: round orange balls.

Log   People.

Lohar   Ironmongers.

Maiyan   A pre-wedding ceremony, in which the bride and the groom are rubbed with a dough of flour, mustard oil, and turmeric.

Muklawa   A post-wedding ceremony concerning the bride, after which the marriage can be consummated.

Pag   Turban.

Palung   Bed or charpoy.

Piri   Low stool.

Poon   Meritorious gift or charity, similar in concept to *daan*.

Raj   Bricklayer.

Rasam-Rawaz   Social customs and procedures of conducting life-cycle rituals and ceremonies.

Rokna   Literally, the blocking of the groom by the brides' family. Similar to engagement, though not as public an event.

Salwaar   Baggy trousers.

Samosa   Savoury triangular pasties.

Satsung   Religious function.

Sikhya   Sermon given during a wedding ceremony to the couple, usually by an older person, or by the priest himself.

Stridhanam   The concept of exclusive female property according to Hindu law.

Suniar   Goldsmith.

Tarkan   Carpenter.

Ticka   A piece of jewellery for the forehead.

Tola   10–11.66 gms of gold; 1 oz=31 gms, 1 oz=2.25 *tolas*. The price of a *tola* or gold, fluctuates with the value of the British pound, one *tola* at present costing between £90 and £100.

Vadaigi   A money gift given to the father-in-law of the bride, normally by the bride's father, almost always as a farewell gift after the wedding ceremony, but just before the bride is sent off to her marital home.

Viah   Wedding.

Wari   Groom's family's gifts to the bride.

Abbreviations used

BD	brother's daughter
BW	brother's wife
F	father
FB	father's brother
FBD	father's brother's daughter
FBW	father's brother's wife
FZ	father's sister
HZ	husband's sister
M	mother
MB	mother's brother
MBD	mother's brother's daughter
MF	mother's father
MM	mother's mother

ONE

Introduction

This book is primarily an ethnographic account[1] of a twice migrated community[2] of East African Sikhs during a particular phase of settlement in Britain in the late 1970s and early 1980s. It is about a single group of urban though traditionalist settlers with a common history of migration from India to Africa to Britain, and who:

(a) belong predominantly to one caste group, that of the Ramgarhias (the artisan caste);[3]

(b) were already part of an established community in East Africa, where they had developed considerable community skills prior to migration;

(c) moved from urban East Africa (Ghai 1965: 93) to urban Britain having been concentrated in a handful of towns in East Africa;

(d) were mainly public sector workers[4] forming the middle level of the three-tier system in the plural society of East Africa (Mangat 1969: 131; Ghai 1965: 94);

(e) were technically skilled because of early recruitment policies which only allowed skilled labour into Africa (Morris 1968: 62);

(f) despite both their absence from India for over seventy years and the lack of home-orientation have maintained many of the values and traditions they migrated with in the early twentieth century;

(g) have arrived in Britain with considerable command over main-stream skills (e.g. language, education, familiarity with urban institutions and bureaucratic processes) and also a certain amount of capital, which makes them relatively prosperous and one of the most progressive of the non-European migrants. Their lack of a 'myth of return' and the fact that they are 'twice migrants' is of central importance in explaining their progress, as well as certain features of their social organization.

East Africans are therefore experienced migrants who had developed considerable community and technical skills prior to migration, and who also had powerful community ties which they have been able to reproduce in Britain since the late 1960s. They lack a strong orientation to a home country, and are settlers who combine facets of both progress and traditionalism in their settlement in the UK. A number of highly-qualified East Africans migrated to Canada and the US around the mid-1960s, whereas the public sector workers and some businessmen holding British passports moved to the UK.

This book has two main aims: first, it attempts to document salient features of a settler population. By focusing principally on marriage and dowry patterns in its latter part, it analyses major features of the organization of the community, namely community values, its structure, economic organization, the influence of a strong communications network, the consequence of the lack of a 'myth of return' and so on, to formulate a picture of the field of social relationships in Britain. Second, it addresses itself to developments that have taken place as a result of settlement in Britain and to mechanisms of change which should furnish some clues about its potential nature amongst other South Asian minorities in relation to their length of stay in Britain.

In the following, I shall refer to the main features of the East African Sikh community to put them into the context of the wider minority of South Asians in Britain of whom they are a part, but from whom they differ in certain fundamental ways.

East Africans *vis-à-vis* direct migrants

From the outside South Asian migrants in Britain are generally seen as a homogeneous community, yet there are clear differences among them of class, caste, experiences of migration, origins (from urban or rural areas), etc. All of these play a determinant role on their orientation and settlement. The complexity of different communities within the South Asian grouping is generally not given enough weight due to the assumption of an entity called 'South Asian culture'. Yet there are direct migrants for whom migration to Britain has been their first move from the Indian sub-continent, often from rural areas to urban ones, and there are twice migrants like the East African Sikhs.

East African Sikhs form one part of the total population in the UK from East Africa which is at present estimated to be around 181,321 (1981 Census).[5] The majority of them arrived in the UK from the mid-1960s onwards, their pattern of migration being different from that of direct migrants from the Indian sub-continent and Pakistan (Ballard 1973; Ballard and Ballard 1977; Saifullah Khan 1976, 1977; Helweg 1979; Anwar 1976; Dahya 1973; Jeffrey 1976; Robinson 1984). They are twice removed, having left the Punjab during the early part of the twentieth century as indentured labour to build the Kenya-Uganda railway (Mangat 1969: 32) and thence to the UK in the 1960s, having been seriously affected by post-independence Africanization policies.

In Britain, East Africans, mainly Ramgarhia Sikhs, constitute a minority within a larger minority of Sikhs consisting of other caste groups with a large number belonging to the Jat caste. The Jats have mostly migrated from the Indian sub-continent and have been in Britain often for much longer than the East Africans. In the latter case, residence in Africa for over sixty years has resulted in the loss of their ties with India, unlike the direct migrants, who maintain them more intensely. They were, thus, orientated towards staying in the UK permanently, right from the point of entry. This is in contrast to other South Asian migrants (Saifullah Khan 1977; Dahya 1973; Aurora 1967; Anwar 1979; Helweg 1979; Jeffrey 1976) who were home-orientated and who made frequent visits to India for reinforcement of their cultural values. East Africans based abroad belong to a community that has multiplex relationships, being interlinked; also they have a developed infrastructure in Britain. They formed a settler community which lacked a crucial feature common to South Asian minorities: that is, the myth of return. The latter was a powerful organizational feature of migrant communities in structuring their attitudes and orientations towards settlement in UK. In spite of increasing lengths of stay and after uniting with families, the myth of return was often still retained by direct migrants as 'a central charter for the maintenance of Sikh ethnicity in Britain' (Ballard and Ballard 1977: 41–2). Brooks and Singh (1978–79: 22) further emphasize its importance, stating that 'the myth of return is of overriding importance when considering the perspectives and actions of migrant workers, particularly those from

the Asian ethnic groups. . . . The successful retention of the myth of return is necessary for this emphasis on the minimising or prevention
of contact with the wider society.' Dahya (1973: 241) too makes similar
points, in classifying Pakistani migrants as 'transients', whose stay
abroad is of a temporary nature. He states (1974: 82): 'Like Indians . . .
Pakistanis emigrate not in order to earn a livelihood but to supple-
ment the economic resources of their families of origin . . . to improve
their existing landholdings and/or to extend them, to improve their
family homestead by building a *pakka* (literally, solid) house and so
on.' Robinson reaffirms this in describing directly migrated South
Asians in Blackburn, who he states have 'restricted aspirations while in
the UK, centred upon the myth – or reality – of an early return to the
sending society. This factor, when allied to structural constraints, has
ensured that the group remains encapsulated in its neighbourhood, in
its place of work and in its place of learning' (1984: 254).

Eventual return home remained the ultimate goal even though the
final return might either have been constantly postponed or indeed
might never have taken place. Migration was seen as an interlude, the
country of origin and kinsmen resident there acting as a controlling
influence on the motivations, actions, and attitudes of South Asian
minorities. For example, Jeffrey (1976: 145) in describing Muslim
Pakistanis in Bristol stated that 'values carried over from Pakistan
influence patterns of interaction in Bristol, links with kin at home
contain obligations and necessitate a constant orientation in the
direction of Pakistan on the part of migrants, and their investment
patterns and intentions to return have an impact on the lifestyles they
choose. Features mentioned above are consistently salient in descriptions of the settlement patterns of South Asians in Britain at the time.
Such characteristics however, do not apply to East Africans, who do
not fit into a number of commonly held stereotypical assumptions
about minorities. They are neither home-orientated nor view their
stay in Britain as a sojourn, since their migration to Britain was always
of a permanent nature.

Despite their absence from India for a long period and their lack of
ties to a home country East Africans have remained traditionalist. This
also applies to other East African Asians like the Gujeratis who have
remained culturally conservative and intensely religious (Tambs-
Lyche 1980; Michaelson 1979; Shah 1979). They are almost 'Victorian

Sikhs' as an Indian Sikh informant suggested, having maintained some of the fundamental traditions with which they migrated from India. This is not to suggest that their cultural values have been ossified and remain static because they have changed in response to their country of residence. But they do observe many of their traditions stringently, more so than newly-established migrants. Their conservatism manifests itself in the ritual elaboration of their marriages, in the gift exchanges that take place according to traditional rules, and in the injection of the wages of brides into their dowries, thus converting female wealth into a traditional framework, and so on. These themes are discussed in detail in Chapter 6.

The perpetuation of some central cultural values more strongly than in the past has occurred despite such features as changes in domestic organization, with an increasing tendency toward nuclear families which set up separate residences away from an extended family; the entry of women into the labour market as wage earners, the dispersed nature of the community, the lack of a myth of return on arrival, and also the absence of control exercised by a kinship group from a distance.

East Africans' orientation towards staying in the UK permanently is obvious from other features of their social organization. For example, their arrival in complete family units, often consisting of three generations, of grandparents, parents, and children, make them unique in relation to international migration, which is invariably of a much younger age group. In the majority of cases, even if the household heads arrived first, the families were united within a couple of years. The phases of settlement described by Ballard and Ballard (1977) for Sikhs are not relevant to them since the community has not gone through the early stages of bachelor households characterized by austere living, to the later stages of fully-fledged family life with the arrival of families in the 1960s and 1970s. The arrival of East Africans as family units has led to their rapid settlement in the UK, alongside the reproduction of strong communication links established during their stay in Africa. The longer process of settlement applicable to South Asians who had migrated directly was automatically telescoped for them. This contraction of phases of settlement, together with their strong communications network has catalyzed the establishment of ethnic services within a short period

of their arrival, even though in comparison to direct migrants East Africans were latecomers, arriving in the late 1960s. The former have been here since the labour shortage period following the Second World War and only started the process of consolidating families in the late 1950s and early 1960s, with people of Bangladeshi origin doing this even later, in the early 1970s, even though their menfolk have been here since the earliest days of South Asian migration. This period also coincides with the arrival of Ugandan Asians in 1972 as refugees ousted by General Idi Amin. I shall not delve into their settlement patterns here, since these have already been well documented (Kuepper, Lackey, and Swinerton 1975; Plender 1972; Humphrey and Ward 1974). East Africans in my study, because they were mainly public sector workers based in Nairobi, are either from Kenya, or have arrived prior to the 1972 Amin episode. Having stated this, I should emphasize that some of the features described in this book for East African Sikhs are also of relevance to other East African Asians in general, whether they be refugees from Uganda, Kenya, or Tanzania; and whether they are Hindus, Muslims, or Gujeratis, etc. (Fernando 1979; Tambs-Lyche 1980; Michaelson 1979; Robinson 1981, 1984; Shah 1979). Their past experiences and common position in East Africa as middlemen gives them a large number of shared characteristics (Brooks and Singh 1978–79: 20).[6]

Despite their late arrival in the UK, their common experiences have given them skills which they are able to utilize in the establishment of communities here. In East Africa they were concentrated in a few towns, and were highly urbanized; they were employed by an equally small number of organizations, their children had been to a select number of 'Asian' schools in the main towns, etc. Since they were already part of an established diaspora before migration to the UK, they have been able to reproduce not only community ties and skills, but also establish institutions like temples (*gurdwaras*) and caste associations rapidly on arrival to further consolidate the community. Their skills have helped them to establish themselves much more rapidly than direct migrants who have not possessed the same expertise, linguistic facility, and communications network to develop community structures at the same pace. All this has further helped reaffirm their East African identity.

In that country they had been able to maintain their community intact through traditionally-arranged endogamous marriages (Bharati 1967: 284; Morris 1967: 276). This helped group formation and the development of the community along caste lines, and also led to the perpetuation of the traditional values with which they migrated. Cross-cutting kinship ties developed through marriage alliances in East Africa, and the great overlap of contact concentrated in urban areas had been conducive to the building of a powerful network there which is now to be found in the UK. It is this that is drawn upon to mobilize the community for specific projects and for generating support in relation to particular issues which are of especial concern to them, and for arranging marriage alliances.

Along with the community expertise, East Africans were skilled technically prior to arrival here due to the selective nature of early recruitment policies of the colonial British government in East Africa. It only allowed in the skilled labour needed to build the Kenya-Uganda railways (Morris 1968: 62; Mangat 1969: 61; Ghai 1965: 96). Morris (1968: 62) states that immigration rules in East Africa were so difficult that 'no alien was admitted unless he could fill a post that was for the benefit of everybody'. For this reason, East Africans in Britain possess developed community and technical skills acquired before settlement here, and, in a large number of cases, even before settlement in Africa.

Since those who have arrived here have mainly been public sector workers, they have not necessarily occupied low-grade jobs or semi- or unskilled industrial work (Phizacklea and Miles 1980; Rex and Tomlinson 1979; Castles and Kosack 1973; Brooks 1975a/b), being more occupationally dispersed in different spheres of work than is suggested by the general literature on migrant workers. The emphasis on the working class and also 'underclass' nature of migrants (Rex and Tomlinson 1979: 275) is also not always relevant to East Africans as a whole, though it clearly applies to some of them. In London, East Africans have pursued the types of jobs they had in Africa, filling administrative civil service jobs as well as factory and professional ones, reflecting a cross-section of the community. In the Midlands, in relation to the local employment situation, East Africans are to be found in heavy industrial work though not on the same scale as migrants coming direct from the Indian sub-continent. East Africans do not conform to the types of employment patterns portrayed in the existing literature, being much more diversified throughout the UK, though with a strong tendency towards occupying public sector employment niches, as in East Africa.

Another facet of the East African community that is unlike that of other minorities, is its geographically dispersed nature. A feature of minority settlement frequently mentioned is residential segregation and concentration in inner city areas, leading to the formation of 'ethnic ghettos' (Anwar 1979; Castles, Booth, and Wallace 1984; Rex and Tomlinson 1979; Dahya 1973, 1974). East Africans are residentially dispersed even though they reside in areas of high immigrant population. Despite this, a strong communications network operates within the community, the consequences of which will be explored in Chapter 3. However, it should be stated here that it is precisely the community ties which have helped perpetuate cultural values and religiosity which have further catalyzed the revival of Sikhism amongst the general Sikh community resident in Britain for much longer. The injection of a more culturally conservative though progressive (that is in their attitudes towards residence in the UK and their command over mainstream skills) community with a clear East African identity into a much less developed and more diverse home-orientated one has precipitated over the past decade the resumption of Sikh symbols. This has led to a stricter organization of temples and the establishment of ceremony along more defined lines, with a stronger emphasis on their Sikh identity. It has been helped by tight community links, which are useful in mustering support for setting up internal community organizations. Ballard and Ballard (1977: 47) have also referred to this trend amongst the Sikhs, attributing the conservatism of East Africans to their lowly Ramgarhia status.[7] They state that since they 'traditionally ranked lower than the Jats, the Ramgarhias have long sought to improve their status by following the rules of religious orthodoxy more closely and they continued their strategy both in East Africa and Britain' (p. 38). However, a point that has not been sufficiently developed in their case is that they are highly organized, which, combined with their common East African experiences, has led to the formation of a distinct East African Sikh identity which is not entirely based on religious orthodoxy but is secular in nature, being a product of residence and consolidation in East Africa as a Sikh community. It also reflects their middle-class status in comparison with the predominantly working-class situation of direct migrants. These factors partly account for greater conservatism despite more westernized urban ways, and also the market skills which make them successful settlers. This book thus deals with a traditionalist twice migrant community which possesses community skills as well as those needed for operating within urban institutions in the UK. They have in the past acquired such experiences through having worked within the apparatus established by the British in East Africa in the fields of administration, employment, education, social services, etc. Familiarity with colonial British institutions and urban life prior to migration in conjunction with their greater command of the English language facilitated the dispersal of East Africans all over the UK, away from areas of concentrated Asian population. In this respect, they differ from direct migrants who have lacked experience with European institutions, having migrated from rural areas in the sub-continent (see Saiffullah Khan 1979a).

Another facet of the East African community which differentiates them from direct migrants is that their stay in Africa and the loss of a myth of return over a period of nearly sixty years, has, as I shall explain in Chapter 2, led to their arrival in Britain with a certain amount of capital. The retention of their resources in this country allows them to maintain a higher material standard of living. The picture for direct migrants was different, especially in the earlier stages of settlement in the UK because of their concern for building properties in their country of origin where their status and prestige networks rested (Ballard 1974, 1983; Ballard and Ballard 1977; Pettigrew 1972; Helweg 1979, 1983; Brooks and Singh 1978–79). In fact, a frequent reason cited for migration is improvement of family status. Dahya (1974: 113) explains that remittances to Pakistan clearly indicate 'that for the present the immigrants' priorities are geared to raising their status, and that of their families in the society of origin'. Robinson (1981: 167), Helweg (1983: 437), and Ballard (1983: 120) describe similar situations. The latter two authors in particular have explored the impact of these remittances on the areas of origin of migrants resident in the UK. East Africans went through this stage during their stay in Africa, and by the time they moved to Britain were motivated to staying here permanently. Their social status scales and positive reference groups are all within the UK, as is the audience which monitors their actions, and towards which their behaviour patterns are geared.

In many respects, East African attitudes are similar to those described by Jeffrey (1976) for Christian refugees from Pakistan, though unlike those of Muslim migrants who share traits common to direct migrants. The latter are home-orientated with 'strong social and economic use of remittances to build pukka houses and to establish some sort of business' in Pakistan. Residence abroad for them is considered to be temporary and 'the economic benefits which accrue are intimately tied up with prestige at home' (p. 48). Christians, on the other hand, see themselves as refugees, being almost permanently exiled from Pakistan, and are committed to staying in Britain, having escaped an oppressive situation where they felt 'foreign and vulnerable' (p. 178). Migration for them was the only way out.

East African Sikhs have similar attitudes towards staying in Britain, but for very different reasons. They were not refugees (other than Ugandan Asians) but, like Christians, their ties to a homeland were weak, and they too arrived in family units with aged parents (p. 148). They visited India infrequently, unlike direct migrants, who maintained stronger ties with the sub-continent. In common with Christians' attitudes towards Pakistan, East African Sikhs have similar unfavourable views towards India as a place for them. It is seen as difficult to live and work in because of 'corruption', and 'conniving' ways of Indians, and poor social facilities. However, even though they are oriented towards staying permanently in the UK they none the less, do not in general have the Christian settlers' interest in emulating British cultural values and attempting to gain acceptance into indigenous British society by stressing their similarities. As Jeffrey states, 'for the Christians it may be said that they *want* the boundaries between themselves and British people to be weak: they are keen to be accepted by British people in a way that the Muslims are not' (p. 150). This attitude differs markedly from East African Sikhs, who are keen to upgrade their market and social skills as related to British public domains, though they remain conservative in their private cultural ones, being stringent observers of traditions (like the Muslims) in certain respects. Their emphasis is not on assimilation through emulation of British Anglo-Saxon cultural values, but on maintaining what they see as their Sikh ethnicity, while interacting with the British in the public sphere. This occurs despite weak ties to a homeland and their urban skills, making them different from the Christians, who want to underplay their Pakistani ethnicity and the differences between themselves and the British. The Christians do so even though 'to the outsider, the domestic styles of the Muslims and Christians are very similar' (p. 154). This contrasts with East Africans, who emphasize their own ethnic identity not by maintaining a distance from white British people but by being emphatic about their own separate identity. However, just as the Christians attempt to seek 'acceptance into British society and are rejected by them because British people do not see "Christian" as a relevant ethnic marker' (p. 159), a similar situation applies to East Africans. Even though they do not have the same interest as the Christians in gaining entry into British society and define their identity independently of British cultural values, they none the less get classified alongside other South Asians as 'Hindus', 'Asians', 'Indians', 'Pakistanis', 'coloureds', and so on, in the eyes of the indigenous British.

In other words, the East African emphasis on their separateness from direct migrants from the sub-continent by stressing their 'East Africanness' through their greater urban skills, sophistication, interest in maintaining Sikh ethnicity, and religious orthodoxy, is not recognized by the white British, who do not perceive finer internal divisions amongst people of South Asian origin. For them these differences are not apparent, even though their 'westernization', material wealth, and fluency with the English language may be noticed by those who come into contact with them in public and statutory institutions. So East Africans get included just like the Christians into the very groups they seek exclusion from, by maintaining their separate caste associations, marriage circles, communications network, and so on. Their exclusion of other South Asians through the above-mentioned community mechanisms is only effective in relation to the internal dynamics of the community. It is not operative in communicating their separate identity as East African Sikhs to the indigenous British: their urban and community expertise does not help them override such labels as 'Hindus' or 'Pakis', and also general British prejudices.

A factor which exacerbates the situation for people of East African Asian origin is that of the racism which is suffered by minorities in general. Racism is a commonly-shared experience, and East African Asians are affected by it in much the same fashion as other minorities, whether it be in its institutionalized, or in its more diffuse, forms. This subject has been covered well by the authors of *The Empire Strikes Back* (CCCS 1982) and was not a major theme of investigation of my own research. However, it should be pointed out that, like the Christians who emphasize their differences from Muslim Pakistanis and their similarities with the British, yet are rejected by them, the same situation applies to East African Asians as mentioned above. Despite their lack of interest in culturally assimilating and despite the stress on their separate East African Asian identity, their subjection to racism and discrimination is on the same footing as that of other South Asian and Afro-Caribbean minorities. Hence, even though people of East African Asian origin emphasize their differences and maintain a distance from direct migrants in relation to caste, class, and previous history and experiences of migration, external forces which are operative on South Asians act in general against them, and just as powerfully. Their urban experiences, middle-class position, westernized market and community skills are rendered impotent in blurring the derogatory stereotypical notions held of them as a Sikh group, part of the wider minority of 'Asian' and 'Black' communities. However, having stated this, it should be stressed that even though they suffer from racism in much the same fashion as other, especially black, minorities, their negotiation of it is dependent on their class position, which on the whole differs from that of most direct migrants. These are mainly working class, though they share features which are similar to urban migrants from the sub-continent, some of whom are middle class like East Africans.

Racism is also an important factor in the definition of the East African Asian identity, though not the only one. Ballard and Ballard (1977: 54) in discussing the Sikhs in general state that 'racism has precipitated a reactive pride in their separate identity'. Although this is true of East Africans, it is not altogether the case, because the maintenance of a separate East African identity in Britain is also linked to the establishment of a clear-cut group status in East Africa. They formed a separate community which consisted predominantly of one caste group which was consolidated as a community for over sixty years in Africa; it became prosperous and confident, and was able to maintain itself as a caste and class group, which had exposure to the 'pace-maker', efficiently-organized community of the Ismaili Muslims led by the Aga

Khan, which had well-developed community organizations and services (Morris 1968: 55). The ability of the East African Sikhs to maintain their identity in Britain is an aspect of skills acquired in having developed as a community away from a home base in the foreign environment of Africa. Their experiences as 'twice migrants' have led to a stricter adherence on their part to their identification with cultural values in the changed circumstances since migration to UK, in spite of racism. Support structures developed during their stay in Africa have not only helped manufacture their 'East Africanness' but have also aided the perpetuation of their identity as 'staunch Sikhs' in the South Asian diaspora, independent of the original country of origin.

In this respect, they are markedly different from first-generation Sikhs in the UK, who 'have tended to organize themselves in terms of the narrow loyalties of their homelands – based on caste and kinship', and for whom 'internal divisions of religion, language, region, and caste as well as village-based alliances are still of overriding importance' (Ballard and Ballard 1977: 54). These are precisely the factors cited as crucial to the maintenance of the ethnicity of South Asian groups in the existing literature, based on research carried out in the 1960s and 1970s. An almost opposite situation exists among East African Asians, who have remained traditionalistic, conscious of their caste group, and have maintained their ethnicity, despite both the lack of ties to their homeland and also the absence of strong kin ties with relatives resident in the Punjab. East Africans' stay in Africa weakened close kinship links, though it strengthened ties with other Sikhs who are distantly related, or not at all. The consolidation of people of one caste group, who in the traditional set-up would have been dispersed in different areas of the Punjab, resulted in a great deal of homogeneity and cross-linkages which had not existed prior to migration to Africa. It is part of that community that has settled in the UK.

Caste and class: internal dynamics versus external identity

Of other traditional features that have gained prominence in the UK, caste has become an important principle of organization of many minorities of Indian origin, and one which is gaining in importance. The significance of caste among the Gujerati communities from East Africa in the UK and their consolidation as caste groups while resident in East Africa have also been described by Michaelson (1979), Shah (1979), and Tambs-Lyche (1980). The caste status of East African Sikhs has been emphasized in the UK, not because of their own consciousness of it, even though in East Africa it was crucial in marriage arrangements and the maintenance of caste endogamy. Since they themselves were the majority Sikh group in East Africa, there being almost 90 per cent Ramgarhia Sikhs (Macleod 1974: 87; Bharati 1972: 1934–38), their caste position was not a defining marker of their ethnicity because their status as Sikhs assumed much more importance. Caste boundaries have become more defined in the UK as a result of interaction with direct migrants from the sub-continent who, as Ballard and Ballard have also mentioned (p. 54) are more conscious of their caste and village ties, being more knowledgeable about a functioning caste hierarchy. The East Africans' position in Britain is the new one of becoming a minority caste within the majority Sikh population of Jat origin, though there are other minority castes such as Khatris, Ahuluwalias, Ravi Dasis, Bhatras, etc. In a way, the caste consciousness of East Africans i.e. their 'Ramgarhianess', is interactive ethnicity (Wallman 1979: 6) produced as a result of contact with a more diverse range of caste groups within the UK, who have experiences that differ from their own East African ones.

This process is especially prominent in areas such as Southall and the Midlands, in which there are large concentrations of Sikhs of different caste groups. It is, however, not only a caste phenomenon but also a class one. The perpetuation of their separate caste and class identity through stressing their 'Ramgarhianess' and their 'East Africanness' reflects not only their different caste position but also their class one as relatively prosperous, skilled, urban middle-class settlers.

The definition of these two positions is also dependent on the context. Their East Africanness, reflecting their class position, manifests itself particularly clearly vis-à-vis interaction with the indigenous British, to stress their differences from the directly-migrated, predominantly working-class groups, whereas their Ramgarhianess, reflecting their different caste position, is most salient during interaction with the dominant Sikh community. Having stated this, it should be emphasized that in areas of high concentration of Sikhs, caste and class positions amalgamate to define the East African separateness from direct migrants, the projection of differences being a product of caste and class combined. Hence their caste status is of especial relevance to the ethnic context but not in relation to inter-action with the indigenous British, who do not perceive internal differences between the different caste groups, and between twice and direct migrants.

However, it should not be assumed that the boundaries between twice and direct migrants remain static, because they do weaken to include different caste groups, especially during times of crisis, and for political mobilization for specific issues. For example, after the army action in Amritsar in June 1984, and during the much-publicized Mandla versus Lee case[8] which resulted in the successful classification of the Sikhs as a 'race' in Britain in 1983, the protest demonstrations that took place in central London included Sikhs of different origins and caste and class groups, even though East Africans were most prominent as initiators, of the latter march in particular. Community support was mobilized on the basis of their common 'Sikh' identity because these issues affected and angered the Sikhs as a group. In such instances, boundaries coalesced for a particular purpose to include people who in other circumstances would have been excluded (Wallman 1979: 4–5). During times of difficulty a con-solidated Sikh identity, ignoring the narrower confines of caste and class divisions which otherwise remain important exclusionary and inclusionary mechanisms, becomes paramount.

But even though boundaries fade in relation to particular national and international issues of universal concern to the Sikhs, on the whole, these remain key features of the internal organization of the community on the British scene, because the East Africanness of the East Africans and their common past experiences make them perceive themselves as different from directly migrant South Asians. Their group experiences determine whom they interact with; who gets access into their social networks; who is included in the kindred of recognition, etc. This is not to suggest that East African Asians as a group have shared community institutions in which they all partici-pate, because this is not the case, since the various communities are organized along caste and religious lines within that broad category. It is to suggest that there is an overeaching East African identity which is as apparent among East African Sikhs as it is among East African

Gujeratis, Muslims, or Hindus. So different categories of East African Asians are included because of similarity of experiences, whereas South Asians from the sub-continent are excluded because of dissimilarity of past experience, even though there may be other shared cultural values, such as a common religion or area of origin.

Racism and the lack of awareness by the British of the different South Asian groups includes them in the very groups from which they maintain their separateness. Thus, their exclusion of other South Asian groups is only relevant to the internal organization of the community. However, with length of stay in Britain, even though caste and class divisions will become more salient than ever, conversely, there will also be increasing strategic unity for effective political action, in conjunction with other 'Black' and 'Asian' groups. This is the result of the growing political sophistication of the community, especially amongst the younger generation of East African Asians who are almost entirely British products and who are forming over-reaching and more inclusive identities for collective action in relation to mutual interests. For the young in particular, their East Africanness is becoming less relevant as their 'British Asian' identity gains strength.

Pointers to the potential nature of change

Processes of change among minorities, as can be seen from the case of East African Asians, have not followed a single path of absorption into the majority communities, but have resulted in complex responses to settlement in the UK. In their case, there have been adjustments to accommodate change in various spheres of their social organization in combination with maintenance, in fact, reinforcement, of certain traditional norms. These have not remained static, but have been modified in response to changed conditions in Britain. For example, flexibilities have been introduced into the criteria used for spouse-selection and marriage arrangement (see Chapter 5) in order to increase the marriage pool of suitable British Sikhs, and also to take into account their changing attitudes. A result of this has been the perpetuation of the external group identity through the introduction of internal changes, thus maintaining caste endogamy and the 'East Africanness' of the group. In this way there is both change and perpetuation of their East African identity in Britain. On the other hand, conditions in the UK which have brought about changes in domestic organization, such as the increasing nuclearization of families, neo-local residence after marriage, and the entry of women into the labour market, have resulted in the reinforcement of traditional institutions in Britain (Chapter 6). The escalation of the dowry system, and their emphasis on caste exclusiveness are aspects of change which have not led to the abolition of traditional values and the assumption of British cultural ones, but have resulted in both traditionalism on the part of East Africans and also progress in other spheres of their lives. These are all facets of their British Asian identity.

In a way, a two-fold identity has emerged, one based on the internal dynamics of the community as a result of interaction with directly migrant South Asian groups, in particular, with other Sikh castes, and one which is a product of interaction with the indigenous British. My suggestion is that the greater emphasis on their separate East African Sikh identity has not developed entirely in the face of 'white rejection' (Ballard and Ballard 1977: 47) though this is an important determinant, but that the growing orthodoxy, caste and class consciousness, positive assertion of their 'Sikhness' etc. are also products of the strengthened internal organization of South Asian communities, in which boundaries are being continuously redefined with settlement in the UK. However, the East African Sikh emphasis of their East Africanness through their class status and their urban mainstream skills is also related to their interaction with the British who do not perceive finer differences between them and directly migrant groups. In comparison with direct migrants who do not possess their community caste and class cohesiveness, and common African experience, being both more home-orientated, heterogenous, and less established abroad as communities, they succeed. South Asian responses to settlement in UK are complex as is the nature of change, because the latter is as determined by their situation in the UK as it is by past experiences, especially in the case of the East African Sikhs, who were part of an established South Asian diaspora prior to migration to the UK.

In the following chapters this book will deal with a particular category of South Asians who possess the technical, community, and urban skills necessary for living in urban Britain; who were relatively prosperous on arrival here; who are here to stay; who lacked a 'myth of return' on arrival; who are occupationally and geographically dispersed; and who have remained traditionalist despite their 'Westernized' skills. They are progressive settlers who have remained culturally conservative by making adjustments in their value systems in response to UK conditions. Their orientation and social organizational features should make us rethink a number of stereotypical assumptions made of 'Asians' and minority communities.

Field situation and access

Before starting my account, I should present some details of my field situation.[9] Before moving to do fieldwork in Southall, I had started to attend *satsangs* (religious functions) at the two main temples there. In doing this, I became friendly with members of some of the families I later became involved with because they had seen me around the temple regularly. Some of them told me of accommodation that I could rent: I would be told of families who had spare rooms to let and who would be trustworthy enough to be suitable for an unmarried Sikh woman living on her own in Southall.

After two months of visiting Southall and the temples, I found a room with the help of a family in the older part of Southall, with another family in old Southall known to be decent. Most people refer to Southall as consisting of two parts: the older part or *purana* Southall is the area south of the railway bridge, which had the earliest Indian settlers, as opposed to the *nava* or newer Southall north of the bridge, which has all the newer Asian shops and also some of the more recently bought houses.

In the early stages of fieldwork, I did not depend on my landlady's family for contacts. I made no attempt to follow up its network of relations until I had established myself in Southall. I maintained the very formal relationship of tenant and landlord because I really did not want to have the status of a family member. The reason for this is that I did not want my movements to be restricted. I chose not to become a 'daughter of the house' because that would have meant that, although I would have access to the family relationships in a more intense way, I would, none the less, be subject to all the restrictions placed on a family member. I had to be out until late at night and went out to meet all kinds of people because of the nature of my work.

I wanted to explore families other than the one I lived with. However, as time went on I came to know the family well and would occasionally visit my landlady's relatives. By this time, she had come to know a bit more of my research and had got used to my unusual habits. Also, I had often attended *satsangs* at which her relatives had been present and they would often tell my landlady about this. Thus, they actually accepted my role as a researcher.

My fieldwork is a 'network study' since this was the most practicable way of working in a large town with a population as geographically spread as the East African Sikhs. Also, methodologically, it was the only way of being certain to get the right criteria included in a manageable number of households. If I had used a statistical sample, there was the possibility of leaving out important criteria in a universe of such small size.

Although in the initial stages of fieldwork, I came to know families with whom I had more intense contact through the temple, gradually I got to know other families partly by just being around in Southall, and also by attending religious functions at different homes. Thus, I built a network of relationships based on these families, who would introduce me to other people. After about six months in the field, I decided to focus on thirteen of a number of families I had come to know. Before this time, I used to follow up any family with whom I was at ease. Therefore, I did not select a particular number of families to study either by, for example, looking at the voters' list, or by concentrating on a particular street, but explored a network of relationships. However, in choosing to concentrate on the core thirteen families, I looked for certain features which partly represented the general background of the East African Sikh community, and which were also related to the theme of marriage and dowry.

All the families I focused on lived in two boroughs. Eight of them actually lived in Southall while the rest were scattered around the surrounding suburbs. In relation to occupations, I looked for professional men, office and factory workers, people who had an interest in the building and construction industry, and businessmen. Within my sample, one of the household heads works in an administrative job, two of the household heads are professional men, three are involved with the building trade in different capacities (one works on a freelance basis, another is employed by a large building concern, and the third has his own well-established building firm). In terms of the size of family, there was a variation between a typical nuclear family of four members, to the eight to nine members of the larger families. As far as marriage was concerned, I was interested in families with marriageable young people of both sexes, and ones in which there were newly-married couples. I was especially interested in families with old grandmothers because they told me the most about changes in the dowry system and marriage ritual. Seven of the households in my core sample had an old parent or parents living with them. Five of the thirteen families had young daughters of marriageable age with whom I was in constant contact. Three of these girls actually got engaged during my fieldwork and one of them was married during the marriage season. I would often meet friends and young cousins of these families whose marriages I could attend. There were three newly-married couples in my sample – one of these got married during my fieldwork, another was married five months before my stay in Southall, and the third had been married for over a year.

To form a more general picture of the East African Sikh community, I shall also refer to families who were in what I consider to be my wider sample. These are families on whom I did not concentrate but with whom I had contact with over my fieldwork. I refer especially to those I came to know by attending weddings, by being with them immediately before the marriage period. These are my 'wedding families'.

TWO

Structure of the Asian community in East Africa

My reason for going into the background of the East African Sikhs is to describe characteristics and features that were developed in East Africa,[1] which have played a vital part in determining the nature and behaviour of the East African Sikh community in Britain.

Early settlement of East African Asians

After many negotiations by the Imperial British East Africa Company with the Government of India, the decision to construct the Uganda railway 'upon Indian methods and chiefly by means of the labour of Indian "coolies"'[2] was taken in 1895 (Mangat 1969: 32, quoting from the *Final Report of the Uganda Railway Committee* 1904). It was thought that the 'railway could not be constructed at any reasonable cost and speed' unless Indian labour could be freely recruited. Around 1896, the first group of 1,000 indentured workers, including a proportion of blacksmiths, carpenters, and masons, arrived in Mombasa. The terms of their contract included a maximum term of service of three years, at the end of which a man was entitled to a free passage back to India, or could remain in East Africa. They earned a minimum wage of RS 15 per month plus rations, quarters, and medical costs. The total expenditure per labourer was RS 30 including all the above-mentioned.

Recruitment of labour from the Punjab in particular started in 1897. This carried on till 1901, during which period 32,000 Indian workers were recruited for service. The attraction for the labourers to migrate to East Africa lay in the higher earnings that could be earned there for the same type of work as they did in India. In later years, as East Africa developed, it came to be known as the 'America of the Hindus'

(Mangat 1969: 61). After the five years it took to build the railway from Mombasa to Kisumu on Lake Victoria, only 21 per cent of the labourers, 6,724 of them, decided to stay, and 2,000 (6 per cent) continued to work for the railways. The rest either returned home or were invalided due to the difficult conditions of work, 2,493 dying of disease.

So by 1905, as the railway system became better established, and the East African interior opened up, the Indian role in skilled and subordinate employment assumed increasing importance. Although the majority of indentured workers had returned to India, the railway itself (which was not fully complete until 1931) continued to depend largely on Indian personnel for its functioning. By the 1900s, the Uganda Railway employed Indians as clerks, artisans, station masters, cashiers, and surveyors; they were also to be found in almost every government department, including the Post Office, the Police Force, and the Public Works Department (PWD), which was set up when Nairobi became the administrative headquarters of the East African Protectorate. The PWD's workshop depended on Ramgarhia artisans for the construction of government offices and for outfitting them with furniture.

The Indian role in middle-grade employment was not only restricted, however, to government services, since their activities as skilled staff and artisans steadily expanded, both in private employment and in business. With the arrival of European settlers, Nairobi and other places became concentrations of major commercial activity. European-owned mechanical workshops, garages, and furniture shops mushroomed, increasing the demands for skilled Indian workers, especially Ramgarhias. Many more were recruited at this time by private firms via agents in India, while others came at their own expense, hearing of the wealth to be made in Africa. These also included more educated Indians, such as doctors and lawyers. The more adventurous of the skilled Sikh immigrants later launched into a variety of business enterprises, as contractors, outfitters, builders, and mechanics. As a result, they fed into the activities of the major Indian commercial community in East Africa, the Gujerati population, which was also expanding during this period. Thus, the first two decades of this century witnessed a rapid growth of the Indian role in the interior of East Africa, as channels of communication opened up. This was 'spearheaded by the old-established traders and the officially spon-sored artisans' (Mangat 1969: 77).

The growth of the Indian role in East Africa during this period also accounted for the rise of a variety of Indian institutions. By this stage, Ramgarhias, like other immigrants, had begun to settle down. They had opened up schools, and social and cultural facilities like the Ramgarhia Associations, *gurdwaras*, and Sikh clubs. However, by the 1920s, European hostility towards the Indian community resulted in conflicts between them. This led to the restriction of Indian partici-pants in the development of East Africa to the limited fields of subordinate employment and commerce. Administrative and agri-cultural development were thought to be a European preserve, trade and craftsmanship were relegated to Indians, while Africans were encouraged to work in the European agricultural system and to supply cheap labour in the towns that were developing in response to European and Indian activities. This occupational compartmentaliz-ation of the East African population did not change until the 1950s and 1960s. 'The communal system of representation, the policy of land reservation and segregation, the provision of separate social services for different races formed the backbone of the three-tier system that became so characteristic of East Africa during the later colonial period' (p. 131), writes Mangat.

East Africanized Asians after the Second World War

This period saw an overall improvement in the social and economic status of Indians as the rigid racial divisions of the earlier colonial period softened. It was also after this time that a younger, more highly-educated generation of Indians was beginning to enter the professions. An important contributory factor, as far as the Ramgarhias were concerned, was that there was in the mid-1950s a general increase in the rate of their earnings due to the abandonment of the racial salary structure within the three-tier system. This meant that there was a marked rise in Indian incomes, though top executive and administrative posts were still not open to them.

Another factor that will be explored in the ensuing chapters for those Sikhs who migrated to the United Kingdom, is that by the 1950s the 'myth of return' which was prevalent in the earlier days was dissolving, further orientating them towards living in East Africa and thus retaining their capital there. This was not so in the earlier days, as is obvious from the literature. To quote an example from a petition made in 1902 by Europeans settled in Nairobi, calling upon the government 'to encourage European Colonization ... because the further immigration of Asiatics were entirely detrimental to the European settler [and] in particular to the native inhabitant. ... Further the money earned by the native in this country remains here whereas the Asiatic takes all his earnings to his native country' (Elliot to Lansdowne, 21 January 1902 (Foreign Office Records 2/805)). R. C. Thurnwald (1935: 283) also describes a similar process: 'A teacher, for example, who earns 200 shillings, sends 100 shillings home'. At this stage contact maintained by Indians with their places of origin was greatly facilitated by generous 'home' leave being granted every four years by major commercial firms and the government.

With the weakening of the 'myth of return' and the overall improvement in their economic status, the structure and attitudes of the Indian community changed considerably. The extensive urbanization of communities, members of which had emigrated directly from Indian villages, gave rise in East Africa to a new generation of East African-born people who were exposed to a system of education modelled on the Western pattern, to higher standards of living, and who were also developing a greater consciousness of their place in the countries in which they were residing. 'In essence, they initiated a process of *East Africanization* of Indian immigrants and the gradual decline of their initially strong links with India' (Mangat 1969: 141, my emphasis).

However, the increased involvement of the South Asians in East Africa also led to their growing isolation as a distinct racial and cultural minority. The factor that aided the isolation of the Indian population was the high degree of urbanization. For example, in 1962, 85 per cent of the Indian population was living in the five largest towns of East Africa. There were more South Asians living in Nairobi alone than in the whole of Uganda and Tanzania. The reason for this level of urbanization was that in Kenya and Uganda, South Asians continued to be prevented from owning and cultivating prime quality land such as that of the 'White Highlands' until the 1960s, thus denying them any openings in the agricultural sector. This restriction was reinforced by legislation passed in the three East African countries, preventing South Asians from setting up businesses outside specified cities and townships. This also prevented them from establishing a foothold in the rural economy; and the Asian concentration in urban centres further intensified 'the organization of the Asian community into a number of tight, closely-knit communal groups, and hence increased its isolation from other races' (Ghai 1965: 93).

The urbanized pattern of South Asian settlement in East Africa is in complete contrast to the pattern established by Indians in Mauritius, Fiji, and South Africa (Benedict 1961; Mayer 1961; Kuper 1960) and also in Guyana, where they lived and worked in agricultural settlements. It is important in terms of a consideration of marriage in the UK because the East Africans developed a taste for urban status symbols, as is obvious from the items in their dowries, and the marriage procedure. Thus when they migrated to Britain, they moved from one urban environment to another, unlike their first move from a rural background in India. The majority of Indian Sikhs who have migrated directly from India to the UK have followed the latter course.

The compartmentalization of the Indian community into religious, sectional, and caste groups has been described by Morris (1967, 1968), in examining the importance of caste in East Africa. He states that 'the need for caste exclusiveness was so strong that in spite of an environment almost wholly unfavourable to it, [it] was one of the most important structural principles in organizing Indian social life in East Africa' (Morris 1967: 276). Unlike other overseas Indian settlements in which caste barriers softened in the course of time, in East Africa this did not happen, even though the traditional hierarchy of the caste system in India and the relationships of dependence due to division of labour were not in evidence in Africa.

Morris also suggests that the home orientation of the Indians was critical in determining their behaviour in East Africa. Marriages were traditionally 'correctly' arranged, first, because spouses of the right category could be imported from India without difficulty due to the good communication links, and, second, because of the feeling that on their eventual return to India, they would have to fit into the local system. Thus, caste endogamy was always an important factor in the organization of East African society. For example, Bharati (1967: 284) states that 'endogamy is so complete and its workings so unchanged

from those in the Indian sister communities in South Asia that it remains the *only* criterion for caste among East African Asians.'[3]

The important consequence of the above is that although a traditional caste system did not appear in East Africa, different communities were able to maintain separate identities through the formation of caste associations and communal caste facilities, around which a distinct community could be formed. These caste categories grew large in Africa because members of one sub-caste which in rural districts in India would never have associated with another, since they often belonged to different regions, were brought together. By 1955, 'except in the eyes of Europeans and Africans, who regarded all Indians as members of one community, the castes and sects had solidified into formal elements of the structure of the Indian community' (Morris 1968: 55).

A final point that should be mentioned at this stage, whose importance will become clearer later in relation to the organizational skills of the East Africans in Britain, is that in East Africa they had had exposure to an efficiently organized community, that of the Ismaili Muslims led by the Aga Khan. Morris (1968) states that it acted as a 'pace-maker' for the rest of the East African Indians, who tended to imitate this progressive community in developing communal facilities and an individual identity. In doing so, they not only established a great deal of communal feeling but also acquired organizational skills that were further utilized in the UK (e.g. for developing their communal East African organizations).

Second migration

I will now turn to the developments which led to a large number of East African Indians moving to Britain from the mid-1960s onwards. By this time there were 372,000 Asians in East Africa (Ghai 1970: 99). Kenya had the largest number of wage earners of the three countries, forming around '70 per cent of the economically active Asian community' (Ghai 1965: 94). The reason for this was that there were a preponderance of employees working for the public sector, which was especially highly-developed in Kenya since Nairobi had the headquarters of all the government[4] and major private concerns.

Commercial enterprise was not as developed among Kenyan Asians as it was among the Ugandan and Tanzanian communities.

An interesting feature of the South Asian labour force is that, as mentioned, there were hardly any unskilled persons amongst its ranks. Another factor the significance of which will become clear in later chapters concerns Asian female employees. A trend[5] that was beginning to establish itself in East Africa in the 1960s was that there was a dramatic increase of female employees in the Asian labour market. In Kenya, the number of South Asian female employees had gone up from 600 in 1948 to 3,750 in 1962 (Ghai 1965: 95) forming 10 per cent of the total Asian labour force. They were employed as clerks, secretaries, teachers, and nurses, an occupational profile similar to that of the younger Sikh women at present in London. Thus in East Africa, South Asian women added to the already well-trained and skilled Asian manpower. A point that is related to this is the high standard of education present within this labour force. For example, the Asian contribution was especially large in 'medicine, law, engineering, pharmacy, accountancy, business management, etc.' (p. 102). Education was especially highly-valued by the civil service/ public sector employees 'conscious of the range of bureaucratic jobs opened by further schooling' (Rattansi and Abdulla 1965: 116). This is the type of background from which the Sikh families who migrated to Britain came. The western-orientated education[6] system was an important force for social change in East Africa since it played a key role in the transition, almost within a generation, of the South Asian population from a traditionalist rural society to an urban one adept at handling British institutions.

It can be seen from the above that, by the 1960s, the Asian labour force provided highly-skilled personnel, both middle-level administrators, and professionals. Thus when the three East African colonies were given Independence, the impact of a policy of the Africanization of public services was felt especially strongly by South Asians. Employment opportunities of public sector workers were especially affected, since the process of Africanization was accelerated in such areas. The categories of Asian employees hardest hit by Africanization were the clerks, the typists, middle and junior-level administrators, and technicians. Those who were being sacked from the civil services had little scope to find jobs elsewhere in East Africa, since private firms were reluctant to take them. These circumstances led to the migration of South Asians to countries abroad. A number of the more highly-qualified East Africans migrated to Canada and the USA around the mid-1960s, whereas the public sector workers and some business-men holding British passports moved to the UK, especially around the late 1960s. Thus, migration to Britain has been selective of a particular category of Sikhs, since most businessmen acquired local citizenship, having large investments within East Africa. Ugandan Sikhs have a different pattern of immigration, since of course they were ousted by General Amin.

A final point that should be mentioned here and which relates to the financial advantages that the East Africans started off with in Britain, is that around the politically vulnerable time of Independence, they were beginning to export capital 'resulting in a fall in domestic investment and a large outflow of capital abroad' (Ghai 1965: 105). This especially applied to the public sector employees who later migrated to the UK, since they were transferring part of their incomes into banks in the UK by the early 1960s. This accumulated capital gave them the added advantage of being able to buy their homes soon after arrival, in the majority of cases.

To summarize, by the 1930s and 1940s, the East African community began to lose its home orientation as it became more established within Africa. This initiated the phase of the East Africanization of the Sikh community, while retaining its distinct characteristics and status symbols. They had been able to preserve their cultural identity for the reasons explored above. One was that they always maintained caste endogamy, making caste as important a feature in the organization of East African society as in Britain at present.

In East Africa, they became economically prosperous in the post-war period, albeit within the middle range of the three-tier system. They had moved from being skilled artisans indentured to build the railways to successful entrepreneurs, middle and high-level administrators, and technicians. By the 1960s, the community was highly-skilled, educated, and fairly prosperous. It was also urbanized, being concentrated in a handful of towns, since Asians were prevented from taking part in the agricultural economy. As a consequence, by the time members of it moved to Britain, they were already well-versed in handling some British institutions because they had migrated from one urban environment to another. The policy of Africanization had most affected the public and private sector employees. These were the Asians who moved to Britain and who were by the early 1960s transferring part of their incomes to banks here in response to the political instability of East Africa.

THREE

The East African Sikh community in Britain

The previous chapter has dealt with the background of the East African Asians in Africa, to show that those who have migrated to the UK belong to an established community, part of which has transplanted itself here.

This chapter will focus on the characteristics and structure of the East African Sikh community, to show that they have become a minority within a much larger Sikh one that was already in existence before their arrival in Britain. As a result, there has been a reversal in the position they held in East Africa, where they themselves formed the majority Sikh community.

One consequence of this contact with non-East African Sikhs from whom they differ in relation to class and caste, has been a definite emphasis on their 'East Africanness' and also their 'Ramgarhianess'. Not only have they become more conscious of their more middle-class position, being prosperous settlers, but also of their Ramgarhia caste status which is traditionally inferior to that of the dominant Sikh community in Britain, the Jats.

Differences related to their occupations in the past; to their urban experiences in Africa; to their orthodox views of Sikhism; and to their cultural conservatism manifest themselves most prominently in areas like Southall and the Midlands, where contact with other Sikh groups is intense. The separate position maintained by East African Sikhs is obvious from their settlement patterns, their caste associations and temples, and their distinctive symbols, which are almost universally applicable to their being different from the directly migrant Asian groups.

Dispersed nature of the community

A feature of minority community settlement that is consistently mentioned in the literature is that of concentration in particular areas resulting in the formation of 'ghettos'. Anwar (1979: 11) in describing the Pakistani community emphasizes this, when he writes: 'extensive research shows that individuals with similar cultural origins tend to cluster together and thus become residentially segregated from the rest of society . . . it allows people with similar values to maintain their group norms to preserve a sense of ethnic identity and to feel a familiar social network.'

Such a situation does not apply to the East African population. Although a large number of East Africans have settled in London, they have in fact spread out into most of the large cities like Birmingham, Wolverhampton, Leeds, Coventry, and Cardiff. Unlike other South Asian minorities (Dahya 1973; Anwar 1979; Saifullah Khan 1976; Werbner 1979; Robinson 1981), they have not gone through the phase of concentrating in inner city areas on arrival here and then dispersing into the suburbs with increasing length of stay, but have tended to disperse on arrival. Some families have followed the chain migration pattern and have settled near close kinsmen, though not necessarily in areas with a high immigrant concentration. Their dispersal has been aided by their familiarity with urban institutions and greater command over the English language on arrival.

Although there are some areas where East Africans have clustered, they are in fact to be found in most London suburbs. Even in Southall, East Africans live in the surrounding areas and not always around the main centre. Southall is often generally talked about in derogatory and stereotyped terms, yet the facilities it provides are marvelled at. The general East African opinion is that it is a place to visit and have fun in, but not to live in. For this reason, people travel from all over London and other areas outside Southall, to shop and attend functions organized by kinsmen and friends.

East African Sikhs are aware of the fact that they are more adventurous about setting up home away from their relatives and from other immigrants in comparison with the Sikhs from India, who have tended to live in areas with a large immigrant population, i.e. close to either their kinsmen or to other Sikhs. A large number of East

African Sikhs have never initially moved into such areas and still maintain superficial contact with them. They say that they prefer to maintain a distance because they are in this way not involved in the petty quarrels of related families and can therefore lead their own individual lives without their behaviour being monitored by kinsmen. It is nonetheless considered important to have relatives within driving distance in case of emergencies.

Some of the families who had on arrival in this country lived with their more settled kinsmen have stayed within the same area, but have bought their houses at a distance, for example, 5 miles away from their relations. This pattern is found consistently. For example, a set of related families of four brothers who all live in the same borough have the following pattern. One of the older brothers arrived in London in 1962, and was the first one to buy his house in the borough. Two of his younger brothers, who followed three years later, lived with him for a year and later bought a house jointly, at a distance of 4 miles, but within the same borough. The youngest of the two brothers went off to buy his own house two years later, some 5 miles away from the second brother. During this time, the oldest brother had arrived from Nairobi. He lived with the youngest brother for eight months and then bought his house 4 miles away. A similar pattern of kinsmen who all live in one area but are, in fact, dispersed all over the borough is a common occurrence. A number of the distant kinsmen of this set of brothers also live in the same borough, but again at a distance. At family occasions or at their religious ceremonies, their relations would gather not only from within the vicinity but also from a large number of other areas.

This aspect of the East African Sikhs was striking to me throughout my research. I would constantly meet people who were either related or were friends, but themselves lived in many different areas. Thus, even though the families are dispersed, they would, in fact, keep in touch with each other and know of the whereabouts of other East Africans. This is possible, first, because of their past contacts in East Africa and, second, because of large numbers of functions they attend in common. I shall develop this point presently, because a number of these contacts is not based on kinship.

This pattern of settlement in London is to an extent related to the one in East Africa. The majority of families I met in Southall were from

Nairobi, and also from particular parts of that city, such as the earliest Indian settlements of Landhia, Pangani, Eastleigh, Ngara, and River Road. Some of these areas contained the government quarters for Asians. As the East Africans moved up the job hierarchy into the European-held positions, so they moved up into the European housings areas of Parklands, South Nairobi, Westlands, Karen, etc. A similar pattern is reflected in London in relation to the areas East African Sikhs have chosen to live in. Families who live in the middle-class suburbs of London had already moved into more prosperous parts of Nairobi before emigrating to Britain because by that time they were occupying better positions in government services. These are also precisely the people who are now living in the more dispersed areas because most of these families had the resources to buy more expensive houses on arrival in London. In East Africa, household heads of the Southall families often occupied skilled and technical jobs which were rated much lower than the prestigious administrative jobs in East Africa.

Occupational structure

The East African Sikh community consists of skilled workers such as carpenters, factory staff at the lower level, office workers of all kinds, predominantly at the middle level of administration, and, finally, professionals and businessmen. A large number of the people in Southall are skilled workers for building concerns, as carpenters or are involved in factory work, partly because of the large amount of industry present in that area and partly because of the nature of the settlement pattern. East African Sikhs who on arrival in London lived with their relations in Southall often found it more attractive to work in factories as opposed to doing an office job because of higher factory wages. People who did not live in these industrial areas often did not get a chance to explore this avenue and went into office work right from the start. However, the majority of people who are office workers here are so because they were already involved in the administrative sectors of the government agencies in East Africa.

The office workers consist of clerical staff, secretaries and typists, executives at the higher level in organizations such as the Civil Service, the Local Authorities, the Post Office, banks, the Crown Agents, private firms, etc. The majority of East African Sikhs I met belonged to this category. Some of the middle-aged men who had worked in the public sector in Africa are working here at a level much lower than the one in East Africa. For example, one of my informants who had the position of the Chief Assistant Accountant of the East African Railways is employed as a clerical officer by the Civil Service. The reason for this is that such men have been prematurely retired from their first jobs in Africa and have had to find employment in another country at quite a late stage in their lives. These disadvantages account for their acceptance of lower-status jobs than the ones they were accustomed to. Also, these men felt that they had received a hostile reception when they applied for office jobs because of their colour and also their turbans. A number of the private firms had never employed turbanned Sikhs before.

The younger more highly-qualified men also work for government concerns, but they have also diverted into a large number of fields and a more varied range of organizations. They are often in more technical fields, working as engineers, architects, electricians, draughtsmen, and a whole range of occupations connected with the building and construction industry. I refer here to men who are mostly over the age of thirty-five, who are more educated than the older ones and who have sometimes acquired part of their qualifications in this country. Also East African Sikhs have produced a large number of professionals especially in three fields: medicine, architecture, and engineering. Within these fields there are endless varieties of types of doctors, engineers, etc. A number of the senior Registrars and Consultants in British hospitals who are Sikhs are from East Africa. The two Indian QCs, one of whom is now a Circuit Judge, are East Africans, although one of them is not a Ramgarhia.

In general, although the younger men are diversifying into a greater range of fields like pharmacy, photography, accountancy, biochemistry, business management, etc., the traditional professions of medicine and engineering are by far the most popular and prestigious. Enormous importance is placed on acquiring professional qualifications. High-status people within the community are not the businessmen but the professionals. This is important in terms of marriage because the most desirable grooms are the turbanned professional men, not the sons of the rich businessmen, the majority of whom have not acquired professional qualifications.

East African Sikhs are increasingly opening their own businesses. The most popular of these are travel agencies, and businesses dealing with cars and related products. There are at the moment a large number of spare parts shops, garages dealing with car repairs and maintenance, and car retailing. The wealthiest of the East African businessmen I met were involved in these types of businesses. They are also opening supermarkets, chemist shops, confectionery and newsagency shops, electrical goods stores, etc. This is a fairly recent development. East Africans have always had an interest in the building trade and for this reason there are a number of small-scale building contractors within the community.

The majority of East African Sikh women go out to work.[1] Those who had been educated up until the 'O' Level stage in East Africa are mostly involved in some form of office work, as clerical assistants, secretaries, typists, etc. Ancillary medical professions like radiography, nursing, and physiotherapy, are also popular among women.[2] Most of this also applies to younger women, but they are also increasingly entering a wider range of occupations. Although there is interest in educating girls at least until first degree level, it is still uncommon to find professional women either in numbers similar to that of the men, or in terms of the level of qualifications the men have achieved.

To summarize, it should be emphasized that migration to Britain has been selective of a particular category of East African Sikhs – government staff. Professionals and businessmen form another group, but the majority of the latter chose to stay behind in East Africa. In this country this pattern has been further reproduced. The majority of East African Sikhs either work in offices or are involved in the building industry, both as professionals and as skilled workers. The community is known for its large category of professionals which is rapidly being expanded because of the emphasis on higher education. Also, there is a developing interest at present in setting up one's own business.

Financial advantages

It has already been stated that the majority of East Africans had worked for government concerns in East Africa, with a few having their own businesses which they sold before migrating to Britain. It had been possible for them to accumulate a certain amount of capital in East Africa because most people who worked in the public sector did not own any form of property. There were several reasons for this.

One was that housing was free, as it went with the job. The situation has been reversed in this country because people tend to buy their own homes.[3] The other important factor was that the uncertainty created by political instability in East Africa since the late 1950s prevented South Asians from investing there because they were a particularly vulnerable category. The consequence of the volatile environment of that time was that people were already thinking of migrating. A number had explored the possibilities of sending money abroad to a European country. Some had already established accounts with certain banks and building societies in the UK which had branches in East Africa to facilitate house buying and banking in this country. In this way they were already channelling part of their incomes and savings into the UK prior to arrival in this country. This was especially so among the people who arrived in the late 1960s and early 1970s, because, by then, some East Africans had already established themselves in this country. Therefore, they could pass on information about the problems of settling here, for example, information about dealing with the financial institutions and about generally getting around in London.

The majority of East Africans had some property in India because that is where their savings were being sent during the earlier stages of their stay in Africa. At that time, it was generally thought that they would return to settle there, because that was considered to be home. The second generation of East Africans did not think in these terms because their ties with India had weakened considerably. They were settled in Africa and that is where their savings were retained.

All East Africans had some form of permanent employment in East Africa. This meant that they had a regular source of income which helped to build up their savings and that could be used directly on arrival in this country. On top of this, the majority were given some compensation for having their jobs Africanized, and have pensions paid to them in this country. Their pensions, their previous savings plus their incomes from their second jobs in Britain have given East African Sikhs certain financial advantages in this country. For this reason they have been able to buy their own homes soon after arrival in this country because they have had the capital to do so. Unlike immigrants who have migrated directly from India and Pakistan, East African Asians have not been through a period of austere living in order to remit a maximum amount of money abroad, especially during the early stages of settlement. Hence, they have settled down rapidly, because migration to the UK was thought of as a permanent move. In material terms, they have rapidly established a standard of living close to the one they were accustomed to, minus the domestic servants and the big houses.[4] Also, their incomes from their jobs in Britain have helped them to retain some of their previous savings. This is possible because the majority of them have their dependants within Britain because they have arrived in family units. This has released them from diverting their savings abroad to support dependants.

Influence of family units

Arrival in family units is of vital importance in explaining the social organization of East African Sikhs, because it is one of the reasons which has accounted for the rapid establishment of an East African community in the UK. One consequence of arrival in family units is that old parents and grandparents are all present within the family, and as in the traditional household in the Punjab, grandparents and grandchildren still have the same intense relationships. This differs from other ethnic minorities, where aged parents and the young children are often left behind in their villages of origin.[5] The presence of old people makes it easier to transmit cultural norms to the young ones; it was very common to see grandparents talking to their grandchildren about life in villages in India, and about the problems of living in East Africa during the early days of settlement. Stories and legends about the Sikh gurus were constantly being recounted, sometimes with little success, because comics and television pro-grammes seemed to be more important to the children. However, in the households that had grandparents, the children could always converse in fluent Punjabi from a very young age. This was not true of the children who have spent a large part of their lives in this country without grandparents, and who have been cut off from the main centres of the Sikh population.

During weddings, the women would constantly turn to grand-mothers to find out about the procedure for conducting particular rituals. Thus, old people help to perpetuate the customs the East Africans had come with from India. This is one of the reasons for the existence of a number of traditional ceremonies still being practised by the East Africans, even though the 'modern' Indian Sikhs in India have abandoned them. The latter consider the East Africans to be very orthodox, especially in relation to their marriage practices.

The completeness of the family unit is one factor which plays an important role in maintaining the conservatism of the East African Sikhs. Pressure can be put on people to conform by a large number of people within the UK because East Africans conduct their social life with others and their status models are within the society in Britain. There is no traditionalist audience present in the Punjab or in East Africa to influence their behaviour here. The presence of relatives within the UK combined with the strong network of East African contacts act as an excellent control.

East African Sikhs not only have their immediate family present in this country but also most of the kinsmen whom they consider to be important. Often the genealogically close kinsmen like the FB (father's brother), MB (mother's brother), MS (mother's sister), etc. who have never left India will not come into the category of close kinsmen because of the lack of contact with them during their stay in Africa and the UK. East Africans tend not to go back to India regularly to cement and reaffirm these ties. This especially applies to the younger generation. Hence, important kinsmen are those ones who have lived in East Africa, even though these may be distantly-related kinsmen and not important in the traditional set-up.

Another consequence of arriving in family units is that women have arrived at the same time as the men. This is important in relation to marriage because women are precisely the people who know about social customs (*rasam-rawaz*), i.e. procedures of conducting life-cycle rituals, the gifts to be exchanged at marriage etc. This knowledge plays an important part in retaining the traditional identity of the East African Sikhs. The other striking aspect of the East African women is that the majority of them go out to work and have done so since arrival in this country. Most women did not work outside their homes in East Africa which meant that they did not have an independent source of income of their own. The few women who worked there were either in the teaching profession or in one of the medical fields, with some in white-collar jobs. These women were mainly under the age of forty years. Although it was quite common for other women to work outside their homes in East Africa, it was unusual for so many of them to work. Their situation in Britain is a complete contrast to that of directly migrant women, the majority of whom are from rural areas and were not wage earners prior to migration. Women's incomes have further added on to the financial advantages of the East African Sikhs.

Arrival in family units includes young people of a variety of ages within the community. The importance of having such a cross-section of young people in relation to marriage is that there is a pool of people from which to find spouses. There is, therefore, neither the need to go to India to get married, nor that to import fiancés from there. Only in rare cases do East Africans resort to India to find spouses for their children. These are cases of girls who acquire a bad reputation, or are not considered to be good-looking. I met few young men for whom wives had to be found from India. The East African communications network helps to prevent the importation of fiancés from the sub-continent because, first, their contacts here can be activated to help them find spouses, and, second, they openly express their disapproval of such activities because they can marry amongst themselves.

To summarize, I have explored the consequences of arrival in family units and the financial advantages of the East Africans. Since the families are complete, there are no dependants to support outside the UK. Second, there are often a number of incomes within a family. Women and old people who were previously dependent on the household heads now either contribute to the household budgets or support themselves, because they have independent incomes of their own. All this has led to a general increase in the earnings of the East African families which is partly responsible for the increase in the dowry system. A consequence of the more balanced age and sex ratio of the East African Sikh community is that of having young people of all ages within this country, which makes it possible for them to restrict their marriage circles to the community already resident here.

The strong communications network

The fact that the East African Sikh community was already an established one before its members moved to the UK has been crucial in helping them establish a strong communications network here. The contacts developed in the past are precisely the ones they use at present.

In this section, I shall focus on the role of the temples and also the many religious ceremonies that are individually organized, to demonstrate that they help perpetuate the existing network of East African relationships, but also strengthen communication links by incorporating new contacts.

The 'religiousness' of the East African Sikhs and their ability to organize themselves rapidly to build temples is commented on frequently, especially by direct migrants from the sub-continent. East African Sikhs have been initiators of the *gurdwara* movements and have been responsible for generating a greater interest among the Indian Sikhs in the Sikh religion. Before their arrival in the mid-1960s, properly-conducted religious ceremonies were almost non-existent even though Indian Sikhs had been in this country a long time before East African migration began. Since their arrival, temples are being run more efficiently and there has been a dramatic increase in temple attendance. The reason for the rapid growth in the number of temples in Britain is partly connected with the links they have established in the past which can be further activated in this country. On top of this they have knowledge acquired in East Africa which enables them to make a success of such ventures. Most of them are well-versed in the scriptures and know precisely how a ceremony should be conducted. This is considered to be common knowledge by East Africans, as opposed to the Indian Sikhs who seem to know less about religious affairs, leaving them to the expertise of the religious specialist or *giani*. It is common to find a *Guru Granth Sahib* (the Sikh holy book) in East African homes; thus, they have miniature temples inside their homes by converting a room where the holy book can be kept. Prayers organized on a basis similar to that of the communal temples are conducted in a vast number of East African homes every day. The women, especially, are already experienced in religious affairs from their East African-based knowledge, and are often the ones responsible for looking after the temples in their homes. They have a huge number of *satsangs* of their own.

Once a temple is established, it attracts people from a large number of areas. East African families constantly grumble about the large number of religious ceremonies and other occasions that they have to attend, almost every other weekend. Despite all the complaints few stop attending them. The younger people refer to this as an obsession their parents have for attending 'religious functions'. They are not area-focused, with people travelling from all over London and outside it. Relatives will especially travel to other towns if a close kinsman has organized a ceremony.

The temple is an important feature of the East African Sikh community, because the occasions that are organized there bring together a large number of people from different areas. On top of this, within East African homes people organize their own functions which make use of temple personnel. There is an overlap of people who attend these functions, because most East Africans have a common set of friends and relations. Although kinship links are important to them, equally important are their ties with the East African community or, as they say, the 'East African *log*'. It is for this reason that people tend to associate with a large number of people beyond their immediate kin. Access to other East Africans is facilitated through the temple functions which are really products of the already existing pool of relationships developed in East Africa. Thus, they are less kin-orientated and more community-orientated. I rarely heard words like *bhaiband* and *biradari* (brotherhood) to describe the people with whom East Africans interacted. More important seemed to be that the people they should associate with are from East Africa. This is not to say that kinship relations are not important, because on specific occasions like marriages, relatives do gather together and kinship terms of address, are then used. But kinship ties are less important in their daily lives and the general decision making. This may be due to the fact that the majority of East African families are nuclear ones and relatives often live at a distance. On top of this, I would frequently meet people who had a set of relatives with whom they did not interact because of a past quarrel, yet both parties seem to function quite efficiently without each other within their own social scene. All this questions the commonly-held stereotype that South Asians tend to reside mainly in joint or extended families.

In the following, I shall illustrate what I mean by the overlap of contact between East Africans and the strong communications network. For example, a travel agent's family who was within my core sample was known to eleven of the thirteen families in my sample. However, it took me well over nine months in the field to figure this out. My landlady knew of the travel agent's family because she and her parents had lived in the same set of railway quarters in Nairobi as did the travel agent's wife's parents. Thus they were practically brought up together and attended the same temple (Landhia). In this country, the travel agent's wife is in the same *kirtan* and prayer group as my landlady's eldest sister, so they go to temple functions together. This is typical of people who already knew each other in East Africa and who have maintained contact in this country. Some of the other families within my core sample knew this family because the travel agent himself is a member of the local association. Not only do people know of his activities in this country but his past background in East Africa. For example, one of the sons of a family within my core sample had worked with the travel agent in the same airline office in Nairobi. At that time he did not have a successful business of his own. Although he lives in Hounslow, I met a large number of families outside the area who had known him in East Africa and who met his family at the many weddings they attend in common. During the marriage season, I met his family at five weddings, three of which were at the Shepherd's Bush temple. None of these weddings were of a member of their kin group, but they had been invited because they had known either the bride's or the groom's family in East Africa.

The example mentioned above is typical of an East African family which is known to other East Africans because of the common functions they attend and the previous contacts they had in East Africa. This pattern occurred all the time. I would observe that most East African Sikhs can in some way trace each other even if they do not know a specific individual or family on the first meeting. They always find out later by asking a friend or relation, and the person concerned will be put rapidly into context. This quick recognition by East African Sikhs living in this country by reference to their past background was extremely striking because the community is like one big family: everyone can easily be fitted into a map of relationships and friendships.

In the above, the contacts of one family have been described. I will now refer to an event which brought together East Africans Sikhs from all walks of life and from different areas, to illustrate the close-knit nature of the community. This was the funeral of one of the oldest of the East African Sikh men in the UK who had been active in the Ramgarhia movement in East Africa since its beginnings. His sons and grandchildren all live in the same borough and are prominent in an association there. This old man had worked for the railways in Africa. He had been responsible for starting a dispensary in Nairobi to provide free medical care for Sikhs, and he had helped to set up Sikh schools and scholarships for bright children. News of his death spread quickly among East African Sikhs on the day it happened. I heard about it in Southall from the families who associated with the Southall Temple during the evening because one of them had been to a wedding where the news had already spread. By then, not only had most of the Southall families heard of it but some had already been to the old man's sons' households to pay their respects. Prayers had already been started at the local temple. East Africans from as far afield as Kent, Croydon, and Lewisham, and the families that I was acquainted with in Ealing (i.e. outside my main sample) were already beginning to attend these prayers, which were concluded on the funeral day some three days later. Most of these people had found out either through the temple or through their friends and relatives who had phoned to inform them of the news. On the day of the funeral, East African Sikhs turned up from all over Britain. There was a mix of professionals, factory workers, businessmen, and administrators. Any East African who wished could attend the funeral because no invitations were sent out. This was not considered odd because on a sad occasion it is customary to visit the bereaved household, even if only to sit and listen to the prayers that have been started in the household. Thus 'community feeling' cuts across kinship ties and was based on the relationships that had been built over the long stay in Africa. A positive effort is made to maintain these links. An East African Sikh is extremely hospitable to another East African even when there is no direct tie of friendship or kinship.

The communications network and the regular contact the East African Sikhs maintain through the temple has enormous implications for marriage. For example, people do not have to rely on their kinship network to help them find spouses for their children. Since there is frequent contact with other East Africans, word passes around quickly once the young people are of age to be married or have come 'into the market', i.e. as soon as they have started work or are at a stage when their studies have been, or are about to be, completed. Around this period, they make a concerted effort to attend public functions to be 'seen'. Such functions initiate marriage alliances because people find out about the availability of eligible young men and women and also widen the arena from which marriage partners can be selected. A go-between is not required but there is a preference for a close relative or friend of either spouse to vet the families and start proceedings before the core members of the families actually meet. Thus, spouses can be selected on a more individual basis because people move around freely among East African Sikh circles and so the bond of the kinship network is not so powerful.

Another important function of the temple is that it brings together people from all walks of life. It has been stated earlier that East African Sikhs attend a number of temples within London although they may attend one more frequently because it is in their area. For example, Shepherd's Bush Temple is attended by people from all over London and it is considered to be the 'smart' temple. It is at the temple that professional people can meet skilled workers or, to use an extreme example, a carpenter has access to a QC. There is a mix of people interacting with one another on common ground. Even though people do not have the time to visit each other's homes, especially in London where they live far apart, they can keep in touch with a large range of people, some of whom they do not know well enough to invite into their homes. I refer here to the large number of people who East African Sikhs know but who are neither close relatives nor friends, i.e. people with whom they have been acquainted for a long period. It is precisely this interaction by East Africans with other East Africans that gives them a powerful system of communication.

To sum up, East African Sikhs are intensely religious and have provided the impetus for the interest that has been generated in religious affairs within the general Sikh community, over the last decade. They have thus acquired the reputation for being '*gurdwara*-orientated' since they are greatly concerned about affairs related to these organizations. Their vast previous contacts help them to muster the support needed to initiate the building of temples and other such projects. The relationship of the temple has been examined in relation to the wider community because it is such an important feature of the East African community and acts as a centre which brings together a large number of East African Sikhs from different backgrounds. It also helps to strengthen an already existing set of contacts which have helped create a powerful communications network in this country. This is particularly important for the women of the community, in contrast to Muslim women who are much more homebound.

The consequence of not having a 'Myth of Return'

In this section, I shall deal with a characteristic of the East African Sikhs which particularly distinguishes them from the other 'Asian minorities', and which is crucial to the social organization of the community. This is that all the families that I come across during my fieldwork have no desire to return, to visit or live in, their place of origin or 'roots'. In fact, there was never any mention of returning to a 'homeland'. There is talk of migrating further to the USA and Canada among some families, but never of returning to the Punjab to retire and enjoy the property that the majority of East Africans hold there. This is also now the case among other South Asian groups, especially the younger generation.

The property they own in India is that they have built with the earnings they had from East Africa at a time when they too were 'home-orientated' and had every intention of returning to settle in the Punjab. However, over their long stay in Africa, the Punjab became increasingly distant. Even by the 1940s, East African Sikhs were beginning to build houses and businesses in East Africa because their prestige and status scales were no longer in the Punjab, but within the African community.

By the time the East Africans moved to the UK, ties with India were minimal, in the sense that India was visited only occasionally for short holidays to meet kinsmen, and especially to shop. Even from Britain, East Africans go for such visits, but make the same comments about India on their return, i.e. 'it is nice to be there for a short period and shopping is fun' but that there is 'filth, corruption, adulteration of food, bad transport facilities, nosy, interfering relatives' and so on. Only rarely did I hear the Punjab's cultural heritage being talked about. Their attitude is that 'the only culture the Punjab has is agriculture'. In fact, the constant topic of conversation is the difference between their lives in Africa and the UK from that of the Sikhs in India. East African Sikhs are supposed to be decent and hospitable towards one another: their children are considered to be less knowledgeable about handling family relationships in comparison with the Indian children who have been brought up in joint families and have learnt of the power relationships within them. The Punjab is talked about in derogatory terms by the majority of East African Sikhs, except by the old people, who remember nostalgically the comforts of village life as it was when they left India in their youth. However, they talk positively about their stay in Africa as a time that was both happy and prosperous for them. Again, this is sentimental talk, emphasizing the 'easy' lives they led. Yet, I never came across any East African Sikh family who wished to return either to East Africa or to India; there is no feeling that ultimately they will be returning to their places of origin. In fact, second generation East Africans are hardly bothered about any assets in the Punjab. There is no continuing 'myth of return'.

This particular aspect has a crucial influence on East African Sikh society. The published material on the ethnic minorities has always emphasized the importance of the 'home background' of the immigrants in determining their behaviour in this country. Their actions were supposed to be geared to the reaction of the inhabitants of their places of origin. The status hierarchies they were involved in were the ones in their homelands, visited at regular intervals to display the newly-acquired wealth from abroad. Also the comforts and luxuries at home were compared to the harsh and unfriendly atmosphere in Britain. Settlement abroad was seen to be a temporary phase, at least initially. It was supposed to be a period of spartan living to accumulate savings to be channelled into the homelands to build properties there. There has often been an assumption that in the end they would return to their homes. This is obvious from the existing material on the ethnic minorities in the UK and from descriptions of their areas of origin in the sub-continent (Aurora 1967; Dahya 1973; John 1969; Ballard 1973, 1983; Ballard and

Ballard 1977; Saifullah Khan 1977; Helweg 1979, 1983; Robinson 1981, 1984).

None of this applies to the East African Sikhs, whose past experiences have taught them that they cannot return to the Punjab. The typical remarks which I heard over and over again are that: 'We built property in the Punjab; what did we get out it? Our relatives have eaten it up, or it has decayed. We have been beaten once, and have made our mistakes, but we won't let it happen again.' The common stories are that they had built houses in the Punjab which had been fully furnished by the women with all the prestigious 'imported' household goods bought in Africa, in the hope that they would retire in comfort and be able to use their homes on their shorter visits to India. These houses would be locked up and the furnishings would be packed into trunks on returning to Africa. East African Sikhs constantly complain that their interfering relatives had broken the locks and had not only made use of their properties but had also stolen their personal belongings. Hence, the properties had either decayed or are still in the process of doing so through not being inhabited or through kinsmen taking them over without their consent. All this was already happening during their time in Africa. As a result, they have realized the uselessness of building properties in the Punjab.

The other common occurrence among East African Sikhs was that many of them had left Africa to settle in India but had returned either there or had re-migrated straight to Britain within a short period. The reason for this is that they had been unsuccessful in finding employment or in setting up in their own businesses. For example, an informant within my core sample had migrated to India from Kenya. In partnership with his brother-in-law, he had set up a workshop making spare parts for sewing machines. The business lost heavily right from the start because he found it impossible to function within that system never having been either a part of it previously or having dealt with 'the corruption and underhand means of doing business'. He re-migrated to the United Kingdom within a couple of years.

The example mentioned above is a common one. Within my core sample of thirteen families, something similar had happened to eight of them. After retiring from Africa they had gone to India, but had returned, having wasted their hard-earned savings on trying to survive without a permanent income to support them. They had lost large sums of money on various business enterprises because they did not have the 'know-how' of the Indians who reside there permanently and are able to cope with them. As a result they found it difficult to penetrate the existing network of business relationships. Knowledge acquired from such experiences seems to have made them all the more certain that they are here to stay, and that they have no 'roots'.

The consequences in cultural terms of not having a sense of belonging to a particular place, of being neither East African nor Indian, are often talked about, especially by the younger generation of Sikhs. For this reason, during periods of racial tension invoked by particular incidents, there is little talk of returning home. Although such times are very straining, the assumption is that they will have to stick it out in Britain and see themselves through any hostile period. However, some young people do talk of migrating further, to the USA or Canada, and this trend is already underway.

One of the effects of never having had a 'myth of return' in the British context is that it has released them from the control exercised by a home community. This has given them freedom of action, because decisions are made individually in relation to the society here. Since East African Sikhs are dispersed over a large number of areas, everyday life can be conducted very much according to the individual's taste, although close relatives with whom they have regular contact do have some influence as do the East African circuits that have been established all over Britain. However, their influence is not as strong as that of the close-knit community in East Africa in the past where Sikhs clustered in the Asian areas.

Since East African Sikhs maintain strong links with each other and have relatives and acquaintances all over the place, gossip and news spreads quickly over large parts of the UK. This is one reason for their conservatism, because the audience to which their actions are geared is in this country. Since they circulate almost exclusively within East African Sikh spheres, this in fact helps to perpetuate their conservatism because the people they most want to emulate are other better-endowed British East Africans.

The other consequence of not having had a 'myth of return' in the UK, and of remaining within East African Sikh circles, is that any identity crisis among the younger generation can be sorted out with relative ease within the context of this country. For example, young

Sikh men who rebel against wearing a turban and keeping their long hair can soon be made to realize that the majority of other East African Sikh men wearing a turban manage to function quite efficiently within the wider society, so why shouldn't they? A conscious effort is made by parents to introduce their children to successful turbanned Sikhs who can be emulated and who can help to pressurize their children into maintaining the Sikh symbols. Also, contact with other young Sikhs, because of good links helps sort out such crises. Unlike Indian Sikhs, who used to forgo the Sikh symbols in the UK and then resume them as soon as they were in the Punjab, the general East African Sikh feeling has always been that they should not let go their Sikhism and give up their symbols because they are in the UK to stay. The absence of ties to a homeland has not diminished interest in retaining identity and religious beliefs, because of the presence of their monitoring groups in this country; orthodoxy is thus perpetuated.

Despite their traditionalist attitudes, they are progressive in other ways. For example, East African Sikh women (or indeed Sikh women in general) have a considerable degree of freedom compared with Muslim and non wage-earning women, who are more home-bound. This was clear from the recent marches to the Indian High Commission protesting against the military invasion of the Golden Temple in June 1984. The British media indeed focused on the huge and vociferous presence of the women. Nor is there any *purdah* system, nor any clear-cut segregation of the two sexes. Men and women talk quite freely to each other in public. This permeates to the young people. Both young men and women are expected to become educated and have successful careers in Britain while maintaining the Sikh symbols and keeping an active interest in the Sikh religion.

To conclude, the East African Sikhs did not have a 'myth of return'. As a result, they were orientated to living in this country permanently. This lack of interest in returning to a homeland accelerated the process of not only establishing links in this country, but also of cementing ties that had already been formulated in the past during their stay in Africa. This has helped create an expansive communications network. A consequence of not having had a 'myth of return' is that East African Sikhs tended to retain their resources in this country, from the beginning.

East African traditionalism and Ramgarhia consciousness

The 'Ramgarhianess' and 'East Africanness' of the East African Sikhs is particularly clearly projected in Southall where the Ramgarhia movement initially gained momentum. It is here that they first came into contact with other Sikhs, predominantly Jats who had migrated directed from India and Malaysia and who formed the majority Sikh population. The people now active in running all the Ramgarhia Associations and indeed many other temples are, in fact, East African Sikhs. According to the Indian Sikhs, effective temple organization is a definitive East African Sikh characteristic. They also stress that the majority of Sikhs in Britain before the arrival of Ramgarhias were clean-shaven. In fact, the few Ramgarhias around at this time also cut off their hair. One of them told me:

> 'When I first came to this country, there weren't any Ramgarhia families around. We used to live like the Jats because they were the only Sikhs we knew. We used to work with them, we went to the pubs with them, we drank heavily, we started to talk like they did, and we cut off our hair because they had done so. Also, because it was difficult for turbanned men to get jobs. Since the East Africans have arrived, we have associated with them and have started to go to the temple.'

This person is, in fact, a founder member of the Ramgarhia movement, who now wears a turban, as do all his sons. He is a vegetarian and does not drink any more, thus observing stricter dietary rules in accordance with the Sikh religion. He is active in the temple committee and went through the initiation ceremony a second time during the development of the Ramgarhia movement. Thus, he says, he has 'completely reformed himself'.

This is a pattern that I have come across frequently, and it is a constant theme of conversation among East African Sikhs. Men who were formerly clean-shaven and who never associated themselves with temple affairs are now staunch Sikhs. The majority of East African men wear turbans. This is a source of great pride for them because their distinctive style of turban (referred to as the *pag*) is the 'hallmark' of an East African Sikh. It distinguishes him from an Indian Sikh and makes the East Africanness of the wearer obvious. An East African can distinguish between an Indian Sikh and an East African one, even if they are 'miles off'. The Indian Sikh turban lacks a point at the top and is often in a printed or coloured material. The East African Sikh, on the other hand, nearly always wears a white turban with a point, though some of the younger men do wear plain-coloured shades, such as black, navy, brown, maroon and grey. I am told that the reason white is a popular shade is that during the Second World War it was hard to find printed fabrics in East Africa because of the restriction on imports. It was during this time that the white turban was worn extensively, initiating the trend that has persisted up until now.

I should mention here an example of the importance of the white turban as a distinguishing mark for an East African. A smart informant who is an Indian Sikh wears a white turban in the East African style because he has made East African friends in the UK. East Africans have often gone up to speak to him, thinking he is one of them, and have been confused on realizing that he has no connection with Africa. They soon drop him from the conversation. Thus, for an East African Sikh, a white turban is an important symbol of group identity.

The greater emphasis on maintaining external Sikh symbols, and the religiosity of the East Africans,[6] runs parallel to the positive perpetuation of their Ramgarhia identity, especially obvious in Southall. On the whole, only Ramgarhias attend Ramgarhia temples; thus their caste status is clearly represented. The Singh Sabha Temple, on the other hand, attracts all kinds of Sikhs, irrelevant of caste, though it is mainly Jat-based. This also applies to the Ramgarhia Association, though the simple fact is that if the name of the caste group appears in the title of the association, it is almost automatic that only members of that caste will attend it.

It is clear that non-Jat Sikhs from India, including Indian Ramgarhias were far more aware of their caste position in the UK, especially in relation to the caste system in India, because they have actually lived there. For that reason, they are more conscious that their caste status is inferior to that of the Jats. East Africans, on the other hand, are extremely aware of their 'East Africanness' (and in Southall their 'Ramgarhianess') but were not so aware of the traditional position of Ramgarhias in a caste hierarchy because they have been away from India for a long time. Their caste status was not as important to them in East Africa because there was no caste system there to fit into. Thus, although the word 'Ramgarhia' gained currency in Africa, 'Ramgarhianess' was not thought of in derogatory terms because it was not related to a caste hierarchy in which Ramgarhias ranked lower than the Jats, but was propagated positively in terms of achievements and wealth.

The reason the Ramgarhia identity is being perpetuated so strongly in Southall is that there is already a well-established Jat population in existence, forming a majority of Sikhs. Ramgarhias who knew nothing of their caste status have found that contact with the Jats and other castes from India has made them aware of their origins, because they are constantly being asked to define not only their caste, but also the region they came from in the Punjab.

Many Ramgarhias say that no-one cared for this in East Africa. They assumed that they were all Sikhs and the issue of caste never arose because East African Sikhs were predominantly Ramgarhias. The Jat population there was strong, though numerically much smaller. It was a very different picture from the one in the UK. In Southall, even young children have been teased by Jat children about their caste. They have been told that they are '*Guli-Karas*' (*Guli* is part of the plough made of wood and also an implement used in a game called *Guli-danda*). The Jats in the villages used to get the Tarkhans (one group of the Ramgarhias) to make this piece of equipment for them. The children have questioned their parents as a result, and they in turn had to find answers for them. In this way, Ramgarhias have been made aware of their identity as a caste in a hierarchy.

The interesting situation in the UK is that there are a number of Sikh castes present which have come here from different parts of India and the world. For example, there are Jats from Malaysia, Singapore, and India; Chamars and Bhatras from India; Khatris from Rwalpindi; and Ramgarhias from East Africa. There was little contact or competition in Africa from any other Sikh caste group, but in the UK, there is a complete reversal of the East African situation because the Ramgarhias no longer hold a majority position and they are increasingly becoming aware of this. During their stay in Africa, their awareness of their caste level blurred considerably. Thus, young Ramgarhias I met outside Southall have not been aware of the fact that they are Ramgarhias. But they are certainly aware of their 'East Africanness' and consider themselves to be more 'refined' and 'progressive' than Sikhs from India, but this is never articulated in terms of caste, but in relation to their middle-class position. Yet the Ramgarhias who have had contact with other castes, as in Southall, are quite aware of their own.

I should re-state the following: first, Ramgarhias in the UK are mainly Sikhs from East Africa. The Southall Ramgarhia Association is controlled and attended mainly by East Africans. Second, they have tended to make associations which are private organizations and which can select their members. Third, Ramgarhias are in a minority in Britain and have migrated at a much later stage than the Jats, a large number of whom have been present in Britain since the Second World War. Fourth, they have become more acutely aware of their caste status, i.e. 'Ramgarhianess', since their arrival in the UK, due to contact with Sikhs from India who are mainly working class and belong to different caste groups. Their East Africanness, projected through their middle-classness, is also a reaction against their classification by the indigenous white population as 'Pakis' or Hindus, with whom they on the whole do not associate.

Conclusion

This chapter has examined some of the features of the East African Sikh community in the UK to show that although it is geographically dispersed, this does not hinder the strength of community feeling that has been generated here due to connections developed in East Africa. It is a society that is linked by all kinds of relationships formulated in the past.

East African Sikhs have previously worked for the same organizations, their children have been to a handful of schools, and their families have been linked by marriage alliances and through their businesses. These links have not only determined their occupational structure in the UK, but have also resulted in a network of contacts which has given them enormous organizational ability. The strength of their East African relationships has helped them establish a strong communications network here which, combined with their religious orthodoxy has led them to become initiators of *gurdwara* movements, thus helping them to rapidly establish temples. In so doing, they have provided the impetus for a greater interest in Sikhism through the injection of religious orthodoxy, traditionalism, and also in maintaining more external symbols amongst the general Sikh community than had previously existed.

Furthermore, East Africans have arrived in the UK in complete family units, which has ruled out the need to support dependants abroad. This gives them certain financial advantages on top of those acquired as a result of having had their jobs Africanized, i.e. their pensions and compensation. The presence of families in the UK also allows them to restrict their marriage circles to those East African Sikhs already resident here since there is a large pool of young Sikhs to select from. This has eased the process of spouse selection which is aided enormously by the balanced age profile of the community.

An important feature that combines with the arrival in family units is their lack of 'home orientation', since ties with India had weakened considerably during their stay in Africa. Unlike the other Asian minorities, this has in the East African case, ruled out any control that may be exercised by an audience abroad. A consequence of not having had a 'myth of return' on arrival is that they can retain their resources in this country. These are reflected in their immediate interest in improving their homes on arrival here; in moving to 'bigger and better' houses in the more prosperous suburbs, and in buying consumer durables. Thus, they indulge in conspicuous consumption that is particularly obvious at marriages. Their financial advantages and the increased earning powers of their women have resulted in the elaboration of their marriage and dowry system which represents a facet of their East African identity which has become all the more prominent in the UK.

For the first time since migration to East Africa, they have come into contact with a dominant Jat Sikh population, which has made them more conscious of their different class position and caste status, and whose Indian experiences differ considerably from those shared by East Africans. As a consequence of their minority position greater stress has been placed on their 'East Africanness' and 'Ramgarhianess', which are projected positively in terms of their wealth, education, urban sophistication, and more stringent adherence to Sikhism and ritual procedures. This separateness is further perpetuated through their shared symbols, their lifestyles, forms of dress, their associations, and the exclusive East African circles in which they move. Thus, they maintain their group identity, which can be observed from their marriages, which emphasize their differences from that of Indian Sikhs and other South Asians who have migrated directly from their countries of origin.

FOUR

Internal organization of the community

The previous chapter has presented a general picture of the important characteristics of the East African Ramgarhia Sikh community in the UK. This chapter will examine the internal organization of the community by focusing on my universe of study, the basis of which is my sample of families.[1] It will describe the occupations of household heads in the UK as related to those they had in East Africa; the periods of their arrival in this country; their housing situation; and their family organization. I shall also look into the role of East African women, to emphasize their independence and their strong orientation towards working outside their homes. The significance of these factors will become clearer in the ensuing chapters on marriage and dowry.

Occupations of the household heads

I have stated in previous chapters that the Sikhs in East Africa had worked for a handful of organizations, such as the Railways, Public Works Department, the Post Office, the major banks, and private building contractors. As can be seen from *Table 1*, eighteen out of the thirty-one household heads in my sample had worked for government organizations, primarily in white-collar jobs, and only four had private businesses of their own.

In Britain, there has been a trend towards working for the private sector, and especially setting up businesses. There is a move away from government service, though there is still a strong focus on white collar and technical work. This applies to fourteen of the thirty-one household heads in my sample, seven of whom work for a government concern, and seven for private ones. Also, nine household heads are in skilled occupations, as opposed to four in East Africa. This

Table 1   *Occupations of household heads in the UK and East Africa*

	government body (e.g. railways, post office, PWD, etc.)	private concern office and technical work	skilled craftsmen	own private business	
core sample of 13 families	9	2	1	1	occupations in East Africa
wedding sample of 18 families	9	3	3	3	
total sample of 31 families	18	5	4	4	
core sample of 13 families	3	2	3	5	occupations in UK
wedding sample of 18 families	4	5	6	3	
total sample of 31 families	7	7	9	8	

increase in skilled employment especially applies to East African Sikhs resident in Southall where there were jobs readily available in local industries at the time of their arrival in the UK. The reason for it is that a number of the younger men who worked in administrative sectors of government concerns in East Africa went either into factory jobs or become carpenters with big building firms because of the higher wages offered at that time in these jobs in comparison with administrative ones.

Eight of the thirty-one household heads have set up their own businesses in the UK. Of those in my core sample, one household head who had worked for an airline in Kenya in an administrative capacity has now established a successful travel agency. Similarly, of the professional men, the engineer has a shop and also his own concern dealing with the design of heating systems for buildings. In

Nairobi, he had worked for the Public Works Department (PWD) as a draughtsman. He arrived in Britain in the late 1950s to improve his qualifications, and worked for a private building concern until 1970, before deciding to go to India to set up a business there. But he returned within a month because of the corrupt dealings of his Indian business partner.

The second professional man, the architect, works for a local authority, though in East Africa he had acquired his training while being employed by a private architect's firm. In Britain, after attending college for a couple of years, he worked for a number of different firms. He does a considerable amount of private work, designing extensions for houses, and it is his ambition to set up an architectural firm of his own. He is also one of the young men involved with drawing up the plans to extend the present association.

Another informant who had previously worked for the Railways in East Africa has a flourishing building concern of his own in Southall. On his arrival in this country, he worked as a foreman for a construction company, a job which taught him the trade. In 1963, he set up his own business, then went to India to settle there with his family. But he could not cope with the situation, and re-emigrated in 1956.

A similar pattern was followed by the family I lived with. The household head migrated to India after having worked for the Railways in Nairobi, as a clerk. He went to India to set up a business in 1964 with his brother-in-law, making spare parts for machines, but the whole venture proved to be unsuccessful and he came on to the UK. For eleven years, he worked as a carpenter for a building concern in London. He now works on a freelance basis as a carpenter, developing his own building concern which deals with the installation of central heating, building extensions to houses, plumbing, and decorating. He is an example of an East African who had an office job in Kenya but has moved to a skilled manual one in Britain. Similarly, another household head in my core sample who had an administrative job in the Post Office in Nairobi has become a metal worker in a factory.

The rest of the office workers in my sample have remained within the administrative sectors in the UK, but have changed the organizations they work for. For example, one household head who worked as a clerk in the Post Office in East Africa now works for the Crown Agents in a similar post. Another one who worked for the East African Railways now works for British Airways in an administrative capacity.

Similarly, East African Sikhs who did carpentry jobs in East Africa either for private or government concerns have carried on doing the same type of work here. Unlike the office workers, they have not changed professions, though some have set up their own small businesses having acquired experience after working for a few years for big contractors.

To summarize, East African Sikhs in Britain are diversifying into a bigger range of occupations, a number of which are nonetheless concerned with the Ramgarhia talents. They are also working for a larger number of organizations, thus breaking the East African homogeneity of occupation and organization. Although their concentration on white collar and technical work, both in the private and public sectors, is still strong, there is a definite tendency in the UK to set up private businesses. This is a move that takes them away from their traditional background in East Africa of being government employees predominantly in middle-range and skilled jobs.

Periods of migration

In general, as can be seen from *Table 2* most East African families migrated to Britain in the late 1960s. Only two men in my wedding sample and five in my core sample arrived before 1965. Of the latter, two are professionals who both migrated to further their studies. The engineer had already been married in Kenya, and his baby daughter and wife joined him two years after his arrival in this country. By this time he had already bought a house and was working and studying part-time.

The architect arrived in 1961. A couple of years later, having completed his studies he acquired a house and brought his parents over in 1966. Soon afterwards he went to India and got married there, to an East African Sikh girl. At the time of his arrival in Southall he says his was the only house in the road in which each tenant had rented one room each. In the rest of the houses, there were Sikhs from India who lived in very crowded conditions, twenty-five men per house, sleeping in each other's beds according to their work shifts, because their main concern was to send money home.

Emigration from East Africa to the United Kingdom in the late 1950s and early 1960s was mainly of students, who came either from wealthy families who could provide financial support from East Africa for their studies here, or were those who funded their own education by working part-time. The non-students in my sample who had arrived around this time all initially worked in factories or became carpenters. Later on, two set up their own businesses. All these men brought their families over to the UK within a couple of years of migration. These were among the first East African Sikh families to arrive in Southall. For this reason, they forged a close bond with each other and any other East Africans around at the time, because of their common background.

Table 2   *Periods of migration to the UK*

	before 1960	1960–64	1965–69	post-1970
core sample of 13 families	2	3	6	2
wedding sample of 18 families	–	2	12	4
total sample of 31 families	2	5	18	6

Within my core sample, nine of the thirteen household heads arrived in this country before their families, who joined them within a maximum period in the East African case of a couple of years. This migration pattern is different from the one traced by Ballard and Ballard (1977: 33) for the Indian Sikhs who brought their families over in the 1960s. In this case household heads started to arrive predominantly after the Second World War, when there was a demand for unskilled labour for industry. These men lived in all-male households in the centre of cities. The decision to bring their wives and children over was only taken after their being here for a considerable length of time. As stated in Chapter 1, this does not apply to East African Sikhs, for whom the decision to migrate permanently had already been taken before the actual event. Household heads arrived in this country before their families so that they could look for employment and provide housing. The families would then arrive to more settled circumstances. I did not come across any East African man who thought that the move to this country was a temporary one and that he would ultimately return 'home' after having earned a certain amount. Migration to the UK was viewed in terms of settling here permanently.

Housing

All the families in my total sample are house owners. Four of these own two houses each. As can be seen from *Table 3*, most of them own three-bedroomed houses (twenty-four of the thirty-one families in my

Table 3   *House ownership:*
(a) *size of houses*

	3 bedrooms	*4 bedrooms*	*over 5 bedrooms*
core sample of 13 families	9	1	3
wedding sample of 18 families	15	2	1
total sample of 31 families	24	3	4

(b) *times of purchase of first house*

	before 1960	*1960–64*	*1965–69*	*post-1970*
core sample of families	1	3	7	2

sample); three own four-bedroomed houses and four live in houses with five or more bedrooms. In most cases, houses were bought within a couple of years of arrival. Six of the household heads in my core sample had already bought their houses, before sending for their families. In some cases, families arrived as complete units and stayed with relations who were already settled in the UK, before buying their own houses, within a short period.

In terms of the maintenance of these houses, in every case in my sample, they have been redecorated. New fittings and extensions have been built onto the house to extend existing space. Two of the families own two adjoining houses, and the central wall has been demolished on the first floor to make one large house. In these two cases, both houses have undergone major extensions to double the space. Central heating was installed in all the houses after the families moved into them. The redecoration and other changes made in the houses were done without professional help in most cases. Extensions to the back of houses are popular and are considered to be more worthwhile than moving to a larger house.

The house of one of my informants was originally considered to be a slum property, for it lacked a bathroom and washing facilities. Like a number of the other houses in the area, such a property could be bought more cheaply than better houses in surrounding areas. Before he moved into this house in 1968, the owner built a bathroom, a toilet, an extension at the back to serve as a dining room and a wash room, a larger kitchen, cupboards, and shelves. He also installed central heating and hot water facilities. The whole house was totally redecorated. This is quite a typical case of restoration of older property, made easier by Ramgarhia caste skills. No outside help is required because relatives include electricians, plumbers, and carpenters, all of whom can pool their resources. The household head himself in this case is a carpenter who can put his skills into practice. The only building costs amounted to the purchase of the raw materials, which could be bought cheaply, as most of the men have access to them at low rates, being in the building trade themselves.

Most of the small Sikh building concerns and private building work that is done in Southall, in fact, feeds the demand within the area to have houses extended and renovated, making it very much an ethnic service.

Another example of renovation of older property on a larger scale was that of the architect. He bought an old house soon after his arrival in Britain, and renovated it completely, rented it out, and moved into his present house. His second house has been greatly extended. He has built two huge rooms in addition to the existing space, and has reclaimed land to increase the size of his garden. His is a typical case of the more educated East African men putting their skills into practice at a higher level. They can get planning permission more easily because they can design their own plans. Such men are responsible for drawing extension plans for the other East African houses and providing professional help for obtaining planning permission. The actual building work can then be done individually by the house owner.

The above are just two examples of the huge amount of renovation of old houses that is taking place and has taken place in the past, in East African Sikh homes because of the building skills of the Ramgarhia caste group. The wealthier men have now moved on to their second and third homes in the more prosperous suburbs.

Family organization

A high proportion of East African Sikhs live in nuclear households. This applies to eighteen of my total sample of thirty-one families, including seven of the thirteen families in my core sample. The significance of this feature will become clear in later chapters because it has influenced not only the structure of women's property, but has also resulted in shifts in power in favour of the brides themselves. They are now exercising greater control over their own dowries than ever before.[2]

The trend towards nuclear households is especially accentuated among the younger couples who either move into their own homes directly after marriage or do so within a couple of years of marriage. Also, it is now common to find unmarried East African men with houses of their own. In fact, ownership of a house enhances their chances in the marriage market. This development has arisen in the UK, and was not in existence in East Africa, where joint households were more common.

Before describing the joint households in my core sample, clarification of the difference between supplementary nuclear and lineal joint households, using Kolenda's (1968) classification, is needed. In my sample, a household that I consider to be supplementary nuclear is one in which there are old parents who live with a nuclear family but do not contribute to the household finances, because they have retired from work. This should be qualified because, according to Kolenda's classification, old people are not earning and are therefore dependants. However, in the UK they draw pensions and can look after their own interests. They could, in theory, go off and live separately on their pensions though I have never come across or heard of such a case amongst East African Sikhs, which is the reason for classifying them as dependants. They are attached to households but they do not contribute directly towards the household budget, keeping their pensions to themselves.

A lineal joint household, on the other hand, is one in which there are two couples between whom there is a lineal link, e.g. a married son and parents. In such a case, property is held jointly and the parents as well as the son are earning members of the household, i.e. they contribute to the household budget. In my core sample, there were two lineal joint families. In both cases, there was jointly-held property. In one case, the son and father are partners in their building business and live in the same household, i.e. two adjoining houses with a central wall that has been demolished. In the second case, the father and sons pursue their separate professions but own their house jointly. In this household, the older woman works, while the daughter-in-law stays at home because she has a small baby to look after.

In two of the households in my sample, the retired parents live with their sons. In the architect's household, both his old parents have retired. They do not contribute to the family income nor do they have a share in their son's house. This is what I consider to be a supplementary nuclear household, because the old parents are dependent on the son. In the second case, the son runs a corner shop. The father is too old to work but he has provided the capital to set up this shop with the money from a building business in Nairobi which he sold before emigrating to the UK.

In another case, two married brothers and their widowed mother live together. The older brother, who owns the house, has two children, while the younger one had just got married at the start of my fieldwork. He was at that time looking for a house to purchase and was therefore viewing his stay with his brother as a temporary measure. Towards the end of my fieldwork, he moved into his own house. His widowed mother, who works for an airline canteen, lives with him but is not dependent on him, as she has the income from her own job which helps to pay her own expenses.

All the other households in my core sample are nuclear ones. One is sub-nuclear, because the husband died in 1974. Three of the four children are earning members of this family. The widow does not work at present although she worked in the past for six years in a factory which manufactured biscuits. Both her sons contribute to the family income while the widow gets some state benefits. The earning daughter did not directly contribute to the household budget, but was busy preparing her dowry. Her marriage took place during my fieldwork.

In two other households in which there are earning daughters they do not contribute towards the family income, although these girls sometimes do the shopping for their younger brothers and sisters or occasionally lend them extra pocket money. The general picture is that the sons contribute to the household budget whereas no contribution is expected of earning unmarried daughters in any of the cases in my sample.

In the following, I shall refer to joint property held by the families in my core sample in the UK, East Africa, and India.

One of the household heads in my sample had a building business in Nairobi. He ran this himself, while his sons worked for government concerns. He had a house in Nairobi which he sold along with the business when he migrated to the UK. None of the other families in my sample had had property in East Africa. All the ones who worked for a government concern had houses which accompanied their jobs, e.g. Railways and Post Office quarters. The others all lived in rented property. Unlike the situation in Britain, where nearly all the East African Sikhs I met were house owners, this was not so in East Africa. The only people who owned houses there were businessmen and the building contractors who had built houses of their choice because they could afford to do so. Thus, there was no developed concept of real property ownership in East Africa although nearly all of them were at that time building houses or buying land in the Punjab.

The property held in India is property which the fathers of the people in my sample had built during their stay in Africa. For example, in the case of the architect, his father had built property in India from the money he earned in East Africa. This property, in Jullunder, means little to his son, who owns two houses in Britain, although his brother and he will inherit it at some stage. In another case, the father built property in Ludhiana with his Railway earnings from East Africa, then died during retirement in India. All his sons live abroad, two in Britain and one in Canada. They all own houses in their country of residence and have no intention of returning to India to settle permanently. Their widowed mother cared for the property until she migrated to Britain in 1977.

It should be emphasized that although nearly all the families in my sample own property in the Punjab though not in East Africa, this is not of importance in determining the organization of household activities in Britain. The younger men in my sample had little interest in the Indian property, nor did they have a clear idea of the precise amount of land they owned. They were not bothered about the state it was in, and would say their relatives were looking after it. Thus, operationally this property is of little use to East Africans settled in Britain, since couples tend to buy their own separate houses soon after marriage. In fact, it was never mentioned, unless asked about, because their fathers had it built with the East African earnings while living in Africa when they were more home-orientated. However, one kind of property held in India that is well looked after is that in which the parents of the men in my sample reside. There were two such cases of dependent parents residing permanently in India, both sons owning property here.

I have already stated earlier that there are only two cases in my core sample where property is held jointly in the UK, by father and son. Also, business in which the male siblings together have a share is also not as common as in the sub-continent and in East Africa in the past. There seems to be little joint property held by male family members.

This fits in well with the tendency to nuclear households among East African Sikhs. It is common for a number of closely-related households to live nearby, in one area, but not in the same house. For example, one of the families I associated with had a number of relatives living close to Southall. Two of my informant's brothers and two sisters all lived in the vicinity. The grandmother would visit the children often, bringing *prasad* (offering) for them from the temple, and there was a huge amount of visiting to and fro within the related houses. Co-operation in this case was mainly between the maternal kin of my female informant. For example, when her husband was in Canada during my fieldwork, her brother would visit her often to look through her post for her and see how she was managing. In an emergency, relations would gather quickly. This also happened during a religious ceremony, e.g. at a *satsang* organized by a younger sister-in-law of my informant, all the older sisters-in-law helped to cook and organize the function. Hence, a lot of labour was rapidly gathered, and tasks could be shared, so that it was not an overtaxing task to prepare meals for the 200 individuals expected at the *satsang*. The men set up loudspeakers to transmit the *kirtan*, one of the older sisters-in-law made the *samosas*, another one made sweetmeats, a sister organized the group of singers for *kirtan*, and so on, so that the woman of the house had little to worry about. This was a situation that I often came across among the families in my sample. Since this was a female *satsang*, not considered to be a large affair, co-operation was only within the extended family.

However, at bigger events, like a wedding or *Akand Path*,[3] East African Sikh connections in general help to raise labour power to organize functions. People would often turn up to help with any task that needed to be done. For example, at an *Akand Path* of an informant, most of her relatives living around the Southall area, i.e. her mother, mother-in-law and father-in-law, her husband's brother, etc. were all present to help with the organization. On top of this, other association members that she knew, e.g. the ladies from the *satsang* groups, and her friends in Southall, all helped with the work. Similarly at weddings, people would turn up to help with any task that needed to be done. At one of my informant's home, her brothers' wives and children all moved in a week before the marriage of her daughter to help with the endless number of tasks that need to be done during this time. Three days after the marriage, when all the mess had been cleared up, they all moved back to their homes. In this case, even though the relatives were not living near Southall, they would make regular visits to see her, especially when help was needed on specific occasions.

Hence, East African Sikhs have an extensive network of contacts on whom they can rely. This includes kinsmen, as well as other Sikhs with whom they shared their lives in East Africa. This particular aspect is very striking because although the households in the UK are simple, being nuclear ones, they are involved in a complex kinship network within extended families, thus forming kindreds of co-operation. However, it should be stressed that non-kinship-based East African connections are relied upon for help and co-operation almost as much as the extended family. In a way, these form a kindred of recognition which may not be actively co-operating but which is, nonetheless, important in terms of marriage, because spouses are selected quite rigidly from within East African Sikh circles. Thus, there are many households of potential marriageables who have been in contact with each other in the past and who are interacting as friends, neighbours, attenders of the same associations and social functions.

East African Sikh women and their attitudes towards work

My purpose in exploring the role of the adult women is to assess their independence and work orientation because both these features are important in terms of marriage and dowry. East African Sikh women in Britain are key actors, playing a more influential role than in East Africa in organizing marriages and in making their dowries in the case of the brides.

Enormous pressure is put on them by other women in their group to work and earn a living, yet none of these women had worked outside their homes in East Africa. Old women who do not go out to work often complain that they had never worked in East Africa and that they are too old to work, but even they will be told off for 'sitting at home doing nothing'. It is common to find women over the age of fifty who go out to work. One of my older informants used to work in a laundry sorting out various garments as they were cleaned; another works in a potato crisps factory on the grading belt; another one worked in the canteen at the airport and so on. When these old women retire, they often look after the children of their daughters-in-law while they go out to work.

As can be seen from *Table 4*, seventeen out of the thirty-one married women in my total sample were earning members of families, and have been so since arrival in this country. This accounts for nine adult women in my core sample and eight women in my wedding sample. I have excluded the three unmarried earning girls in my core sample, two of whom are still studying on a part-time basis. One started work as a laboratory technician after having failed her 'A'

Table 4   *Occupations of women*

	factory and unskilled work	*administration and office work*	*homework (e.g. sewing)*	*do not work*	*semi-professional and professional*
older women (wives of household)					
core sample	6	2	1	4	–
wedding sample	5	1	2	10	–
total sample	11	3	3	14	–
brides					
brides' occupations	–	15	–	5	3

Levels, another is a clerk typist, and the third, who got married during my fieldwork, had an office job with a local firm.

The focus on administrative work is especially clear from my sample of brides in *Table 4*. Of the eighteen working brides, fifteen are involved in office jobs as clerks, secretaries, etc. Of the others, one is an optician, another a pharmacist, and a third a trainee accountant. The majority of brides have had part of their education in this country. None of these young women are involved in any form of factory work, which is a very different picture from that of the older married women in my total sample, the majority of whom do unskilled factory work. For example, one of my informants works for a sausage factory, and two work in the catering section of two airlines packing food trays, etc. The latter type of work is especially popular because of the fringe benefit of a 90 per cent reduction in the total cost of an air ticket. Home sewing is another area of work, though it is not popular in Southall because of the low wages and the availability of better-paid unskilled factory work. Of the three women in my total sample, one sews skirts for 20p each, another makes underclothes for babies and is paid 20p per dozen, and the third occasionally does some sewing for a hospital.

An interesting point is that a large number of the women had changed their jobs several times. One of my informants did some home sewing when she first arrived because her children were small. She then started to work for a factory which made cells and batteries.

While working here she got her younger sister employed within the same section. After a year, she moved on to an ice-cream factory, a job she got with the help of her husband's MBW. She did not much care for this job, so she found one with the catering section of an airline with the help of a former neighbour of hers in Uganda, as this woman, too, works in the same section. The reason it is possible to change jobs with such frequency in Southall is that news of any vacant positions spreads quickly through the community.[4] Since there are other Punjabi women working in these factories, even the women who cannot speak English fluently manage to get work, because ones already employed will introduce them to their bosses and supervisors. Also, the higher density of the Sikh population in Southall helps women make friends outside their family circles on whom they can rely for help with further employment. Often these contacts are other East African women.

This is important in the arrangement of marriages because women often find out about eligible young people through the information they get from East African workmates. For example, the MBW of a bride in my sample arranged her marriage through regular contact she had at work in an airline's canteen with the groom's sister, who was on the same shift. Similarly, an accountant bride in my sample was found an accountant groom by her FBW who worked with the groom's MBW in the same sausage factory. The matchmakers in both the cases mentioned above were women who had access to information at work on potential marriageables. This widening of their network through their work situation also applies to other spheres. As the women develop further contacts with other East African women, making their East African friendship as important a criterion as their kinship relationships, they might rely on non-kin to help them find jobs, i.e. by the time they were looking for their second and third jobs. I did not come across this outside the Southall area, for although most of the East African Sikh women I came across worked outside their homes, they were not in touch with other Asian women with the same sort of intensity as the Southall ones, nor could they change jobs with the same frequency, since so many of them were involved with office work. Work seems to be easier to find in Southall, although it may involve unsocial hours.

I have stated earlier that the majority of East African women started work soon after their arrival in this country, around the late 1960s, when most East African families arrived. The Sikh women in Southall before this period did not work with the same frequency as at present. One of my informants wanted to do a job then but her husband was against the idea of her working outside the home. However, after living here for three years, she pressurized her husband to let her work because, increasingly, other women were working, and she could use them as role models. Women in one of my core families who arrived before the mid-1960s still do not work, first because they had never got used to the idea and second, because the household head has a prospering building concern.

Of the non-earning women in my core sample, one also does not work because she is rich, being the wife of a prosperous businessman. She is involved with the *kirtan* groups, and is therefore constantly at some *satsang*. This also applies to the retired women who take an active part in running the temple and in organizing the female *satsangs*. There is a great demand for the services of these *kirtan* groups. Of the other women who do not work, one is too old and has retired, and two do not need the money because their children have grown up and they themselves are settled.

Once a woman has worked she finds it hard to stay at home. Not only is she losing a vital source of income which partly earns her her independence, but also the company of other women. One of my informants had three of her four children in the UK. She went to work soon after their births, leaving them with a baby minder each time. Her husband objected to this, but to no avail. A number of people consider this to be greedy behaviour, because they feel the children are too young to be away from the mother. However, the young women were said commonly to be doing this, and children in the process were seen as being neglected. However, in my core sample the only such case was the one mentioned above. A more common case was one in which the young mother would leave the children behind with a retired grandmother. Also, older children help to look after younger ones, which freed the mother for work outside the home.

East African Sikh women move around quite freely in Southall. There is no restriction of their movement, unlike with Muslim women, since none of them is in any form of *purdah*, and a great many are actively involved in temple activities. A pattern that is common amongst Sikh women which also applies to four women in my core sample, is that they can either drive or often have access to a car to attend the endless *satsangs* and religious ceremonies. In a number of cases, older daughters who drive often provide the transport for the vast number of things the women do on their own in the company of other women. For example, at the time of a marriage, most of the pre-wedding ceremonies were almost entirely 'women-orientated'. A few men would be around the house but did not participate in any of the activities. The singing sessions were attended mostly by women, women were invited to look at the dowry, and they also turned up to help with the wedding preparations.

   In sum, East African Sikh women have a considerable amount of freedom and spend a lot of their time on women's activities. The reason for this is that a number of the Southall women, in particular, have expanded their contacts because they work outside their homes. Consequently, they have developed friendships which are outside their kinship network. These are important not only for informing them of general activities in Southall but sometimes prove to be useful in marriage arrangements, because of the accessibility of information about eligible young people. Also, the fact that they are economically independent has led to an increase in their freedom of movement. Women in East Africa were on the whole more dependent on husbands to take them places and were, therefore, not as well-informed.

Conclusion

This chapter has described the internal organization of the East African Sikh community by referring to my sample of families in Southall. The first section, on the occupations of the household heads in the UK, refers to the trend towards going into business and working for the private sector in both skilled and white-collar jobs. For East Africans who have previously worked primarily for government organizations in East Africa, this is a shift away from that background, though the focus on white-collar and technical work has persisted.

   The second section, on the time of migration to Britain, shows that the majority of East African families arrived in the late 1960s. Earlier East African migrants were students who had come to further their education. Unlike Sikhs who have migrated directly from India, East Africans have arrived either as complete family units or have united a few months after the arrival of household heads. This process was further accelerated by the lack of a 'myth of return' because their decision to migrate to the UK was seen as a permanent and not a temporary move.

Related to this, the majority of East Africans bought their houses soon after arrival in this country. In a number of cases, household heads had purchased houses before their families joined them. I have referred to their enormous interest in improving and extending their homes, often utilizing their traditional Ramgarhia skills. Since they consider themselves to be settlers, their earnings are consumed and retained in this country.

A consideration of features of family organization shows that most East African Sikh households are nuclear ones. This is a trend which is even more prominent among the younger couples. Despite the simplicity of household organization, East African Sikhs are involved in a complex net of relationships based both on the extended family and previous East African connections. The latter is their kindred of co-operation, the arena from which spouses are selected, since East African Sikhs tend to marry where familiar.

The final section dealt with East African Sikh women and their defined interest in working outside their homes, since most of them are earning members of their families. The older women are mainly in unskilled factory work whereas the younger ones are to be found predominantly in administrative jobs. The general independence of Ramgarhia women combined with their earning powers, makes them central figures in weddings especially as related to gift exchanges. This is particularly crucial in the case of the earning brides who are now themselves important contributors to their dowries.

A further consequence for older women of working outside their homes, especially around Southall, has been a broadening of their contacts with other East African women. These spread far beyond their kinship network, giving them accessibility to information both about general East African activities and also about marriageable young Sikhs. This often proves to be useful in matchmaking and marriage arrangement which is the subject of the next chapter.

FIVE

Arrangement of East African marriages

The preceding chapters have dealt with the background and significant features of the organization of the East African Sikh community in the UK. I have shown that the community has established itself as a distinct group which has for various reasons become more conscious of its past background than ever before, i.e. of its 'East Africanness' and also of its 'Ramgarhianess'.

The following chapters will consider the changes in marriage and dowry patterns since migration to Britain, especially in relation to the elaborations and modifications that have arisen in response to British conditions. Although trends are emerging within East African Sikh marriages which will assume more importance in future, further influencing the structure of the community, at present, the traditional criteria of spouse selection and kinship organization follow much the same pattern as that of North Indians (Lewis 1965; Gould 1960; Madan 1965; Karve 1953; Van der Veen 1972; Berreman 1962; Pocock 1972; Vatuk 1972).

Rules and preferences in marriage arrangement

The factors considered important in the arrangement of marriages can be divided into rules which are explicit and strongly-held, and preferences which are less rigidly observed. Some criteria which were classified as rules in East Africa, e.g. the four *got* rule and regional endogamy, have become preferences in the UK.

The first classical rule of caste endogamy applies to East African Sikhs as it does to North Indians, i.e. that marriage should take place with the Ramgarhia caste, *saadi biradri*[1] (Rowe 1960: 299–311; Gould 1960: 476–91; Gould 1961: 197–300; Vatuk 1972: 91) During my fieldwork, there was severe opposition to a marriage between a Jat bride and a Ramgarhia groom. The bride's kin threatened to kill the groom since this was a hypogamous marriage. The Jats in the Sikh caste hierarchy rank higher than the Ramgarhias (Macleod 1976: 103). All the Ramgarhia families involved felt that the bride was neither attractive nor educated enough to be suitable for a professional groom, who could have married a much better qualified Ramgarhia girl. None the less, they were prepared to give in to the groom's wishes because the affair had been going on for five years. Unlike this *pratiloma* (against the hair) marriage, there was another inter-caste marriage which was actually arranged by the parents, of an educated Jat groom to a Ramgarhia bride. The lack of opposition for this marriage could be that it was in tune with hypergamy being an *anuloma* ('flows with the hair') marriage, in which the higher status of the Jat groom was maintained.

However, there was one case in my wedding sample of a Ramgarhia bride who wanted to marry a Jat man but was prevented from doing so because of parental opposition. The bride's parents had been active in the development of the Ramgarhia movement in Southall and were very conscious of their Ramgarhianess. During my fieldwork she was married off to a Ramgarhia man who fulfilled all the traditional criteria. Twenty-two of the twenty-three marriages in my sample observed this rule. The only marriage in my sample to which there was opposition because it broke all the classical rules was that between a Hindu bride and a Ramgarhia groom. Caste endogamy is, therefore, a basic criterion of marriage arrangement in the UK, as it was in East Africa (Morris 1967: 176; Bharati 1967: 316).[2]

The second rule is that of *got* or *gotra*[3] exogamy. In North India, marriage is prohibited with close cognates (*sapinda*) and agnates (*gotra*). The *sapinda* and *gotra* rules are meticulously prescribed for the Brahmans as of prime importance. Gould (1960: 480) suggests that the higher the ritual status of the caste, the more its kinship organization will correspond to the Brahman *gotra* pattern. Both Mayer (1960: 203) and Madan (1965: 105) have pointed out that *sapinda* rules are not always observed, because people can invariably only remember kinsfolk till the fourth generation instead of the ideal limit of five to seven generations. Among the East African Sikhs, I could not discern *sapinda* rules 'which forbid a man to marry a woman who is a cognate as far back as the fifth generation' (Karve 1953: 53). In fact, I had difficulty in getting them to remember the MMs *got*. Also, East African Sikhs have shallow genealogies, mostly only two to three generations in depth.

I shall not discuss the origin of *gotras*, but point out that in relation to hypergamy, the adoption of *gotra* names is an important part in the process of Brahmanization and reflects high status, just as dowry marriage is a marker of high castes. *Gotra* organization is also one of the highest symbols of ritual superiority of the Brahmans (Gould 1960: 480; Kapadia 1966: 129; Dube 1954: 65; Karve 1953: 59).

The four-*got* rule which states that marriage into the clan of one's M, FM, MM and F is prohibited has become a preference for the East African Sikhs in the UK. Tiemann (1970: 176) states that among the Jats, the reason four and not five or more *gots* are prohibited is that 'effective kinship relationships successively decrease in intensity and finally cease to exist after the third generation', that is, after the family which has been founded by a marriage has reached its ideal size of three generations, demarcated by a grandfather and a grandson (*pota*). After this, marriage can be arranged with the prohibited *got* because the family separates after this period.

In the UK, the rule is that marriage should be avoided with the clans of the mother and father, i.e. the two-*got* rule, whereas the preference is the four-*got* rule. The feeling at present is that less attention should be paid to the *gots* of the FM and MM and only five marriages in the sample of twenty-three observed this rule. The rest were arranged keeping in mind the two-*got* rule. The reasons given for *got* exogamy are the same as those of Jats. Tiemann states that 'the Jat *got* . . . is emphatically a "brotherhood" (*biradri*) by virtue of its male members being brothers. . . . The brotherhood which is meant here is obviously not the brotherhood of caste which does not obviate marriage but the brotherhood which also underlies the rule of *got* exogamy. . . . It is kinship by blood.' But while inside a *got*, this brotherhood is reckoned only in the male line, 'the four-*got* rule presupposes the acknowledgement of brotherhood based on descent through females, i.e. through one's mother, father's mother and mother's mother' (p. 170).

The East African Sikh explanation for *got* exogamy like that of the Jats is that 'brothers cannot marry sisters'. Sexual connections between them are immoral and particularly scandalous. *Got* exogamy is regarded as a criterion by which human beings distinguish themselves from animals. This was why an intra-*got* 'love' marriage which was considered socially unacceptable was talked about frequently during fieldwork. It caused the groom's kin in the UK a great deal of embarrassment and affected the marriage chances of his sister, who was also in London. Her family in East Africa had already tried to 'marry her off' there, but their attempts had proved unsuccessful, partly because of her own reputation as a 'loose character' and partly due to her brother's scandalous marriage, which 'spoiled the family name'. This marriage did not take place in a temple because the *Granthis* (priests) would not agree to such a union, considering it to be almost incestuous and far more shocking than marriage outside the community. This too certainly happens quite often and does not arouse a similar type of emotion. An intra-*got* marriage abuses the patrilineality of the Ramgarhias because in a way such marriages involve an alliance between distant agnates.

The third rule is that of village exogamy which is also typical of North and Central India (Gould 1960: 472–92; Lewis 1965: 160, 319; Mayer 1960: 209; Madan 1965: 110–12; Karve 1953: 117–88; Van der Veen 1972: 81). A village is referred to as a *pind* and to marry a person within it is tantamount to incest, because *pindwalas* are considered to be brothers and sisters. Berreman (1962: 55–9) suggests that the rule of village exogamy is like that of *gotra* exogamy; the abstention from agricultural work by women, the prohibition of widow remarriages etc. which are all signs of high status. The observance of these traditional rules combined with dowry marriage accrues higher standing in North India.

The fourth rule which applies to East African Sikhs in the UK is the asymmetrical relationship between the wife givers and takers which is the basis of both formal and informal hypergamous systems (Kapadia 1966; Dumont 1966; Inden 1976; Thurston 1909; Gough 1955; Ibbetson 1881).[4] I came across three marriages that were gossiped about because each one had involved a direct exchange which had equalized the positions of the inferior wife givers and the superior wife takers. All these were 'love marriages' that had taken place in this country. The observance of asymmetry between the two parties in an alliance is still very much a rule in the UK, in common with North

India, because these marriages would otherwise have been accepted by the community.

Having dealt with rules, I shall in the following consider preferences, some of which were classified as rules in the past but which have in response to settlement in Britain become preferences in order to bring about flexibilities in the marriage system and also widen the pool of suitable marriage partners. This is a clear adaptation within the British scene.

The first preference is that of regional endogamy. Regions are referred to as a *jhillas*, of which those of particular importance to the Sikhs in general are Doaba, Malwa, and Majha (see Map 1 of the Punjab). Regions can often be discerned from the *gots*, e.g. those which either start with the letter 'b' or have this letter in them are nearly always from Doaba, whereas those that begin with 'v' are mostly from Majha. Information about *gots* can easily be scanned before any of the families likely to be involved in an alliance are approached. It is considered perfectly acceptable to get in touch with the families concerned directly a long time before the potential bride and groom meet each other.

There is a status scale between the three main regions since people are seen to possess different qualities. The Majhails[5] rank themselves higher than people from Doaba and Malwa. They say that they are more educated and refined in their habits than people from the latter two regions. Doabais are considered to be the most traditionalist and inclined towards elaborate marriages, whereas the Malwans are considered to be less sophisticated and most quarrelsome. The latter two consider the Majhails or Amritsarias to be the most dishonest. I could not verify these differences because they have blurred considerably during the Ramgarhias' stay in Africa and in Britain.

However, regional differences are important in marriage and were observed in twenty-one of the twenty-three marriages in my sample (*see Table 5*). Thirteen were Doabi marriages; six were of Malwa couples, and two were Majhails; and one was an inter-regional arranged marriage between a Doabi bride and a Majhail groom. Although there is a strong preference for intra-regional marriages, I did come across young couples (not in my sample) whose marriages had been arranged by their parents in the UK, not having observed the regional endogamy.[6] This was not the case in East Africa, because this rule was adhered to more strongly. I certainly did not come across a marriage that had taken place in Africa which had been inter-regional. This rule has in the UK increasingly become a preference because of the flexibility that is creeping into marriage arrangements in response both to the fear and the fact that young Sikhs are marrying outside the community. Individuals who are especially suited to each other in terms of family background, education, and personal attributes will now be suggested for marriage even if they are from different regions. Also, the increasing amount of attention being paid to the personal assets of the spouses and concern about their suitability for each other has further contributed towards making the marriage system more tolerant to inter-regional marriages in the UK than it had ever been in East Africa or in India. On the other hand, East Africans do not have a problem fulfilling the criterion of regional endogamy because the majority of them are from Doaba, an area which has also provided 'the bulk of immigrants to Britain' (John 1969: 15) to East Africa and to other parts of the world.

Table 5   *Observance of regional endogamy*

regions	Doaba (Jullunder)	Malwa (Ludhiana)	Majha (Amritsar)	across regions	marriage outside the community
number of marriages	13	6	2	1	1

total number of marriages: 23

Having described the classical rules and preferences, I shall consider the other criteria which are also important in the arrangement of East African marriages in the UK.

The lack of status differences among East Africans

I shall distinguish between ascribed and achieved status in a way similar to the distinction made between status and standing by Pocock (1972: 52–69). The former refers to traditional criteria which are more fixed (e.g. caste position, region, *gots*, etc.), and the latter to the standing of the family, i.e. the more flexible position of the individual and past family history.

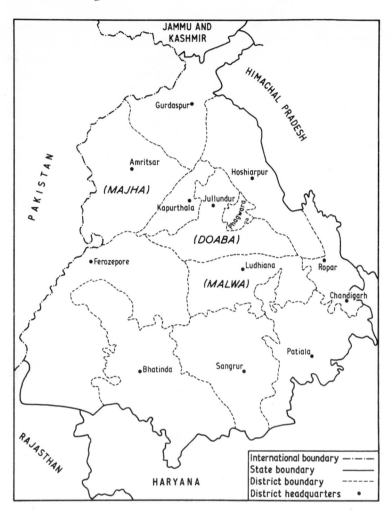

The Punjab after November 1966

Earlier it has been stated that the East African Sikhs are primarily Ramgarhias. Migration to the UK has been selective of a particular category of East Africans resulting in a community here which has a large degree of homogeneity. For these reasons, East African Sikhs can basically marry a large number of other East African families, since these are of a similar standing. For example, I did not come across an élite group like the Desais (Van der Veen 1972: 52) and the Kulin families (Pocock 1954: 196) among them. This lack of an 'aristocracy', and the similarity of background and previous experiences, eases the task of spouse selection considerably in comparison with Sikh migrants from India, who lack this community feeling. However, there are certain status differences, which were more prominent in East Africa but which have been diluted since migration. The East African background still carries some weight and will be talked about at marriage, e.g. previous family wealth, the presence of an illustrious individual, etc. In a number of cases, the past prestige of a family has not survived the migration.

East African society in Africa can be divided into roughly three categories. The first was that of businessmen such as building contractors and shop owners; the second was that of the public-sector workers, i.e. administrative and white-collar staff; and the third category was that of skilled craftsmen (*fundis*) who worked both in the public and private sectors. A family which has lost its past high status is that of the Xs, whose household head was at one stage the wealthiest of the Ramgarhia building contractors. He died in the early 1960s leaving his sons the business and a big fortune. Over a period of a decade, the sons have squandered the money and have been unable to keep the business going. This family is, however, extremely well thought of because of the good deeds, generosity, and wealth of the old man. His daughter in the 1940s received the largest of the East African dowries, well remembered even now. One of the marriages in my sample was that of this man's granddaughter. The past achievements of the old man were made clear to the groom's people during the negotiations to make them realize that the bride belonged to a well-known family with a high standing in East Africa.

Another important family is that of the Ys, whose prestigious status is based on the fact the father came to Britain in the 1940s to receive his education, making him the first East African Sikh to have done so.

He had become wealthy through his education as a highly-qualified engineer as opposed to the Xs, whose wealth was based on business acumen. Although X's sons were sent to the UK for further education, none of them completed their studies. Nevertheless, in the 1960s their value as grooms went up in the marriage market because they were the 'UK returned' sons of a wealthy building contractor. The Ys, on the other hand, did educate their sons, who are considered to be high-status grooms because of their own professional status and that of their prestigious father. One of the professional couples in my sample belongs to this family.

Another important status factor concerns the *Bahu* families who worked in offices right from the establishment of government offices in East Africa. These were people who had received a higher level of education in India before moving to East Africa, whereas skilled craftsmen were recruited for the building of the railways. The latter category produced educated children who became white-collar workers ten to fifteen years after the completion of the railways. Thus, the *Bahus* had an advantage over these people because of their earlier start in the administrative spheres. These families tended to marry amongst themselves in East Africa. They would occasionally give their daughters to the better-educated sons of wealthy businessmen in what could be considered hypogamous marriages which were modified slightly through the groom's family wealth.

Traces of these three broad categories still persist in the UK. I could not discern any other form of hierarchy based on ascription, though I should mention that achievement of either wealth or education is highly valued by East African Sikhs, more so than ascribed status. For this reason, professionals are considered to be the most sought-after young people and are the ones who upgrade their status rapidly. As in East Africa, in Britain these tended to come from the families of white collar workers. The children of building contractors, especially the sons, are notorious for being spoilt by wealth and being 'wine, women, and song' types. This category preferred to marry among themselves partly because they made important alliances which proved useful for business and partly because there was a similarity of background. However, even these families considered it desirable to educate their sons and get their daughters married off to educated sons of administrators' families. The skilled craftsmen similarly married people of an equivalent level. Again a well-qualified son or a pretty fair-skinned girl of such families could be upwardly mobile by marrying into white-collar families.

In Britain, this more clear-cut scale has became confused because people have dispersed not only into different towns but also work for a wide number of organizations. I have already referred to this diversity in the previous chapter. Although the past East African status scale is still strong in Britain, it has, nonetheless, broken down to some extent. Families who have become successful in Britain have taken over high status from the ones established in East Africa. A whole new generation of young people who have had most of their education in Britain has emerged, and to these what was considered important in Africa is not considered so in Britain. For this reason, status differences are harder to discern here. People are friendly with each other precisely because they are East African Sikhs, because there is a need to perpetuate and maintain the East African circle. It should be stressed that a large range of East African families are suitable for each other in terms of marriage because status differences are not at all obvious.

However, differences in individual family background (*khandan*) are important. These refer to personal moral qualities of both the patrilineal and matrilineal kin. A 'good' *khandan* is defined mainly by the absence of scandalous and incorrect marriages, physical disabilities, etc. stressing the importance of previous marriage relations in determining the background of families. To illustrate, a family that I had contact with but was not in my sample, was considered to be inferior even though the sons were professionals and would otherwise be considered prestigious grooms. The reasons behind their inferiority lay in the fact that their MM was referred to as a *Kadesar*, i.e. a non-Sikh woman who had married the MF because he was thought to be slightly mentally retarded. In this case, a physical defect had led to a deviant marriage. All this had happened forty years ago in India. Although the family is prosperous here, with educated sons, I was told that higher-status families would not give them their daughters, though skilled craftsmen's families would not be averse to doing so. On top of this, the sons themselves were short and thin and not the 'sturdy sardar' types. Grooms are not necessarily expected to be handsome but they are expected to be well-built.

In relation to spouse selection, marriageable young people from inferior status families can soon be suggested for families of a similar background because past scandals are well-known among the close-knit East African community. However, if a family with a 'tainted' background manages to become wealthy, upward mobility is not difficult, because status through ascription is minimal and the previous background is overshadowed by newly-acquired prosperity. There are constant cases of this, especially in the UK, where families which were not high-status ones in East Africa have taken over through family wealth and education. However, even here, spouses who are well-educated and from a pure *khandan* have an advantage over those with qualifications and a *halki*, less eminent, background.

To summarize, deviant marriages can affect marriage chances in the UK, though their adverse effects decrease considerably if applied to well-qualified young people. This is again related to the increasing attention being paid at present to the individual assets of the spouses as opposed to general family background, which has lost prominence since migration. This trend is also noted by Vatuk (1972: 77) for urban white-collar migrants in India. Personal attributes, especially of the groom, i.e. earning potential, education, and social manner all far outweigh family ancestry and its present position. It is his future potential as related to his qualifications that plays a vital role in determining the status of a prospective groom. All this is further aided by the absence of defined status differences amongst East African Sikhs.

The importance of East African connections in spouse selection

In Chapters 3 and 4 I have described the East African communications network in the United Kingdom and the awareness people have of their East Africanness. These factors are crucial in spouse selection because of the preference that both spouses should be from East African families. It is felt that marriages between East African young people and those who have come directly from India can prove to be difficult, because of the differences of background and upbringing. Such marriages were only made in the last resort in such cases as those of women who had either acquired a bad reputation or were considered to be unattractive.

For example, one of the brides in my sample had gone to India for a visit during which time her paternal grandfather had got her engaged. She is fat and short, and there had been earlier attempts made to get her 'married off' to East African men, but the two men suggested had refused. This is a clear case of a girl who had difficulty getting married within the East African community here. It was precisely because of this that her parents did not reject the idea of bringing over a groom from India.

Another bride who married an Indian Sikh studying at a university here opposed her engagement violently but gave in under the considerable pressure that was exerted on her. She is an attractive girl, but there were rumours that she was already involved with a man of whom her parents disapproved, which made them extra keen to get her married. The groom selected for her had a higher status than that of a man imported directly from India because he had received some of his education in this country.

The third bride who was married in this way was known to have been out with a West Indian man. This would have made it almost impossible for her to marry an East African Sikh. All the cases described above are of 'difficult' girls to whom it is not easy to marry an East African Sikh. A tension in these marriages in that unlike the East African brides and grooms, Indian Sikhs still retain the 'myth of return' and are thus extremely home-orientated. These grooms are dependent on the bride's family for a considerable period before they settle into a job, buy a house of their own, etc., making their position inferior to that of grooms resident in this country. Furthermore, there is considerable loss of status involved in being *ghar jamai*, even though they may not live with their in-laws. Since most brides tended to live near their parents, the grooms' contact with their parents-in-law was intense, unlike the situation in India in which sons-in-law retain their position of respect by not seeing them on a regular basis (Van der Veen 1972: 76). Residence after marriage for Indian grooms in the UK is uxorilocal, which is as undesirable in India (Mayer 1960: 222) as it is in this country.

This takes me on to the arrangement of 'pure' East African Sikh marriages. As soon as young people are considered to be of marriageable age, i.e. from nineteen years upwards for girls, and twenty-two for boys, word is passed around by the families concerned. This is done both by the brides' and the grooms' parents. The close community ties are especially helpful in this direction, because people tend to meet each other at the many religious functions that they attend in common. By maintaining this regular contact, information is obtained about the pool of eligible young people present in the community, even though a lot of them do not themselves attend these social functions. Nonetheless, people still know of them because their parents and kinsmen are involved in the circuits. In fact, a positive effort is made by parents to mix more intensely with other East Africans in order to search for suitable spouses for their children. If a suggestion is made, messages get rapidly transmitted to the parties concerned. Often if an eligible spouse is seen by the parents themselves, they might get in touch with each other directly, as had happened in the majority of cases in my sample.

This is especially so because go-betweens are almost non-existent in the UK, unlike the North Indian situation. Van der Veen (1972: 58) states that 'the help of the matrimonial agent or intermediary is indispensible'. This is not so among East African Sikhs, who resemble the urban white-collar workers described by Vatuk (1972). The reason for this is that East African Sikhs tend to marry where familiar and marriage alliances are developed from relationships formulated in the past. For example, one of my female informants arranged the marriage of her BD to a groom whose mother attended her fortnightly *satsangs*. In the past, the groom's father had worked in the East African Railways, in the same section as my informant's husband, and they had lived in the same complex of quarters in Nairobi. Thus, they had met each other's kinsmen on a number of occasions in the past. My informant's brother, i.e. the bride's father, was also employed by the Railway though in a different town; but he had often met his future son-in-law's father at his sister's home. Obviously, there was no talk of marriage at the time since the children were still in their early teens. This is a typical example of the use of past East African ties based on work and neighbourhood for marriage arrangement here.

Another example within my sample also illustrates the use of the communications network. The father of a clerical bride arranged her marriage to a groom who had a research post in a government department. The groom's parents had lived in the same area as that of the bride's maternal grandparents and the FZs in Nairobi for over twenty years. As a child, the groom and his family had often visited the bride's kinsmen's homes. During school holidays, the bride's parents would visit Nairobi, which meant that they were acquainted with the groom's family. After migration, all these families settled in South London and maintained contact through common invitations to social functions. Also the groom as an adult kept up his childhood friendship with the bride's older brother who was the same age as himself. Hence, he had often visited the bride's home and had met her before marriage. However, at the time, the bride's father had not considered him to be a potential husband, because he was looking for a more qualified groom. This case will be discussed presently.

However, it should be stressed that this bride, in common with other East African ones, had met her future husband a number of times since childhood because of past contacts. The interlinkage between different East African families gives them enormous familiarity since they have known each other a long time before arranging their children's marriages. This is not say that all brides and grooms have met each other before their suitability for marriage is recognized, but that their parents can easily find out about each other through their shared background and contacts. Marriages are also arranged by kinsmen who will act as the intermediaries, e.g. in one case, a groom's marriage was arranged by his older brother's wife who suggested the daughter of her FB as a bride. In another case, a groom's MZ found a bride for him. She used to attend the Southall Association where the bride and her mother were frequent visitors. In Chapter 1, I have referred to the matchmaking abilities of women through their work contacts. This applied to two marriages in my sample, that of the accountant bride and the clerical officer one.

In the following, I discuss four cases to illustrate the arrangement of marriages and ways in which some of the couples were introduced to each other.

For example, the first wedding that I attended was that of a twenty-one-year-old girl bank cashier who got married to a twenty-five-year-old television engineer groom. I covered this marriage from the bride's side. Her father works in an office locally in Southall. The engagement[7] lasted for one-and-a-quarter years, but after the first meeting of the bride and groom, they did not meet each other individually although they would meet each other often at various social functions in the presence of other people. Since both these families lived within Southall, it was difficult for them to meet each other even if they went out of the area, because gossip spreads rapidly there. Couples often told me that if both the bride and groom lived in different areas, it was easier to meet on neutral territory without arousing suspicion, e.g. in the centre of London after work. Both the families of the couple mentioned above are referred to as *puranay khialaat walay*, i.e. they are more orthodox. They preferred the bride and groom not to date each other. The bride never complained about this and found it quite acceptable. This was a match between families who thought along similar lines.

On the other hand, three of the couples within my sample had open courtships after their engagements. All these three brides married university graduate grooms. One of the brides was an optician who married an engineer, the second was a pharmacist who married a medical groom, and the third was a trainee accountant who married an accountant. These were considered to be more progressive relationships. The optician bride had also known the groom for some time before their marriage, because both the families were connected with the same temple organizations. The marriage itself was initiated by the bride's sister-in-law (BW) who had known the groom's family in East Africa because they lived in the same town. Again in this case there was no need to introduce the couple as they had already met before.

In the third case, the accountant bride's engagement followed a more traditional pattern before the engagement, because she had not previously known the groom. I have mentioned this case in Chapter 4 because her FBW had heard of him through the groom's MBW because they both work in the local sausage factory in Southall. These two women between themselves had arranged the match because the couple was thought to be suited, being in the same profession. The groom's MBW had 'viewed' the bride on a casual visit to the bride's FBW's house, without her knowledge. It was here that the groom was also introduced to the bride, but she, unlike the groom was given no prior indication of the impending introduction. This was something that annoyed her because of what she saw as the 'unsophisticated handling of the whole affair'. She was left in a room with her potential husband to make polite conversation knowing very little about him.

Although most young people are forewarned about such meetings, this method of introducing people was fairly common. The bride and groom would either talk to each other in the presence of close relatives or they would be left alone for a short period. A number of the brides who had never met their husbands before felt that it was just too short a period to get to know someone, though nearly all of them accepted the match after giving it some thought. I classify this as the traditional pattern of arranging East African Sikh marriages because nearly all the young couples are at least allowed a first meeting, which comes about only after checking criteria for suitability, and after both the parties concerned have had a fair look at the young people concerned. If either the groom or the bride have not already known each other then, in the majority of cases, there are further meetings between the couple before the engagement is officially announced. It is for this reason that parents prefer to select a spouse from the circles in which they already move, because the likelihood of the bride and groom having met or known each other without having thought of marriage is enormous, thus reducing the shock of the initial meeting. The accountant bride spent three months after having met the groom twice before she agreed to the engagement, because she was angry at the way in which the initial meeting was forced upon her without her agreement. After the engagement, she went out with the groom frequently and helped him furnish and decorate their future home.

Even in the case mentioned above, the meetings before the engagement were restricted. This did not apply to what was considered to be an avant-garde marriage within my sample.

In the fourth case, the bride, a cousin of the accountant, had a reputation for being outspoken generally, as well as about her views of marriage. It was known to all her relatives that in no way would she agree to a traditional arranged marriage. The feeling was that she would object so strongly she would probably go completely against the system if such a proposition was put to her, and if the groom was to be introduced to her in the normal way. Equally, the groom himself objected to 'viewing' brides. In this case, both of them had similar views, although it is unusual for women to voice them openly. Despite this, the bride's relations were anxious about the whole affair, and felt that she would find it more acceptable if the groom himself were to ask her out after she had been given his particulars. There was a lot of tolerance shown in this case by both the parties because the couple

were particularly well-suited and both of them came from unortho-
dox families.[8] Although this was an arranged marriage, because the
traditional criteria I have referred to earlier were observed, and the
groom was selected for the bride, regional endogamy was, not
observed because of the suitability of the couple. Neither the groom's
nor the bride's parents raised any objection to this. In East Africa, this
match would not have been considered because the bride was from
Doaba and the groom was from Amritsar.

Of the four cases I have described above, three are very much
'modern' marriages, although most of the traditional criteria have
been taken into account during their arrangement. There are,
nonetheless, modifications in the way in which the young people are
left to handle their relationships after these criteria have been fulfilled
and after the spouses themselves have been vetted for suitability. Most
young people were not against arranged marriages but objected to the
lack of flexibility in dealing with their relationships with the opposite
sex.

The more informal way of introducing young people and of
allowing them to meet before their engagements is greatly desired
and talked about by the more progressive of the East African leaders.
This is reinforced by the fear that many young people, especially the
newly-independent girls are not staying within the community but are
'going off' with Muslim and English men. There is, thus, a demand
to lift the traditional restrictions so as to allow more casual contact
among young people of both sexes. This attitude has encouraged
some young people who have met through social functions and
who have developed a liking for one another, to state this to their
parents, who can then initiate the procedure for fulfilling traditional
marriage rules.

Personal criteria of suitability

Above, I referred to the importance of East African connections in
marriage arrangement in the UK and the process of introducing
spouses. I shall now discuss the personal attributes of the bride and
groom, i.e. the criteria of suitability considered important in spouse
selection.

A groom is expected to be anything from the same age as the bride to a maximum of seven years older. Most girls are married in their twenties, i.e. seventeen out of the twenty-three brides in my sample (see *Table 6*). Of the grooms, thirteen were under twenty-five years old, and nine were over this age, as compared with six brides, and one was thirty-two years old.

Table 6   *Age at marriage*

age (years)	19–24	25–30	30+
grooms	13	9	1
brides	17	6	–

total number of marriages: 23

In terms of occupation, although there are broad outlines followed when matching spouses, there are no clear-cut professions that are considered suitable for each other except the medical ones, e.g. a female doctor or a woman in the para-medical fields will be matched up with a doctor groom. Providing the grooms are well-qualified and have steady jobs, brides of all kinds of occupations will be considered for them.

In most cases, brides are less qualified than grooms. The greater emphasis is on their personal qualities and their moral characteristics in comparison with those of the grooms, whose status is judged by their earning potential and education, i.e. socially-defined criteria of achievement.

The control exercised over the amount of education girls receive is reflected in the majority of marriages in my sample. Nine grooms were university graduates and professionals, in comparison with three brides. Graduate grooms mostly marry women who are either in white-collar jobs or in the para-medical fields. As can be seen from *Table 7*, the majority of brides in my sample were office workers. This situation is increasingly changing as the younger, better-educated women are emerging through the university and higher education system of the UK. There is at present a demand for university graduate brides for professional grooms, and a trend towards matches of equally-educated spouses. Also, as most girls are now earning, both

Table 7   *Occupations of brides and grooms*

	university graduate or professional	white collar or office worker	skilled and technical work	own business	not employed
grooms	9	2	11	1	–
brides	3	15	–	–	5

total sample: 23 couples

before and after their marriages, there is greater interest in being trained for a job and on being sufficiently (though not over-) educated to be able to earn a decent salary.

Of the graduate grooms in my sample, one was married to a beautician bride; the second married a student who was in the middle of her HNC in business studies, and two married secretaries. The only grooms married to professional brides were an engineer who married the optician bride, a medical groom who married a pharmacist and an accountant who married a bride in the same profession. Of the non-graduate grooms, one was an accountant who married a computer programmer bride; a photographer and a television engineer both married brides who were bank cashiers, and a laboratory assistant married a secretary. The rest of the grooms were all married to brides who were white collar workers or unemployed. It is difficult to give an indication of particular occupations that are thought to be suited for one another since there is such a concentration amongst the brides in white collar and para-medical jobs. Educational achievement in Britain has become a very important factor in measuring the status of spouses, especially that of the groom.

In terms of the personal morals of spouses, stricter control is exercised on the women who are referred to as 'loose characters' if there is the slightest hint that they have boyfriends, especially non-Sikh ones. A tainted reputation for girls as a result of such relationships diminishes their chances of getting good husbands within the East African community. This does not necessarily apply to men who date European women. They can still be married to respectable brides, especially if they are well-qualified. A lot more 'bad behaviour' is tolerated from the young men than from the women, who are expected to maintain a purer personal standard.[9]

Another important criterion in determining the status of the bride is her appearance, which ranks above her knowledge of household skills, temperament, and education. This feature is important especially to young men who now meet their brides before getting engaged. A highly-educated and accomplished but unattractive girl does not do nearly as well in the marriage market as a pretty girl with a mediocre level of education and from an ordinary family background. Nonetheless, the present emphasis on women's education has made attractive but not well-educated girls much less upwardly mobile than in East Africa.

This reflects changes in the way in which marriage is being viewed in Britain. Although the qualifications of the grooms are ranked higher than their physique and family backgrounds, there is much greater attention being paid to the personal preferences of both brides and grooms. There is therefore a shift from viewing marriage as a match between two families, i.e. the traditional view, to the more individualistic 'western' notion of marriage being a union of two people, albeit within the East African Sikh community. The social emphasis can be discerned from the fact that twenty-two of the twenty-three marriages in my sample were arranged observing classical rules, though there has been flexibility in these. However, the emphasis on personal preferences is also obvious from the greater freedom allowed to couples to court before marriage.

A feature of the personal preferences and assets of the spouses concerns the grooms in particular, i.e. ownership of personal property, mainly a house. This was non-existent in East Africa but has gained prominence in the UK. From the ethnographies of marriage in North India, it is clear that residence after marriage is predominantly with the joint family of the groom, in which the daughters-in-law have subordinate positions (Naik 1947: 253–54; Madan 1965: 128–33; Gould 1968: 413–21; Lewis 1965: 160–95; Van der Veen 1972: 65). However, Vatuk (1972: 69) does mention that neolocal residence after marriage is increasing among urban migrants, being associated in their case with the occupational mobility that has drawn people from rural areas to small town houses. Even so, unlike the East African situation in the UK, there is no expectation of grooms owning exclusive property separate from that of their families before marriage. It is now common for East African Sikh men to buy houses as an investment soon after starting work, even though they may take up residence only after their marriages. This applied to four of the grooms in my sample. A consequence of ownership of personal property has been the further intensification of individual attributes of the grooms. This has changed the criteria of spouse selection, because instead of considering collective property and the status of the groom's family, as in East Africa, parents are now investigating the groom's own possessions and qualifications before confirming an alliance.

The reasons for the higher status of 'propertied grooms' in the marriage market is that brides can thus completely avoid joint family residence. Neolocal residence is guaranteed by the ownership of exclusive property, thus reducing contact with the bride's affines to a minimum. This has led to a reduction in importance of the general family background of the groom. A well-qualified young man with property but from a mediocre *khandan* will be considered to be a good catch on his personal merits.

All this links up with the other characteristics of East African Sikh society that have developed since migration. For example, status differences have dissolved considerably in the UK and less attention is being paid to finer differences of standing. This is due both to the concern that East Africans should marry within the community, and also to the emergence of young East Africans and higher-status families who have achieved wealth and prestige since migration.

Another feature that pushes up the status of the grooms is that they should be 'proper Sikhs', i.e. they should be turban-wearing. This does not imply that they should have untrimmed beards, since the majority do trim them. However, there is at present more interest among young Sikh men in maintaining a full beard than ever before.[10] This trend runs parallel to the increased interest in wearing a turban, especially during the past eight years, and also to the general conservatism of the East African Sikhs. Nineteen of the twenty-three grooms in my sample were turbanned Sikhs. On the wedding day, all the grooms wore turbans, including those normally not doing so. A clean-shaven Sikh may be considered a good catch for a bride from a clean *khandan* only if the girl has herself cut her hair.

Marriage negotiations; procedures of rejection and acceptance

Although a number of boys and girls may be kept in view, on the whole when a spouse is selected and an approach is made, there was usually acceptance shown by both sides. Within my sample, I did not come across a bride or groom who had refused anyone once there was clear interest shown by one side, usually the bride's people. This was especially so if the groom's family approved of the bride. This is not to say that people are never rejected, but the aim is never to be put in a position where one has to reject or is rejected. Early discussions quickly reveal the possibility of a potential rejection. Direct approaches are made to the families of either spouse only when there is a pretty good chance of acceptance. In this way, both the bride's and the groom's sides 'save face' since neither of them are put in an embarrassing situation.

If someone has to be rejected, an attempt is made always to do so either by using a subtle method like suggesting that the young person concerned is still studying and is not ready for marriage, or by traditional excuses of using four-*gots* instead of the standard two, as well as unfavourable opinions of the older people in the family. Often, enough interest may not be shown in a proposal in the first place, mainly by the groom's side, who are the ones who are approached first by the bride's people. When the response is slow, then the bride's people do not pursue any further discussions. One example of this within my sample was one that I have already referred to previously, of a clerical bride who married a research officer. The bride's father knew of a professional groom whom he thought was suitable for his daughter. He asked the groom's FB who had worked with him in the East African Railways to put the proposal forward to the groom's family. The FB felt that the girl suggested was neither well-qualified enough for a professional man (being a white collar worker), nor was she considered to be smart and pretty, although the family background was impeccable. The bride's father is one of the most active members of an association in London, and belongs to an established but orthodox East African family. However, although the family background of both spouses could be considered to be suitable, a match between a professional groom and a clerical bride was thought to be too unequal in terms of personal qualifications. The bride's father was aiming too high for her. For this reason, the FB did not take much interest in the proposal and did not present it to the groom's father as one that was worth considering. Since there was a cool response from the groom's family, the bride's father did not repeat his request, having realized his position in this way. The bride was soon afterwards engaged to a groom who holds an interesting job but is not a university graduate. This was thought to be a more appropriate match for a non-graduate bride. The professional groom later got engaged to a university graduate bride, a much better match in relation to educational achievement. Thus, there was no open rejection by the groom's side and hardly anyone found out about this proposal.[11]

The secrecy surrounding marriage negotiations is due to the fact that news of any possible rejection spreads quickly within the community. A leak is most undesirable for the bride because it spoils her future chances. Also, the bride's family's position is more vulnerable because they tend to make the first move, which gives the groom's people an upper hand. This is not to say that girls and their families do not reject grooms suggested to them. In fact, increasing independence of East African women, both economic and otherwise, has made them more outspoken and 'fussy' about their marriage partners. Most of them take an active interest in the discussions and do reject grooms, although a number of them pretend not to know of the negotiations in public, which makes them appear more passive than they actually are. Girls reject grooms either when they have seen them prior to any discussions of marriage, or when someone is being considered for them. Once an approach has been made to the boy's side by her family and if they accept, then the girls nearly always accept. This is certainly the case within my sample, although I have met girls who have actually met the groom chosen for them and have rejected him. This is something that can only be done once or twice, otherwise people are likely to consider the girl to be *too* fussy. The phrase used most often is '*nak dhay thalay koui cheez nahi andhi*' – 'nothing comes under her nose'. The consequence of this is that people may be reluctant to suggest further grooms because of the fear of rejection.

This also applies to the grooms, though traditionally less fuss was

made if they rejected prospective brides, because it was considered
to be their right to have the final say. Even grooms can only reject
potential brides for a particular period, i.e. while they are considered
to be eligible. Once they are past the age of thirty, their value
depreciates because there are fewer girls suited to them in terms of
age and education, and younger, more eligible men emerge who
are considered to be more suitable. This happend to one of my
informants, who was thirty-two at the time of his marriage. He was
thought to be an especially good catch from his mid-twenties till the
age of thirty, but he kept on rejecting marriage proposals because he
wanted to travel and establish himself. Most people had heard of his
rejections and grumbled about them. During my fieldwork he got
engaged rather rapidly under pressure and was married within six
months. Around the time of his engagement, he felt strongly that he
was foolish in not having considered some of the previous proposals,
because they had been of a better quality than the one he actually
accepted.

The final aspect of marriage arrangement is that I did not come
across any case in which, during the stage of negotiations, demands
for a dowry or a particular type of marriage ceremony were made. In
fact, the grooms' people take pride in their lack of interest in what the
brides bring with them since they are supposedly only concerned
with getting 'decent girls'. It is considered to be uncouth to demand a
certain level of dowry for a particular groom. I shall detail dowries in
the next chapter, but I should mention here that cash is not given at
marriages in great sums, nor is it considered the right of the groom's
side to receive or demand it.

People were surprised when I questioned either the bride's side
about the level of dowry demanded for the groom or the groom's
people about the level of dowry stated. They would emphasize that
'the Sikhs are not Patels who ask for huge dowries' and that they are
only interested in 'a girl who would fit in with the groom's family'.
Thus, there are no negotiations for a particular type of dowry.
However, groom's people do have unspoken expectations because
they are quite familiar with what is given in 'particular families and
circles'. Remarks like 'such and such a family is good at *dayna layan*'
are commonly made, referring to their generosity in gift exchange.
Also, the amount of dowry given to daughters and the procedures

followed in previous marriages within the family concerned are known to a lot of people. Such knowledge is commonly available to both the groom's and the bride's side, so that the implicit expectations of the groom's side are nearly always met by the bride's people. There are also enough stories around to remind people that the position of a bride with a small dowry is likely to be vulnerable in her marital household.

Despite this, I want to emphasize that there are no demands made overtly by the groom's side, nor is there any notion of recognizing their right to demand a dowry. Nonetheless, I did hear of a few marriages which took place in East Africa and in India before the 1950s in which the daughter-in-law was harshly treated by the mother-in-law because her dowry had been considered insufficient. I shall explore this aspect in greater detail in the following chapters.

Conclusion

Important criteria of the arrangement of East African marriages in the UK have been considered in this chapter. The explanations given for the observance of the traditional rules of village and *got* exogamy, caste and regional endogamy, the asymmetry between the wife givers and wife takers, etc. are similar to that of the high-status Hindus in North India. However, certain explicit rules have been modified into preferences since migration, in order to loosen the marriage system in response to circumstances in the UK. Despite the more informal introductory meetings of couples within my sample, the majority of marriages were arranged by the parents, i.e. twenty-two of the twenty-three in my sample.

However, modifications have taken place in Britain. Greater attention is being paid to the personal achievements of the groom and the bride as opposed to the family background, which was given a great deal of weight in East Africa and also in the Punjab. Thus, there is a move away from the collective assets of the family and its general status to the individual accomplishments of spouses concerned.

A point that relates to this is that in Britain there is a tendency to move into nuclear households either straight after marriage or soon afterwards. An asset of the groom which guarantees this is the ownership of a house. This feature has contributed to a major change in the traditional spouse selection procedures by further emphasizing the individual standing of grooms, instead of family status, because a mediocre family will be overlooked in favour of education and a steady job.

Leading on from this, status differences are not clear among East African Sikhs. The situation in Britain is more complex due to greater geographical and occupational dispersal. Nonetheless there are many equal-status families with similar levels of wealth and education due to selective migration from East Africa, making the pool of people from which spouses can be selected quite large. This is an enormous advantage in the arrangement of marriages.

The desire to maintain East African society intact has led to the loosening of the rules of *gots* and regions and to greater tolerance of slightly deviant marriages. A degree of flexibility has crept in to decrease the threat of marriage outside the community and in response to the emergence of marriageable young people who are almost British products because of their upbringing and education in this country. As a result, the personal preferences of the young people are given more consideration as are mutual choice marriages of Ramgarhias wanting to marry Ramgarhias, thus observing the rule of caste endogamy, something which is not difficult for them because a large number not only have a similar status but they also belong to one caste. On top of this they maintain intense contact with one another, which is useful in finding spouses.

This desire to restrict the marriage circle helps to maintain the 'group' or collective identity of the East African Sikh community. This is further reinforced by the preference to marry within the community, thus perpetuating the East African identity through restriction of marriage circles. Although East Africans are conservative, as can be seen from their strong adherence to traditional criteria in the arrangement of marriages, they are, nonetheless, forward and progressive in other directions. The reason for this is that factors such as the absence of roots, greater British orientation, the clear vision they have of staying permanently in this country, etc., all come into play.

Having referred to the general community aspects, at the familial level, changes are occurring which focus on the individual more so than the general family. An attempt is being made not to see marriage so much as an alliance between two families but increasingly as a union between two people. Thus, there is a shift in focus to the couple itself due to the changing values and more tolerant attitudes of the community as it has been established in the UK.

A consequence of the tolerance over marriages inside the community in order to prevent marriages outside will, in future, result in growing acceptance of marriage forms inside the community becoming extended to those outside, i.e. with non-Sikhs, both Indians and Europeans. The paradox is that the weakening adherence to traditional rules of marriage arrangement will lead to great accommodation within East African society of heterogeneous marriages which may further dent the consciousness they have of their 'East Africanness' and their communications network. For example, a marriage outside the community will automatically reduce the kin universe and general East African ties to half, i.e. to that of the East African spouse. As a result, there will be certain changes in the Ramgarhia kinship system which will dilute existing obligations and duties of kinsmen towards each other. This feature will become more prominent and could potentially weaken still strong community solidarity. The homogeneity of East African society established through the perpetuation of previous links in the UK will also be affected. At present, the aim of loosening marriage arrangement procedures is precisely the opposite; it is to maintain the 'East Africanness' of the community through the arrangement of correct marriages within East African circles.

SIX

The dowry system: continuity and change

The previous chapter discussed the criteria for spouse selection and the adaptations in the marriage pattern of East African Sikhs in Britain, which on the whole conforms to the informal hypergamous system of North India.[1]

This chapter considers the dowry system of East African Sikhs, which has undergone changes due to the process of migration from India to East Africa and from there to the UK. These two stages of migration have brought an increased amount of wealth to East Africans, which in the past and at present, has been translated into two important aspects of their society, marriage and dowry patterns. I shall also consider the effects of other factors which have arisen within the community since migration, such as wage earning amongst East African women, which especially concerns the brides who have themselves had an impact on the content of their dowries; and changes in family patterns, especially the developing predominance of nuclear families, the consciousness East Africans have of their 'East Africanness' and 'Ramgarhianess', which has been further accentuated in Britain. Their traditionalism is reflected in the elaborations that have taken place within the marriage rituals and dowry system. First, I will give some background to the North Indian marriage and dowry system.

North Indian and Ramgarhia notions of dowry

Dowry[2] in North India is 'property given to the daughter to take with her into marriage. Technically, it is her property and in her own control, though the husband usually has rights of management' (Tambiah 1975: 62). It is 'wealth given with the daughter to use as the nucleus of their conjugal estate' (p. 83). The legal definition of dowry is more inclusive. Derrett (1963: 218) states 'by a dowry is meant any property or valuable security given or agreed to be given between the parties to the marriage or by any person to any person at, before, or after the marriage, in consideration of it. Wedding presents are expressly excluded from the definition unless they are made as consideration for the marriage.' The above, it seems, includes not only bride wealth but also *any* form of property which is transferred at the time of marriage, and it also abolishes almost all property transactions at marriage. However, the generally-used definition of dowry is a more restricted one referring only to the wealth given along with the daughter at marriage.

Dowry and the prestations that take place at marriage are classified in North India as 'pure gifts' accompanying the 'gift of a maiden or virgin' (*Kanyadaan*) (Van der Veen 1972: 210; Tambiah 1975: 64; Vatuk 1972: 99). The latter is considered to be the prestation of utmost purity.[3] According to Brahmanical ideals, the prestation of dowry and *Kanyadaan* is extremely meritorious, providing no return is accepted. The sheer act of giving such a gift results in the enhancement of an individual's status, suggesting that the acceptance of it decreases the recipient's prestige providing a larger return is not made (Mauss (1954:72)).[4] This is not so in the North Indian context (Van der Veen 1972; Pocock 1972; Madan 1965; Derrett 1963: 409). Dowry marriage seems to be an ideological denial of reciprocity because it is the duty of the bride givers to do this without expecting a return and it is the bride takers' right to be constant recipients.

This is a consequence of the hypergamous marriage system of North India, which is characterized by the existence of an asymmetrical relationship between wife takers (groom's people) and wife givers (bride's people). The former, despite being presented with lavish gifts from the latter, do not face subordination because of the superior status accorded to them within this context. This type of ideology recognizes their status as endless receivers of gifts even long after the marriage itself (Tambiah 1975: 64; Vatuk 1973: 193). Vatuk shows that among the Gaur Brahmans, this gift giving does not stop even when the woman is widowed. The bond between the daughter and the parents 'never ceases' and is 'reaffirmed at every ceremony' through the prestations of gifts to her and her husband's kin. Thus, in the North Indian case, the presentation of 'pure gift' like that of a *Kanya* (maiden) and her dowry has the opposite effect to the one expected by Mauss (1954: 72). The acceptance of such gifts by the wife takers in North India, in fact, reflects their superordinate status.

The main belief on which hypergamy rests is that a woman's marriage is seen as being 'a gift of a maiden' (*Kanyadaan*). The giving of such a pure gift along with material objects is meritorious for the wife givers, providing no return is accepted. This particular aspect is the most important feature of hypergamy, first because it provides the moral basis of the different positions of the wife givers and wife takers, and second because dowry marriage and *Kanyadaan* are publicly validated, being considered the most prestigious form of marriage in North India (Karve 1953: 132; Blunt 1931: 70–1; Madan 1965: 114). They also act both as indicators and enhancers of family and caste status (Pocock 1957a, 1972; Van der Veen 1972; Madan 1965, 1973; Lewis 1958; Vatuk 1973). Dowries are excellent vehicles for 'pursuing the status game of hypergamy' (Tambiah 1975: 72) in which families of lower status but superior wealth can attempt to acquire prestige by arranging marriages with higher-status ones. By so doing, the wife givers are able to convert material wealth into high status through the prestation of dowries and *Kanyas* as pure gifts for the superior wife takers. Hence, there are connotations of generalized reciprocity, since status is the indirect reward for a supposedly pure gift, for which ideally the giver should have no expectation of return.

Dowry, which is most often defined as the property or wealth given to the daughter at her marriage is, according to Goody, a type of 'pre-mortem inheritance' (1975: 1). For this reason he classifies it as 'diverging devolution' (1976: 7), a process by which parental property is distributed to a daughter at her marriage rather than at the death of the holders. In comparing bridewealth and dowry to the different technologies and the sexual division of labour, he suggests that the former is to be found where women make a major contribution to the agricultural economy, whereas dowry is restricted to those societies in which the male contribution predominates. In the latter case, the woman's position is maintained in her marital home by providing property for her in the form of a dowry to keep her in the manner to which she has previously been accustomed (1976: 109). Hence, dowry is also seen as compensation for the loss of inheritance rights as related to the patrimony.

In North India, a developed concept of exclusive female property can be discerned from the classical legal treaties, the *dharmashastras*. Dowry forms the major part of this property complex called *stridhanam* (Tambiah 1975: 71; Vatuk 1973: 63; Madan 1965: 158, 237). Although there is theoretically a clear-cut belief in the concept of female property in North India, in practice, a bride may have little control over large parts of her dowry.[5] This is because the hyper-gamous marriage system puts the wife takers in a powerful position from which an enormous amount of control can be exercised over bridal property. I shall explore this aspect later in connection with a number of factors, one of which is the increased earning powers of East African Sikh brides in the UK, making their dowries more like *stridhanam* because of their own contributions towards making them.

East African Sikh notions about dowry, referred to as *daaj*, show that although the ideology in existence in North India behind giving one also applies to them, the language used to explain the reasons for doing so is not the same. For example, the presentation of a dowry accompanied by a bride is not referred to as *Kanyadaan*, nor is *stridhanam* used to refer to female rights to property. Yet there is a clear understanding that it is a woman's right to receive what is referred to as a *daaj*, which is her share of the inheritance and is similar in content to North Indian dowries. The whole complex of gifts that flow from the bride givers to the bride takers are seen as *daaj*, a pure gift for which no return is expected. *Sanskrit* terms are not used by the Ramgarhias to express or to explain this ideology, though the word *daan* (gift) is constantly used. Similarly gifts will never be accepted by the bride givers from a daughter and her affines in realization of their superior position as bride takers.

For this reason, in conformity with the North Indian situation, there is a big difference in the volume of gifts that flow from the bride givers to the bride takers (Mayer 1960: 234; Lewis 1958: 188). The only gifts that the groom's people present at a marriage are to the bride herself and not to her family in general. If a gift is ever accepted by the bride's family from that of the groom's, a reciprocal one will always be given on the spot, or soon after receiving it. This rule applies regardless of the size of the gift because 'one who gives the daughter should not receive anything' (Karve 1953: 31) not even in the form of services[6]

(Lewis 1958: 169, 188), though the enhancement of the bride's family status is a reward for the prestation of such a gift.

In the following I shall consider the *daaj* in relation to the elaborations and modifications that have occurred as a result of migration from India to East Africa and from there to Britain; and to the force of changes in family structure on the shape of the *daaj*.

The components of the *daaj*

A *daaj* refers not only to the bride's personal property but also to all the gifts that are given by her family to the groom and his relatives. It has four main components.

The first consists of items of clothing for the bride. This is the most important part of the dowry because when I asked the women what they had received in their *daajs*, they would always refer to the clothing content: the number of items they had received. Only upon further questioning would they tell me about the gold and household goods. Even today, when both younger and older women discuss the quantities of the *daaj* they have received or other brides have been given, it is always in terms of clothing. For this reason, I shall focus on this particular component to compare the *daajs* presented since before the 1930s. However, I shall also refer to the other components because these have undergone some important changes.

The second component of the *daaj* is the gold the bride receives from her family.

The third part consists of household goods, including utensils, furniture, linen, quilts, kitchen gadgets, crockery, and consumer items like washing machines, stereo music centres, etc.

The fourth component is referred to as the affinal gifts since these do not concern the bride herself, unlike the previous three parts of the *daaj*. Although a number of categories of the groom's kin are recipients of gifts from the bride's family, the three main people are the groom himself, the mother-in-law, and the father-in-law.

The interesting aspect of East African Sikh *daajs* is that money payments, like bridegroom price, are non-existent. These payments are common among the Desais (Van der Veen 1972: 39) and Patidars (Pocock 1972: 3) and are decided in accordance with the groom's personal prestige and general family status. In the East African Sikh case, the affines are given material gifts in the form of gold and clothes. The main cash gift within this sphere is referred to as *Vadaigi*, and is given to the groom's father when the bride leaves her parental home after the marriage ceremony. In Britain, the sum has not exceeded £101 in any of the weddings within my sample. The amount that is most commonly given is £51. Thus, cash payments and money exchanges are a relatively minor part of the *daaj*. Similarly, there has never been a recognition that a price should be paid for a particular calibre of groom. There is disapproval attached to any demand made by the groom's side for a sum of money or a particular range of material gifts as a price for the groom. News of such demands travels rapidly within the community, which can put the groom's people in an embarrassing situation, resulting in negative consequences at a later stage, because girls from 'good' families will no longer be suggested for these grooms. I did not hear of any open demands for cash that had been made by the groom's side either during my fieldwork, or in relation to marriages that had taken place in the past.

Before describing the *daaj* in detail, I should point out that there is a difference in what is considered to be the *daaj* at present and what it was in the past, both in India and East Africa. In comparing the *daajs* of the women who got married in East Africa and the UK with those who were married in India, I realized that the *daajs* of the latter category of women were meant specifically for the mother-in-law. I refer here to all the gifts that are now reserved for the bride herself, especially clothes and household goods. The mother-in-law did precisely what she wanted with these. She could also redistribute the gold, though it was traditionally recognized to be the most sacred part of the *daaj*, being an important symbol of the marital status of the bride. For this reason, there was strong disapproval attached to the control exercised by the mother-in-law over the gold, though a number of women said that their gold was later used to provide dowries for the marriages of their husbands' sisters.

The reason the *daaj* was no longer given to the mother-in-law was that there have been changes in the marriage procedure in East Africa and the UK. In India, before the 1930s, brides stayed with their parents for three to five years after their marriages. The consummation of the marriage took place after the *muklawa* ceremony, when the bride would go to reside permanently in the groom's house. Most of the older women were married around the ages eleven to fifteen, but had their *muklawa* at the age of seventeen to nineteen. The gifts that they took with them at this stage were ones that they kept for themselves. The *muklawa* even now does not contain any gold because the brides are supposed to wear *daaj* gold, which in the case of older women was in the custody of the mother-in-law until this stage. The other items in the 1930s *muklawa* were utensils, the *piri* (a low sitting stool), and a spinning wheel (*charkha*). These were all items for the bride's personal use. Similarly, clothing items presented were of a much higher quality than those in the *daaj*, since the bride actually wore them, whereas the *daaj* clothing gifts were often in the form of unsewn cloth which the mother-in-law could use for further gift giving.

My older women informants would constantly emphasize that they did not expect to keep any of the gifts given to them by their parents nor did they mind their *daajs* being incorporated into joint family property, because they had little concept of separate property, unlike the UK brides. Although I shall discuss this in great detail presently, the *daajs* of the older women were much smaller than present-day ones, which are more extensive both in household goods and the personal items of the bride. Gold jewellery was also restricted to a maximum of two or three pieces in the form of a ring, a pair of earrings, or a small pendant. None of these women had the gold sets, which were given both in East Africa and the UK, containing a neck piece, a bracelet or bangles, earrings and a ring, all presented in a velvet-lined jewellery box.

East African and British *daajs* are much more like the *muklawa* of the older women, and less like the 1930s and 1940s *daajs*, which were similar to what I have termed the affinal gifts of the present *daajs*. The main parts of British *daajs* consist of property that is exclusively for the bride, and they have more characteristics of *stridhanam* than any of the previous *daajs*. Since affinal gifts are clearly differentiated from the gifts for the bride, there has been a change in the person who controls the *daaj*, from the role of the powerful mother-in-law to that of the daughter-in-law, for whom the majority of the *daaj* gifts are now intended.

To summarize: among the East African Sikhs, there are no negotiations for a particular type of *daaj*. In fact, the groom's people take great pride in emphasizing that they have no interest in the gift exchanges, since they supposedly only want a decent girl. Nonetheless they have expectations of a *daaj* and they know that these will be fulfilled. I did not come across any women who had been married without a *daaj*, because her position in her marital home would have been vulnerable if she had arrived without one. This is one of the reasons the *daaj* is very much a dowry and not a trousseau, which is not obligatory and which often just consists of clothes exclusively for the bride. Also, a trousseau has a restricted number of items whereas a *daaj* contains a large range of gifts. A marriage without a *daaj* would also reflect badly on the *izzet* (honour) of the *khandan* of the bride.

In the general North Indian case, it is considered meritorious (*poon*) to present gifts to the affines along with the gift of a daughter. The presentation of a *daaj* is seen not as a demand by the bride takers but as a legitimate right of the bride. It is said to be *garibidava*, a 'poor man's gift' even though the contents of the *daaj* may be both expensive and elaborate. All this is in accordance with the hyper-gamous situation of North India in which the bride givers are considered to be inferior to the bride takers, especially at the time of marriage. Similarly, a marriage that involves a direct exchange (*bata*) or one in which bridewealth is accepted is, according to the Sikhs, the lowest type of marriage, conforming to higher caste attitudes (Madan 1965: 114).

The underlying explanations for giving a *daaj* are similar to those of the Hindus. The ideology prevalent in North India, related to *kanyadaan* and the accompanying dowry, to the effect that they are pure gifts is also the same, though the terminology used by the Hindus is not followed, since the Sikhs[7] are theoretically not supposed to have followed Hindu customs. The giving of a *daaj* and ostentatious marriage celebrations are forbidden by the Sikh religion due to its anti-caste and anti-ritualistic nature (Macleod 1976: 86), yet the Sikh marriage pattern and their gift exchanges conform to the North Indian Hindu situation.[8]

In addition, the control of the *daaj* has shifted from the mother-in-law, in the 1930s and 1940s, to the daughters-in-law in the 1960s and 1970s. I have differentiated between a *daaj* and *muklawa*, the former containing lower-quality gifts for the mother-in-law to be used for further gift giving, before the 1950s, and the latter containing better-quality gifts for the bride.

Changes within the content and structure of daajs

I shall refer to a total number of seventy-four *daajs*, all of which belong to women within both my core and wedding samples. The families have been described in previous chapters, which have explored their relationships. To demonstrate the changes the *daajs* have undergone, I have divided the time-span from before the 1930s to 1978, when I conducted my fieldwork, into seven phases.

As can be seen from *Table 8*, Phase 1 refers to eight marriages

Table 8   *Countries and times in which* daajs *were given*

| | countries | | |
time periods	India	East Africa	United Kingdom
Phase 1: pre-1930s	8	–	–
Phase 2: post-1930s	3	–	–
Phase 3: post-1940s	5	1	–
Phase 4: post-1950s	2	6	–
Phase 5: post-1960s	–	13	2
Phase 6: post-1970s	–	–	11
Phase 7: fieldwork, 1977–78	–	–	23

total number of *daajs* = 73

before the 1930s and Phase 2 concerns three marriages after this period, all of which took place in India. Few marriages during these two phases took place in East Africa because it was rare to find complete family units. Most men lived in 'bachelor households' and went to India for leave after every four years, during which time single men would get married and married ones would be reunited with their families.

It was only in the 1940s that families started to arrive in East Africa, as the community became more established. In this third phase, post-1940s, there are six women in my sample, of which only one was actually married in East Africa, while the rest were married in India, sometimes to grooms who already had strong East African connections, e.g. a father resident in East Africa.

Phase 4 refers to the post-1950s, in which six of the eight marriages in my sample took place in East Africa, and two in India. By this time, East African Sikhs only married other East Africans already resident in Africa. Phase 5 refers to the post-1960s, and concerns marriages that took place both in East Africa and the UK. I have stated earlier that East Africans started to arrive in Britain in the late 1960s. Some of my informants who were in London before this period remember having been to only a couple of weddings during this time. Phase 6 refers to the post-1970s, during which time eleven marriages in my sample are British ones which took place before my fieldwork. Phase 7 concerns the twenty-three marriages that I actually covered during my fieldwork, from September 1977 to September 1978. As can be seen from *Table 8*, the 1930s and 1940s refer mainly to Indian *daajs*, the 1950s and 1960s to East African ones, and the 1970s to ones in the UK.

Before I describe the *daajs* of this period, I should mention that the clothing content, which as stated is the most important part of the *daaj*, changed in the 1940s, though it has from then onwards remained extremely conservative.

In the early days, clothing items were different from the ones given in East Africa and Britain. A complete outfit, which I refer to as a clothing item, was called a *ter* and consisted of four separate pieces. During and before the 1930s these were the *kagra* (long skirt), the *kameez* (tunic) and two *dupattas* (headscarfs) called *dornay* because they were worn together for extra cover. These garments were worn by rural women, as urban dress took the form of a Punjabi suit, consisting of a *salwaar* (trousers), *kameez*, and *dupatta*. The latter attire is similar to that worn by women in East Africa and at present in Britain. Since the Punjabi suit consists of three pieces, a handkerchief is always added to the package to make it into an even number of four.

Phase 1: pre-1930s *daajs*

The *kagras* in the *daaj* were not made to fit a particular size, meaning that most women could wear them. They could, therefore, be used for further gift-giving by the mother-in-law, unlike the Punjabi suits in the East African *daajs* which were made specifically for the bride.

Earlier I mentioned that the pre-1930s *daajs* were simpler than those presented to women in the post-1940s and 1950s in Africa. In the following, I shall analyse the *daajs* of the women in my sample by referring to the gifts that they themselves received but not those that were presented to the groom and his kin. I shall only refer to these gifts in the 1960s and 1970s *daajs* because of the difficulty in getting older women to remember their own *daajs*, quite apart from recalling the gifts that were presented to the affinal kin. These women married between the ages of eleven to fifteen years and were far too young to remember what these might have been. This also applied to an extent to the 1940s and 1950s brides because they were at the time of marriage and that stage in their lives not concerned with what should be, or was given, to various kin. They could only remember their own personal gifts and one or two special gifts given to the affines.

A reason for this lack of memory was that they only started to learn about it when they were well past their thirties, at which time they made a concerted effort to learn about how to give, what to give at particular times, and also the ways in which, and categories of kinsmen from whom, gifts could be accepted. Such knowledge was acquired by women either around the time of the HZ's wedding or near their own children's marriages. In their marital homes, these activities were reserved for the mother-in-law who was in charge of gift exchanges and who exercised an enormous amount of control over the daughters-in-law till a late stage in their lives. This was especially so in the case of older women because all of them lived in joint families. This is not to say that these women were not aware of the general gift exchanges that took place on an informal basis, but that their rank was a junior one when they first married in comparison with that of the mother-in-law who had more precise knowledge of the presentation of gifts at major functions like engagements, weddings and other life cycle rituals. The force of the joint family was much stronger than at present, as was the authority of the mother-in-law. She was also the focus of the gifts presented in the *daaj* at the time of marriage, rather than the bride herself, who was very young at the time.

Of the eight women in the pre-1930s period in my sample, three were married around the age of eleven to twelve years, and five at the age of thirteen. All of them had their *muklawa* at a much later stage when they moved permanently into their marital homes, i.e. two had it three years later, five had it five years later, and one had it seven years later. Focusing on the clothing items in their *daajs* (see *Table 9*, two of the eight women had five items, five had seven items and one had eleven. All these women were also given a bed and a low stool (a *palung* and *piri*) which were the MB's gifts. All of them received a *muklawa* of five clothing items. Four of them were also given a

Table 9   *Clothing items presented in* daajs

	items									
	5	7	9	11	13	15	17	21	31	41+
India										
Phase 1: pre-1930s	2	5	–	1	–	–	–	–	–	–
Phase 2: post-1930s	–	1	–	1	–	–	–	1	–	–
India and East Africa										
Phase 3: post-1940s	–	1	–	2	–	–	–	3	–	–
Phase 4: post-1950s	–	–	–	3	–	1	1	3	–	–
East Africa and the UK										
Phase 5: post-1960s	–	–	–	–	3	2	1	9	–	–
UK										
Phase 6:										
pre-fieldwork, 1970s	–	–	–	–	–	–	–	7	3	1
Phase 7:										
fieldwork, 1977–78	–	1	–	2	–	–	1	17	2	–

spinning wheel at this time. Other than the one woman who had a *daaj* of eleven clothing items and who was given eight *tolas*[9] of gold, the rest all received under five *tolas*, equivalent to two to three small pieces of jewellery. At this time gold sets were not given, only becoming popular from the 1940s onwards. The eleven-itemed *daaj* is unusually high for that period. The reason for this is that this woman was an only daughter of a wealthy landowner who had three educated sons.[10] All the other women with the smaller *daajs* described their fathers' occupations as *tarkhans*; they did carpentry jobs for the Jat Zamindars in return for grain payments.

A general comment about pre-1930s *daajs* is that although the three spheres of the *daaj* were all in existence, there was little emphasis on giving property that could be considered exclusively as the bride's. The reason for this is that the *daaj* was not aimed primarily at the bride as at present, but was meant for the groom's family, the mother-in-law in particular.

Phase 2: post-1930s *daajs*

The three women in my post-1930s sample were married in India at the ages of eleven, fifteen and sixteen and had their *muklawas* two to three years later.

One woman whose father was settled in East Africa, migrated soon after her *muklawa*. Her *daaj* contained eleven clothing items, eleven brass utensils, five *bistras*, a *palung* and *piri*, and eight *tolas* of gold.

The second woman's father worked as a carpenter in Jullunder and did not have any East African connections, though the groom had an older brother resident there. Her *daaj* contained seven clothing items, a *palung* and *piri*, nine utensils, five *bistras* and two *tolas* of gold.

The third woman had a very large *daaj* for that time, because she was the daughter of a successful building contractor in Calcutta. It consisted of twenty-one clothing items, fifty *tolas* of gold, 101 utensils of which twenty-one were of pure silver, two chairs, a table, a *palung* and *piri*, and five *bistras*. Her two daughters, who were married in East Africa and the UK, had smaller *daajs* to which I shall refer later on, in comparison with the mother. Her husband was not a businessman but was a clerical officer in East Africa.

By the 1930s, the Ramgarhias in India were increasingly developing East African connections. All these brides migrated to East Africa soon after marriage.

Phase 3: post-1940s *daajs*

Of the post-1940s marriages, there were not any in my core sample that took place in East Africa, though there was one in my wedding sample. At this time only a few marriages took place in Africa of Indian-born young Sikhs who had been brought up in Africa and were of marriageable age in the 1940s. This especially applied to the pioneer Sikhs who were beginning to bring their families over from India during the mid and late 1930s.

Although the rest of the marriages in my sample took place in India, at this stage most East African families still had strong Indian contacts, just as Indian families had direct contact with branches of their families in East Africa. For example, one of the brides actually went from Africa to get married in India and returned with her husband soon after marriage. The second bride's father worked in East Africa, though she herself was resident in India before her marriage. The third bride's husband's brothers were already settled in Africa at the time of her marriage and were developing a furniture business in Nairobi.

During the 1930s and 1940s, it was prestigious to marry grooms with families settled in Africa. Stories about the wealth that could be gained in Africa further helped raise the status of the 'Africa-returned' grooms[11] who went to India to marry. Similarly, a groom who had some of his family in Africa, and who had prospects of getting a job there, was also considered to be a good match. One of the brides who got married at this time to such a groom who had a job in India but whose father was settled in Africa, and whom he was expected to join, said that she had heard the African Sikhs boast about the wealth they had in Africa, because of good wages and a plentiful supply of jobs. When she migrated to Kenya after her marriage, she was shocked to find the poor facilities of the African Sikhs had to cope with, e.g. bad housing, lack of schooling facilities, and the difficulty of getting Indian foodstuffs in the small towns the Sikhs were living in as the railway system they were employed in was established.

The *daajs* of the two women who married grooms with East African connections were larger than those of the other brides. Both these brides are related, being daughters of two brothers who were considered to be wealthy since they had worked in Simla in the 1920s as building contractors. The money they had earned there had been channelled into their village. Both these brides had a twenty-one-itemed *daaj* (reserved for the mother-in-law) and an eleven-itemed *muklawa* of higher-quality garments for themselves the day after the wedding. They had twenty *tolas* of gold each in the form of eight bangles, two hairclips, two pairs of earrings, one gold set, and two pendants. Their household goods consisted of fifty-one utensils and eleven *bistras*.

The *daaj* of the woman whose parents had no connection with East Africa and who stayed in India for five years after her marriage before migrating was roughly the same smaller *daaj* of the pre-1940s bride. It consisted of five clothing items, one pair of gold earrings, and seven brass utensils. Her *muklawa*, given a year later, consisted of seven suits.

The *daaj* of the bride whose father worked in East Africa, but who married a groom resident in India who later migrated to Africa, consisted of eleven clothing items, twenty-one utensils, and twelve *tolas* of gold. Her *muklawa*, given three years later, had twenty-one clothing items and four *bistras*.

The bride who went from East Africa to marry an Indian groom had an eleven-itemed *daaj*, a light gold set (four *tolas*), twenty-one utensils, five *bistras*, and a watch. This *daaj* had East African influence since it contained furniture, in the form of four chairs, two cupboards, and a bed. Her *muklawa* consisted of five suits. This was a smaller *daaj* compared with brides who married East African grooms. This bride was from Malwa region. There are small regional differences in the amount of *daaj* given. The Majhails say that Doabis give more in *daajs* in comparison with either Malwains or Majhails. The majority of couples in my wedding sample are from Doaba (thirteen out of twenty-three couples) though the *daajs* of the three regions did not show any obvious differences in Britain, because regional differences in the UK are becoming increasingly muted as regional endogamy weakens.

The *daaj* of the only bride in my sample whose father worked for the Railways and who was married in 1942 in East Africa to an East African groom, consisted of twenty-one suits, no longer referred to as *ter* because the Punjabi suit was then in vogue. *Kagras* were no longer presented as they had been previously to the mother-in-law. The suits were very much bridal property. This *daaj* consisted of one gold set, two large bangles (sixteen *tolas*), twenty-one utensils and furniture, i.e. a bed, a table, four chairs, a cupboard, and a chest of drawers.

East African *daajs* even later on always contained furniture, a component which was never emphasized in the Indian *daajs* because the utensils and *bistras* were considered to be more desirable items. These are still important in present Indian *daajs* given in the Punjab, since they have a higher prestige rating. For this reason the two Indian brides in my 1940s sample who had large *daajs* had fifty-one utensils and eleven *bistras*, but only a *palung* and *piri* for furniture. However, one of these brides was also given a cow and a calf.

Points to emphasize at this stage are as follows: first, the *daajs* of women who married either in East Africa or to grooms with East African contacts were larger than the Indian ones. Similarly, the bride who went from East Africa to marry an Indian groom had a smaller *daaj*, in comparison with the East African bride who married in East Africa at the time, indicating the superiority of the East African bride over the Indian groom.

Second, there is an increase in the *daaj* in the post-1940s, from the five to eleven clothing items of the 1930s, to eleven to twenty-one items. This also applies to the amount of gold given in relation to the increased amount of contact with East Africa.

Third, there was a trend towards giving the *muklawa* soon after the wedding, unlike marriages of the previous decade. This meant that the *daaj* was increasingly the property of the bride and not that of the mother-in-law, although at this stage she was still powerful because all the brides lived within joint families.

Fourth, a factor that will emerge more clearly later on is that furniture was becoming an essential part of the *daaj*, especially in East Africa.

Finally, the pattern of giving a twenty-one-itemed *daaj* had already started, especially in the cases of East African-connected marriages. This size of *daaj* would later become the typical East African one.

Phase 4: post-1950s *daajs*

Of the eight marriages that took place during this period in my sample, two were those of Indian brides and the rest were East African ones.

The fathers-in-law of the Indian brides lived in East Africa at the time but had not brought their families over. Their wives, who were both sixteen years old at marriage, followed them within a couple of years. One of them had seventeen suits in her *daaj*, five in her *muklawa*, twenty-one utensils, two *bistras*, one gold set (ten *tolas*) and a *palung* and *piri* from her MB.

The second Indian bride had what I term as a modified *daaj* because it lacked heavy household items which were difficult to transport to Africa. She had eleven suits in the *daaj*, five in the *muklawa*, and a gold set (ten *tolas*). She did not get any furniture because she was migrating to East Africa but was given two *bistras* and fifteen utensils.

The six East African *daajs* of this decade varied from those with eleven clothing items to large ones with twenty-one items. Some of these brides are either related or have known each other since childhood.

Of the first set of three women, two were not related but were neighbours in Nairobi. The third was a Z-in-law of one of them. The two who had grown up together were both married in *Landia Gurdwara*, the first Sikh temple to be built in Nairobi. They had a similar *daaj* because the temple committee had passed a resolution to restrict the amount of dowry given in the marriages that were conducted there. This applied especially to both these brides, since their fathers were active members of this temple. Both of them also worked for the Railways, as carpenters.

One of the brides had five sisters, all of whose *daajs* are within my sample. Except for the youngest sister who was married in the UK and who had a twenty-one itemed *daaj*, the rest of the sisters married in East Africa and India and had *daajs* consisting of eleven to thirteen suits, five suits for *muklawa*, two gold rings, one watch, five *bistras*, two beds, four chairs, twenty-one utensils and a sewing machine each. The sister married in the 1950s did not get any glass utensils because at the time it was not considered prestigious enough to give cheaper breakable crockery. Brass and steel kitchenware was far more popular.

The background of the second bride has been referred to several times in previous chapters. Her family is in my core sample. Her husband is the wealthy travel agent. She had a *daaj* of eleven suits, one gold set (10 *tolas*), twenty-one utensils, a dining table, six chairs, two beds, and a sewing machine.

Both these *daajs* are similar except that one of them has more gold, because she was the last daughter to be married. The first bride had four sisters yet to be married. In both cases, the grooms were given a gold ring, a watch, and a suit which consisted of a pair of trousers, a jacket, a shirt, a pair of shoes, and one pair of socks. Both these brides were married in the early 1950s.

The Z-in-law of the travel agent's wife was married in the late 1950s.

Her *daaj* contained twenty-one suits, one heavy gold set (15 *tolas*), twenty-one utensils, a sewing machine, and furniture, i.e. a cupboard, two beds, six chairs, and a dining table. The groom was given two suits and a gold ring. This wedding was not at *Landia Gurdwara*.

The second set of women was also related. One of them is in my core sample and the second is her MBD, whose brother's family is also in my core sample. Both had *daajs* of twenty-one suits each, with five suits each for their *muklawas*, but there were other differences. My informant's father was a businessman who had a shop in Kenya selling a variety of sports goods. Also she was the only sister in a set of four brothers. Her MB was at first a carpenter for the Railways, though later on, he built up his own building contracting business. Her MBD thus had a smaller *daaj* in comparison with her own, which consisted of the twenty-one items, twenty *tolas* of gold (i.e. a set and six bangles), a watch, furniture, a transistor radio, six *bistras*, two tea and dinner sets, and twenty-one brass and steel utensils. The groom was given a gold ring, a watch, and a suit. Her MBD had twenty-one items, but only twelve *tolas* of gold, fewer furniture items (two beds and a cupboard), six *bistras*, and thirty-one utensils.

The eighth *daaj* belongs to the wife of a leading member of the Temple Committee in Southall. Her father had died a year before her marriage, which meant that her *daaj* was smaller than it might otherwise have been. It consisted of fifteen suits, plus five suits for *muklawa*, one gold set (11 *tolas*), one watch, two beds, a dining table, five chairs, seven *bistras*, twenty-one utensils, a small amount of glass crockery, and two very prestigious presents for that time, a radio and a record player from her two brothers.

Of the 1950s *daajs*, I want to stress the following points: first, by this time, a trend that had already been set up by the 1940s had become clearer. This is that the clothing items in the *daaj* were no longer for the mother-in-law as in previous decades, but for the bride herself, certainly in East African cases, although the furniture and household goods were incorporated into the joint household.

Second, other than the two Indian brides who had their *muklawas* a year after their marriages, East African brides who all married around the age of twenty had theirs a couple of days after the wedding. Thus, the long time that used to exist in previous decades between giving the *daaj* and the *muklawa* was no longer in existence. On top of this, there was no difference in the quality of gifts presented at both occasions since all the items belonged to the bride.

Leading on from this, the groom's kin were given gifts which were quite separate from the bride's *daaj*. For example, in the eight *daajs* of this period, the important people, the mothers-in-law, were given five suits each in six cases, two suits each in two cases, and two were also given a gold ring each. Similarly, in all eight cases grooms received a suit, a gold ring, and a watch. In three cases, the fathers-in-laws got a gold ring along with a suit and a turban that was presented to all eight of them. Thus, by the 1950s, bridal gifts of the *daaj* had become quite distinct from the affinal ones which were labelled and kept separate from the trunk which contained the bride's *daaj*.

It will become clearer from material to be presented later that the 1950s *daajs* were simpler in comparison to those of the 1960s and 1970s, although an important component of the *daaj* by this stage was the furniture. All East African *daajs* contained bedroom and dining room furniture. Consumer items such as tape recorders and food mixers were still uncommon. Within the household goods sphere, glass utensils were being given in some *daajs* but these were considered less valuable than steel and brass ones. In terms of the personal accessories of the bride, few were presented, unlike the present day *daajs*, where shoes, handbags, and shawls, are included. At most, the bride sometimes had a purse, though rarely a handbag, a pair of sandals and a small amount of make-up.

The final point is that all these brides married either East African grooms already settled in Africa or ones who migrated soon after marriage. None of the East African brides imported male fiancés from India, since there was an increasing trend to find spouses within the East African Sikh community that had already East Africanized in this phase (Mangat 1969: 141).

The *wari*, the groom's gifts to the bride, consisted of under eleven clothing items, mostly around five to seven; a gold set, a pair of slippers or shoes and henna. The *wari* has changed little over time as will be seen later.

Phase 5: post-1960s *daajs*

Of the fifteen marriages in the 1960s sample, only two took place in Britain, while the rest are East African ones (see *Table 8*).

Of the thirteen East African *daajs*, seven brides had twenty-one clothing items, one had seventeen items, two women related to each other (Zs-in-law) had fifteen items each, three sisters of a set of six (to which I have been, and will, refer) had thirteen suits each.

The three sisters all received furniture, twenty-one utensils, five to seven *bistras*, but only a few glass utensils. They had less gold than the rest of the brides in the form of two rings (2 to 3 *tolas*) and a watch. One sister had a light gold set but did not get a watch. Their grooms were all given a suit and a gold ring. These three *daajs* are similar to those given in the 1950s. The incoming Z-in-law of these sisters had a much larger *daaj*, of twenty-one items: two gold sets (eighteen *tolas*), seven *bistras*, a sofa set, a dining table with six chairs, a cabinet, twenty-one utensils, coffee, tea, and dinner sets, and a sewing machine.

A sewing machine was always presented in East African *daajs* because it was the most important piece of household equipment, since these women made all their own and their children's clothes. Similarly, all these *daajs* contained furniture except for the modified *daajs* of brides who migrated to Britain soon after marriage. This furniture was mostly made by Sikh furniture shops which had been booming in East Africa since the 1940s. Some of their business depended on making *daaj* furniture.

Other than the *daajs* of the three sisters, the rest of the women all had gold sets by this stage, sometimes in addition to separate pieces of gold jewellery. For example, one bride received a gold set, plus eight bangles, two rings, and two pairs of earrings which amounts to a total of twenty *tolas*, i.e. the equivalent of two good gold sets. Six of the women in my sample had one gold set only, while five had gold sets plus additional gold jewellery.

Within the household goods sphere, there were small changes in the 1960s because there was an increase in the number of consumer goods given, e.g. irons, pressure cookers, and radios, though luxury items like tape recorders, food mixers, and washing machines were still not commonly given. However, more furniture was presented in the form of sofa sets, cabinets, and dressing tables.

As for the affinal gifts, three mothers-in-law were given two suits (i.e. those of a set of three sisters), while the rest had five suits each. Seven of them also received a gold ring each. The grooms had roughly the same gifts as they did previously, though eight were given one suit, a gold ring, and a watch each. In the 1950s, the groom was given only one suit, and a gold ring not a watch. All the fathers-in-law had a suit, and six had gold rings as well.

The *vadaigi* (the only cash payment given in the *daaj* to the father-in-law) varied in these *daajs* from 51 shillings (£2.50) in six cases, 101 shillings (£5.05) in seven cases, and £11 and £21 in the two British *daajs*. As can be seen from the amount of cash given in these *daajs*, it is never the main part of the gift exchanges that take place at marriage.

The two British marriages in the 1960s were those of a brother and a sister. I have previously described the background of the family in my core sample. The household head, who arrived in the late 1950s, has a successful building concern, and is one of the most prominent members of the temple. His family was amongst the few East African ones to have arrived in Britain at that time. His daughter's marriage was the first one my informants had attended in Britain, and they had collectively helped to arrange it. The reason for this is that East Africans had only started to arrive in Britain in the late 1960s, and started to marry their children off after a couple of years of settlement.

British *daajs* did not differ from those of the East African brides because both these had already prepared part of them before migrating. Nonetheless, they did have difficulty in gathering *daaj*-type clothes in Britain during this time.

Both of them had twenty-one clothing items. One had five suits for her *muklawa* and the in-coming daughter-in-law had seven suits. Both had about seventeen *tolas* of gold in the form of a set and additional jewellery. The out-going daughter did not receive any furniture but was given £300 instead which was used to pay for the deposit on a house. The daughter-in-law got neither the furniture nor the money. Neither one was given Indian cooking utensils because they could not buy these in Britain at the time, unlike the present day, when such things are freely available. Instead they were given cutlery sets, saucepans, tea, coffee, and dinner sets, blankets and bedspreads, etc.

Thus, on the whole both, these *daajs* were similar to the East African ones except that the Indian utensils and furniture were no longer presented. As will be seen from the 1970s *daajs*, the absence of the latter category will become more prominent. Otherwise, the pattern of the *daaj* remained the same, and not influenced by the process of migration, though the volume of household goods was less compared with that of the East African *daajs*.

A final point related to this section is that the fathers of the 1960s brides in East Africa worked mostly for government concerns in keeping with the East African pattern of employment. Only three of the fathers had their own building concerns. The fathers of four of the brides worked as carpenters for the Railways, and two were office workers, one of them working for the Post Office and the second for a bank. However, the *daajs* do not seem to vary with occupations of the fathers. The businessmen's daughters had the same amount of *daaj* as the office workers' daughters. Since I have not actually seen these *daajs*, it is difficult to judge the quality of gifts presented, but the quantity of *daaj* is roughly the same, though the smaller ones in my sample belong to daughters of skilled workers with heavier commitments (i.e. a large number of daughters to marry off) and not to daughters of businessmen.

Two general comments: by the 1960s a *daaj* of twenty-one items, with furniture and gold gifts for the affines, had become the established pattern. This is an increase over the 1940s and 1950s *daajs* in India and East Africa. Second, none of these brides worked outside their homes and were, therefore, not earning members of the family.

Phase 6: post-1970s *daajs*

I shall divide the 1970s *daajs* into those of brides who were married before my fieldwork and those whose marriages I covered during my fieldwork year. Out of the toal of thirty-four 1970s marriages, twenty-three are in my fieldwork sample and eleven took place between 1972 and 1977. All these marriages took place in Britain.

Daajs of the pre-fieldwork marriages in Britain: 1972–77

Of the eleven brides in my sample, two are sisters who married 1972 and 1974 and two are daughters-in-law of the prosperous building contractor I have just referred to. One of them is a Hindu.

The rest of the brides are not related. As can be seen from *Table 9*, all the brides had a minimum of twenty-one clothing items in their *daajs*. Seven had twenty-one items, three had thirty-one items, and one had sixty-one items. In fact, I have never come across a *daaj* given in Britain, of an East African Sikh bride being married to an East African Sikh, which has contained less than twenty-one items. This is the generally-accepted pattern and it is considered most unusual to present an amount lower than that. I shall illustrate from my fieldwork sample later to show that, when a *daaj* containing less than twenty-one items is presented, one of the spouses is always non-East African.

In the following, I shall first outline the larger *daajs* before describing the rest of them.

The sixty-one-itemed *daaj* belonged to an only daughter. Her father worked as an accountant in the Railways in East Africa but is a machine operator in Britain. The bride herself is a radiographer and had worked for two and a half years before marriage. Her husband is an engineer. At the time I started fieldwork, this *daaj* was being talked about amongst my Southall informants because it was so large and also because the groom had often spoken out against the dowry system in public. Yet he had himself accepted a gold *kara* (wrist bangle) at the wedding, which is considered to be an extravagance. Grooms only used to be given a gold ring of one-and-a-half *tolas*, whereas a *kara* which is increasingly being given to East African grooms, can be anything between four and six *tolas*. On top of the sixty-one items, this bride received eleven suits in her *muklawa*, which is a total of seventy-two outfits. Fifteen of these were silk saris, eleven chiffon ones, eleven Western outfits and the rest were a mixture of Punjabi suits and embroidered saris. She had two sets of gold worth twenty-five *tolas*. Her personal accessories included five pairs of shoes, five handbags, five shawls and a whole range of lingerie, dressing gowns, nighties, etc. The biggest increase in the 1970s *daajs* are in clothing and household goods. For example, this bride was given five pairs of bedsheets, five bedspreads, five quilts, four blankets, a fridge, a washing machine, a stereo music centre, a tape recorder, huge Wedgwood china tea, dinner, and coffee sets, an expensive set of saucepans on top of all the Indian utensils and small items like an iron, pressure cooker, food mixers, flower vases, ironing board, etc. The bride kept most of these household items in her parent's home until she moved into her own house, nine months after marriage.

The second bride who had a large *daaj* is the daughter of the travel agent who had become especially wealthy here since his agency business has boomed. Unlike the previous bride she had not worked before her marriage at the age of nineteen. None of the other 1970s brides have had such a large *daaj*. She had thirty-one clothing items in the *daaj*, and fifteen items in her *muklawa*. (Her mother, whose *daaj* I have described in Phase 4 had eleven clothing items in East Africa.) Amongst her accessories, she had twenty pairs of shoes, five handbags, five sweaters, five shawls and a huge range of lingerie. She had five gold sets, one of which was from her FB, the second from her father's business partner, eight bangles, one gold pendant (sixty *tolas* altogether), one diamond ring, and two watches.

This *daaj* also contained a new car as a present from the business partner because he acted as a classificatory FB to the bride. Her furniture consisted of a bedroom suite, a sofa set, two cabinets, a dining table and six chairs, a dressing table, etc. The other household goods included twenty-one steel utensils, five quilts, eleven blankets, a washing machine, a drier, a dishwasher, a cooker, a fridge, a Kenwood Chef, Wedgwood china tea, coffee and dinner sets, and a sewing machine. A few months after the wedding, when the couple bought their own house, the bride was given money for having the whole house carpeted. This is very much the *daaj* of a bride with a rich father who has gained wealth since migration to Britain and who is at present an extremely well-respected member of the community.

Before I go on to describe other *daajs*, I should emphasize that although both these brides had a large number of items in the *daaj* for themselves, affinal gifts were not much above what had been given previously in the 1960s and what was given in the other 1970s *daajs*. For example, the grooms were both given two suits but one had a gold *kara* and the other a gold ring. Mothers-in-law had five suits each, one had a gold ring, and the second a gold pendant. One of the fathers-in-law was dead, but the second was given a gold ring and a suit. I shall develop this point presently to show that although the affinal gifts have shown an increase, they have not done so to the same extent as the bridal ones.

Having described the larger *daajs*, I shall now describe the rest of them.

The second two brides, who married the sons of the building

contractor, also had *daajs* of thirty-one clothing items, two gold sets, sewing and washing machines, and a Kenwood Chef on top of the usual crockery and smaller consumer items. Both brides had worked as secretaries. However, of the two, the Hindu bride whose father is a businessman, also had a bedroom suite, all the dining room furniture and a much larger range of personal accessories than the Sikh bride. The affinal gifts were again not greater than those presented in the average *daajs*. The Hindu *daaj* consisted of two saris and £11 for the mother-in-law, two suits and a gold ring for the groom and a suit and £11 for the father-in-law. The gifts for the Sikh *daaj* contained five suits and a gold ring for the mother-in-law, a suit and a gold ring for the father-in-law, and a gold *kara* for the groom.

A gold *kara*, which had never been given to any of the grooms in the pre-1970s marriages, is a UK custom to which there is opposition from staunchly Sikh families, who feel that the presentation of a gold *kara* goes against Sikh principles. A *kara* should always be made of steel and not gold since it is one of the five Sikh symbols which should be universal to all Sikhs. Five of eleven grooms in my pre-fieldwork marriage sample were nonetheless given gold *karas*.

The rest of the seven *daajs* contained twenty-one items. Three of the seven brides had worked before their marriages. Their *daajs* contained twenty-one items, just like the *daajs* of girls who had not worked. I shall follow up this aspect in the next chapter. At this juncture, I should state that despite the superficial similarity in the quantity of clothing items in the *daajs* of the brides who had worked before their marriages and those who have not, there is a difference in the quality of goods given, in the variety of household and personal items in the *daaj*. These differences begin to show up in the 1970s *daajs* because it was at this period that young girls started to work, having completed part of their studies in this country. In Chapter 4, I have detailed of the types of work these brides and their mothers are involved in, and also their 'work-orientated' attitudes.

For example, the *daajs* of the two sisters of a set of three, neither of whom had worked, contained twenty-one items each (only two silk saris), five suits each for the *muklawa*, two light gold sets of seven and nine *tolas*, eleven utensils, two quilts, two pillows, five *bistras*, and coffee, tea, and dinner sets (but not Minton or Wedgwood ones). Their personal accessories included two handbags, two pairs of shoes, two shawls, two cardigans, and a watch each. Both the *daajs* had the same affinal gifts, consisting of two suits, a gold *kara* and ring for the groom, five suits for the mother-in-law, and a suit for the father-in-law. Other than the groom, no other affines were given any gold.

In comparison, the office worker bride also had the standard twenty-one-itemed East African *daaj* (including nine silk saris), but it was accompanied by five suits for the *muklawa*, five handbags, five pairs of shoes, a coat, three shawls, one gold set plus four bangles (sixteen *tolas*), five *bistras*, a washing machine, a sewing machine, a tape recorder, a stereo, a pressure cooker, a fridge, and Minton dinner, tea, and coffee sets. Affinal gifts included all the standard gifts for the groom, father-in-law and mother-in-law, but all were also presented with gold gifts. For example, for the groom, there was a gold *kara* and a ring, a pair of earrings for the mother-in-law, and a gold ring for the father-in-law.

My point is that the *daajs* which contain the more expensive items like silk saris, washing machines, fridges, stereo music centres, and prestigious china sets, nearly all belong to those brides who have worked and not to ones who have not.

However, I should state that there are other factors that operate to make a *daaj* a large or a small one. For example, a number of sisters nearly always receive smaller *daajs* in comparison with an only daughter. Similarly, the youngest and eldest sisters may often receive larger *daajs*. In the former case, all the other daughters have been married off leaving the parents relatively free to spend more lavishly, while in the latter case, the first daughter to be married sets the standard for the rest. This *daaj* is always a generous one because it is a status confirmer for that particular family. However, I was constantly told that an attempt is always made to give an equal amount of *daaj* to all daughters in order to prevent potential friction, though *daajs* can reflect dramatic changes in family wealth. For example, in one of the families in my core sample, the eldest daughter, married in 1961, was given a *daaj* of only five suits and a pair of gold earrings because the father's business was particularly bad at that stage. Subsequently, her younger two sisters, who married in the late 1960s when the family fortunes had recovered, received the normal twenty-one itemed *daajs*.

In conclusion, East Africans have a clear picture of the minimum of which a 1970s *daaj* should consist. This pattern had already emerged in East Africa in the 1960s, and it has become the established norm in the 1970s and 1980s in Britain, providing both spouses are from East African families residing in Britain. The amount given in the *daaj*, by which one can judge whether it is large or small, is as follows. The least expected of an East African *daaj* is twenty-one items for the bride, a gold set, all basic household goods like crockery, saucepans, sheets, linen, quilts, blankets, etc. For the affines there should be two suits and two gold rings for the groom, five suits and a gold ring for the mother-in-law, and a suit and a gold ring for the father-in-law along with all the other gifts for the rest of the affines. This is a *typical* East African *daaj*. Hence my reference to a smaller or larger *daaj* relates to this particular pattern.

All the 1970s *daajs* (in Phase 6) contained at least twenty-one items. Four exceeded this. Within my sample, except for the one particularly large *daaj* of the travel agent's daughter who had not worked, all the others containing prestigious clothes and household equipment belonged to brides who had worked for a couple of years before marriage. Just by looking at what comprised the *daaj*, when it is displayed, it was possible to work out if the bride had worked or if she had not.

I have also suggested that there are other forces that function to increase or decrease a *daaj*. For example, the *daaj* of the biology teacher who had not worked before her marriage also contained twenty-one items and some expensive household items, but because she was the youngest daughter to be married, the consumer goods could be bought for her by her parents since a lot of her *daaj* had already been prepared a long time in advance. Also, her elder married sisters who can never be gift givers to their parents, can always present gifts to younger sisters, especially at marriage. This bride had thus received most of her prestige items from the older siblings. The affinal gifts were the same as the rest of the *daajs*, consisting of gold gifts for the groom and parents-in-law. On the other hand, the *daajs* of a set of sisters who had not worked contained neither the consumer goods nor gold gifts for affines.

Finally, 1970s *daajs* show an increase in the number of gifts for the bride herself, e.g. clothes, household goods, and personal accessories, but a similar increase is not so obvious in affinal gifts. The latter have remained much the same as those of the 1960s *daajs*, though more gold is presented to the groom, especially if he is given a gold *kara*. The increase in bridal gifts is related to women's earning powers. In the next chapter, I shall describe the contributions of the bride herself to the *daaj*.

Phase 7: fieldwork *daajs*

The previous chapter on spouse selection has referred to the couples that I shall be dealing with in this section in relation to their family background, marriage suitability, occupations, etc. In the following, I shall refer to the *daajs* of the twenty-three brides.

As can be seen from *Table 9*, two of the *daajs* contained thirty-one items, seventeen had twenty-one items, one had seventeen items, two had eleven items, and one had seven items.

It is important to explain the backgrounds of the women with smaller *daajs*. The bride with the smallest *daaj* of seven items was an East African Hindu widow who remarried an East African groom. I covered this marriage from the groom's family who disapproved of it but were prepared to go through with it after much discussion, providing the wedding ceremony itself was conducted according to Sikh principles at the temple. It was difficult to talk to the bride about her *daaj* since she had already been given a proper one at her first marriage which was to a Hindu. For her second marriage she had gold and some saris from her previous *daaj* though she had been bought new wedding clothes for this marriage. Her *daaj* was not displayed. All this is in accordance with Hindu ideology that second marriages for women are always simpler than first ones, making gift exchange less elaborate. The bride did not receive any household goods nor did her *daaj* contain any affinal gifts. Her *wari* was the same as that of other East African brides, and consisted of eleven clothing items, a gold set, eight bangles (sixteen *tolas*), two pairs of shoes, and make-up.

The three other women with smaller *daajs* married non-East African grooms. In one case the bride herself is from India, and married an Indian Sikh groom resident in this country. The arrangements of the marriage were made by her FB who is also a non-East African although he has distant East African kinsmen. I attended this marriage with a family in my core sample.

The bride's *daaj* had been prepared in India before she migrated.

It consisted of eleven clothing items (only one silk sari), a four-*tolas* light gold set, one bedspread, two pillows, eleven steel utensils, a hairdryer, a pressure cooker, and some glass utensils. The MB's contribution consisted of two suits (including the wedding day suit), five steel utensils, a watch, and a bedspread. The affinal gifts consisted of five suits for the mother-in-law, one suit for the father-in-law, a *vadaigi* of £11, and a suit and a gold *kara* for the groom. There were hardly any accessories for the bride, and there was a distinct lack of any of the prestigious household gifts present in most East African *daajs*. Similarly, other than the groom, none of the other affines was given any gold.

I have already explored the case of the third bride with the eleven-itemed *daaj*. Her marriage was rapidly arranged to an Indian Sikh groom, after she had 'tainted' her reputation by going out with a non-Sikh boyfriend. Her father had died seven years before, leaving five children, so this family was particularly badly-off. The bride was the first of four girls to be married. Although she herself worked full-time as a canteen supervisor at Heathrow, she helped with the household expenses from her salary, leaving her little spare cash to spend on herself or for buying things for her *daaj* like the other working brides in my sample. For all these reasons, her *daaj* was a simple one consisting of a light gold set, the basic household items, some glass cookware, one *bistra*, and one blanket, but none of the luxury consumer items. The groom was given a suit and a gold ring. No other affinal gifts were offered.

The fourth bride, with a *daaj* of seventeen items, also married an Indian groom. She belonged to a set of six sisters. Her father works as a carpenter for a building concern, but her mother does not work outside her home. Her older married sisters all had a *daaj* of eleven items. She had a part-time job as a cashier at the airport canteen for one-and-a-half years, and this was converted to a full-time one six months before her marriage. She had used her salary to buy some of the core items of her *daaj*, such as clothes and household utensils. But it was also lacking in luxury items, though she had all the basic household ones like saucepans, bed linen, etc. Her personal accessories consisted of three pairs of shoes, two handbags, three shawls, a gold set (eight *tolas*), a silver set, and a watch. This *daaj* was also lacking in affinal gifts other than those for the groom, a suit and a gold ring. Even though this *daaj* is smaller in comparison with the general East African one, it is nonetheless larger than those given to any of the older five sisters who had not worked before their marriages.

The reason I have gone into the details of the smaller *daajs* is to emphasize that they do not conform to a typical East African Sikh one. This is not to say that a twenty-one-itemed *daaj* is not presented when an East African Sikh marries a non-East African because there are other cases within my sample that do follow the East African pattern. It really indicates that the smaller *daajs* in my sample belong primarily to brides who have married fiancés from India. When an East African marries endogamously, observing the traditional criteria of spouse selection, a *daaj* of *under* twenty-one items is not presented in the 1970s.

The rest of the *daajs* follow much the same pattern as that of the 1970s pre-fieldwork marriages. Out of the nineteen, the two *daajs* that contained thirty-one clothing items belong to the brides who are only daughters, both of whom worked for over two years before their marriages. I refer here to the optician bride and the clerical bride, whose marriage negotiations I have already discussed in detail. Both of them would openly admit that they had helped to make their *daajs*.

The clerical bride's *daaj* consisted of thirty-one clothing items (eleven silk saris, eleven chiffon ones), eleven items for her *muklawa*, six nighties, seven pairs of shoes, and seven handbags. Her gold ornaments were worth over thirty *tolas* in the form of two sets, two heavy bangles, six light bangles, three rings, and five pairs of ear-rings. She had one gold ring, two suits, and £100 from her MB. Her household goods consisted of a sewing machine, a washing machine, a tape recorder, a radio, a stereo set, a car, a TV, a bedroom suite, a cupboard, five *bistras*, five bedspreads, Wedgwood tea, dinner, and coffee sets, etc. The affinal gifts consisted of two suits, two gold rings and a watch for the groom, five suits and a gold pendant for the mother-in-law, and a suit, gold ring and *vadaigi* of £51 for the father-in-law. This is a large *daaj* though the items presented in it have become typical of other East African *daajs* within my sample.

A more modified *daaj* belonged to a bride who migrated to East Africa. This lacked the larger consumer items though all the smaller ones were transported with the bride to Nairobi. She did not receive any money in lieu of luxury items. This was what I classify as a basic twenty-one-itemed *daaj*, since the bride had not worked before her marriage. The *daaj* was also not increased by the fact that the groom was a graduate engineer educated in Britain, who is a partner in a successful family business.

The basic East African Sikh *daaj* was given to three other brides in my sample who had not worked. These were not the modified ones of brides who migrated but those which fulfilled all the requirements of the average East African *daaj*.

The rest of the eleven *daajs* which contained twenty-one items could be divided into what would be considered 'generous' *daajs* as opposed to basic ones, and what would be more 'commonplace' ones.

For example, a 'generous' *daaj* was that of the beautician bride who was an only daughter and who had worked for two-and-a-half years. She married a graduate engineer who owned his own house. Her *daaj* consisted of twenty-one items (eleven silk saris), eleven items for *muklawa*, four handbags, four pairs of shoes, three nighties, two dressing gowns, etc. The household goods consisted of Royal Doulton china tea, coffee, and dinner sets, a silver cutlery set, a fridge, a washing machine, four *bistras* as well as all the general cookware. She had two gold sets and two watches. The affinal gifts consisted of two suits, a gold ring, *kara*, and a gold watch chain for the groom, and five suits and a ring for the mother-in-law. Although the father-in-law was dead, a *vadaigi* of £101 was still given along with the *daaj*.

This was one of the largest and most elaborate of the twenty-one-itemed *daajs* since it had all the consumer items, silk saris and personal accessories of the bride. Her *muklawa* of eleven items was also among the largest within my sample. Sixteen of the twenty-three brides were given a normal *muklawa* of five items, four were given eleven items, two had seven and nine items, and the Hindu widow who remarried did not get one. These large *muklawas* are part of the general elaboration of gifts exchanged since migration to Britain.

A more 'commonplace' *daaj* was that of a bride who had worked in a bank for two years and whose father was a Post Office clerk. This consisted of twenty-one items (ten chiffon saris and five silk ones), a *muklawa* of five suits, one gold set, and six bangles (fifteen *tolas*). Her accessories included three pairs of shoes, two handbags, four nighties, four sweaters, etc. Her household goods contained four tablecloths, two blankets, two bedspreads, two quilts, iron, toaster, camera, kettle.

All the smaller consumer items were present but none of the larger ones.

I want to stress that, although most of the brides in my sample had twenty-one items in their *daajs*, there were differences in the quality and the quantity of the other gifts presented. I have differentiated between twenty-one-itemed *daajs* that contain only the basic items and those that contain the larger, more expensive ones. Yet, there are *daajs* that are lacking in the larger luxury items but which are nonetheless considered to be superior to the normal twenty-one-itemed ones.

For example, the pharmacist bride's *daaj* contained twenty-one very exclusive items, of which four were designer outfits and eleven silk saris. There was also a big difference in the quality of the accessories she had. All her handbags and shoes were worth over £60 each. Her shawls and lingerie were of a much higher quality than those in the average East African *daaj*. In the household goods section, she had all the smaller consumer items like the Kenwood Chef, toaster, sewing machine, etc. but was not given the larger ones like the fridge, cooker, washing machine, and so on. She had about twenty-five *tolas* of gold, i.e. a gold set, ten bangles, three pairs of earrings, and a bracelet. Her cousin (FBD) the accountant bride had roughly the same *daaj* but more gold, thirty-five *tolas*.

Although both these *daajs* are lacking in the larger household items and furniture, the reason these were considered to be 'good' *daajs* of twenty-one items, is that the quality of gifts presented was superb. This applied both to the affinal and the bridal gifts. The groom was given two suits and two gold rings, the mothers-in-law received five expensive suits and a gold ring each, and the fathers-in-law had a suit and a gold ring each.

These two *daajs* are also examples of how little the *daajs* change according to the occupation of the father. The pharmacist bride's father was a civil servant who had died two years before her marriage, and the accountant's bride's father is a businessman, yet the differences in the two *daajs* are not particularly apparent. However, the businessman's daughter did receive a larger amount of gold and a *vadaigi* of £101, more than the civil servant's daughter, who had a *vadaigi* of £51. In the next chapter, I shall refer to this particular aspect at greater depth to explore the effect on the *daajs* of the earning capacities of the brides and the occupations of the father.

A final point is that the only cash gift in the *daaj*, the *vadaigi*, varies little despite the increase in gifts, especially those for the bride. Out of twenty-three *daajs*, fifteen were accompanied by £51, three by £21, one by £11, and three by £101. The Hindu *daaj* did not contain a *vadaigi*. Thus, the maximum amount given is £101 which is often just the price of an expensive silk sari. The amount does not seem to vary in relation to the wealth and status of either the bride givers or the bride takers, since it is a fairly standardized sum. It is also the only cash gift that is reserved for the men of both parties, which indicates that the major part of the gifts exchanged at marriage are extremely women-focused. Similarly, the elaborations that have taken place in the gifts exchanged during marriage are also restricted to female spheres.

Conclusion

This chapter has dealt with the close similarity of East African Sikh notions about *daaj* to the North Indian ideology of dowry and *kanyadaan*: pure gifts for which no return is expected. Marriage with a dowry is considered to be the most prestigious form, as with the high-caste Hindus of India, yet the word *stridhanam* is never referred to, just as *kanyadaan* is not mentioned. However, the reasoning behind the giving of a *daaj* is almost exactly the same as that used by North Indian Brahmans. A marriage without a *daaj* is considered to be the least status-bestowing, since it reflects badly on the *izzet* of the family. I have never come across a Sikh woman who did not receive a *daaj*. This indicates that it is very much a dowry and not a trousseau because it is a gift that should be given almost compulsorily, without expectation of return.

The second section dealt with the different components of the *daaj* to show that major sections within it have remained stable over time, despite internal changes in the types of gifts presented, especially in the household goods sphere.

An important change in the exchange system is that in the case of the older women, there was a distinction between the *muklawa* and the *daaj*. The latter was designated for the mother-in-law who could use it for further gift giving. The 1930s and 1940s brides only had control over their *muklawas* which they received three to five years after marriage. The *daajs* of the 1950s and 1960s in Africa and those of the 1970s in the UK have acquired a different meaning. Affinal gifts had been separated so that the mother-in-law had little control over the clothing items and gold, though household goods in the 1950s and 1960s were absorbed into joint family property. By this stage, there was an increase in the control exercised by the bride which undermined the authority of the mother-in-law. This coincides with Phases 4 and 5 which concern the *daajs* presented in Africa, whereas the previous *daajs* belonged to marriages that took place in India where the joint family system was stronger and at a time when families had not been fragmented by migration. None of these brides set up their own separate households like some of the 1970s brides.

By the 1970s, the UK *daajs* contained fewer heavier household goods, since there has been an increase in expensive consumer items. Similarly, bridal gifts have increased along with a general improvement of the quality of gifts given. This suggests that the *daaj* is, at present, much more like *stridhanam* than it has ever been. This is further strengthened by the total separation of the affinal gifts from those reserved for the bride. This trend of earmarking the affinal gifts started in the post-1950s, though it had by the 1970s become more obvious. Despite the increase in the number of affinal gifts given, the division of this sphere from the bridal gifts has further increased the power of the bride to control the *daaj*, especially in Britain. The aim of this separation had been to allow the bride to establish her own household by clarifying gifts that belong to a daughter and those that are for her affines. All this is partly linked to the increased earning power of the brides in Britain. Since they help to make the *daaj*, they also expect to be able to control it. None of the pre-1970s brides had ever done this.

Changes in the structure and control of the *daaj* reflect the migration process. In East Africa, some of these trends had already begun although they became clearer in the UK as families separated into nuclear units and as women became earning members, and therefore contributors to family incomes. Also, the movement of control from the kinship group of the groom to the bride and the couple itself, with the groom becoming a more important focus of gift giving (the gold *kara* etc.), is related to the themes discussed in the previous chapter on spouse selection. East African society is becoming 'couple-orientated' as opposed to 'kinship group-orientated', with increasing attention being paid to the individual.

In relation to changes in the quantity of *daajs*, the first three phases of the 1930s and 1940s concern mostly marriages that took place in India. All the *daajs*, with one exception, consisted of between five and eleven items. The three twenty-one-itemed *daajs* of the 1940s all had East African connections. Therefore, the increase in the *daajs* given around this time was linked first to a marriage that took place in Africa, and second, to the two Indian brides who married hypergamously in India to East African grooms and migrated soon afterwards.

By the post-1950s, it was rare for an East African Sikh bride to marry non-East African grooms though some of the men still married Indian brides. The community was, at this stage, marrying endogamously within East Africa. The amount of *daaj* given had increased from a maximum of eleven clothing items, to anything from fifteen to twenty-one items.

Phase 5, the 1960s concerned only pure East African Sikh couples, and the custom of giving twenty-one-itemed *daajs* was then firmly established. Such *daajs* were larger than those presented in India in the 1930s and 1940s. The prosperity of the East Africans is reflected in the increase in *daajs* given at that time. Similarly, by the 1970s, there is a further increase in the *daaj* for reasons I have already explained and which I shall explore in the next chapter. In the 1960s in East Africa, although the majority of brides had twenty-one-itemed *daajs*, there were some which were smaller but none that I heard of or that were within my sample that went over this amount. However, in the 1970s and 1980s, a *daaj* of twenty-one items has become almost obligatory for a bride marrying in the UK community; in fact, it is at present common to find *daajs* consisting of thirty-one items and over. Now, when an East African marries endogamously in Britain, a *daaj* of under twenty-one items is never presented. However, when a non-East African man marries an East African bride, the *daaj* is smaller. This indicates the appreciation East Africans have of their superior status in comparison with Indian Sikhs.

Not only has there been an increase in the amount of clothing items in the *daaj*, there has also been a general improvement in the quality of *daaj* gifts. The pre-1950s *daajs* contained gifts that were of an inferior quality to be used for further gift giving, unlike the *muklawa* gifts, which were of a better quality for the bride's personal use. *Daaj* clothes of pre-1970s brides were actually relevant to their lives, and were used extensively by the bride since they formed her total wardrobe. However, the majority of *daaj* clothes presented in the UK are those which the brides use only for special functions. They certainly do not form the major part of the everyday 'western' clothes used regularly by the brides.

Yet despite this, there has been little change in what are considered to be or feel like '*daaj* clothes'. These are the Punjabi suits, and the elaborately-embroidered chiffon and silk saris which are a good indicator of the quality of the *daaj*. Therefore, the *daaj* has remained extremely conservative in its content over time. The feeling among the older Sikh women is that a *daaj* should at present consist of what it has contained in the past, despite occasional protests from younger women who point out the futility of possessing such ostentatious garments. This also applies to the designs and type of gold used for jewellery. There have been only slight changes in the sets presented over the past fifty years just as the amount of gold given to the bride has not increased in comparison with the clothes since the 1960s.

A point relating to the household goods is that expensive consumer items have become an important part of 1970s *daajs*. These were not commonly given in the East African *daajs* of the 1950s and 1960s, which contained furniture instead, a category that is present in only a few of the UK ones. The 1930s and 1940s *daajs* had neither the furniture nor the *consumer* items, since the *bistras*, brass, and steel utensils were considered to be more important. A reason for the lack of heavy household items in the 1970s *daajs* is that the bride can easily take all the consumer items with her when she separates from her affines to set up her own household. It was not possible to do so with furniture and *bistras* because they were part of joint family property. Unlike my fieldwork brides, who expected to move into their own homes within a couple of years after marriage, that is, if the groom did not already possess his own individual house at marriage, Indian and East African brides did not have such aspirations. This type of post-marital residence in the UK has given the *daaj* a completely different dimension from that of previous years.

Finally, the elaborations that have taken place are primarily within the traditional three spheres of the *daaj* and have remained constant over time. Cash gifts have not assumed greater importance, nor are brides being given money for the deposit on a house, instead of the usual material gifts, nor are they getting expensive carpets or antiques etc. This is not to say that the *daaj* has not changed over time because, clearly, a different range of household items is presented on top of the usual Indian cookware. It means that the choice of items thought to be suitable '*daaj* gifts' has on the whole remained orthodox. All these factors run parallel to the general conservatism of East African Sikhs, making them translate their wealth in a traditional way that has not changed markedly over the past seventy years.

SEVEN

Elaborations: marriage procedure and the dowry system

This chapter will deal with the marriage procedure itself, focusing on the elaborations within it, to demonstrate that the simple 1960s marriages were replaced by more elaborate ones in the 1970s. These are products of a more established community. The greater consciousness developed by East African Sikhs of their identity since migration to the UK is reflected in the marriage system, especially in the expansion of ceremonial activity. The re-establishment of traditional rituals and ceremonies that were in existence in East Africa serves to redefine the boundaries of the East African Sikh community in changed British conditions.

I shall further consider the influence of features such as women's earning power, the lack of status differences in East African Sikh society, and the effects of state benefits on marriage and dowry patterns.

Marriages in the 1960s and 1970s

Marriages in the 1960s were often performed without a specialist because any person who could read the *Guru Granth Sahib* or who had some knowledge of the ways in which a Sikh marriage ceremony should be conducted was made responsible for such events.[1] Only a few London Sikhs went to the main temple in Shepherds Bush, which employed a regular *giani*. The cost of having a marriage ceremony in the temple was under £2. Most Sikhs just had a registry office marriage, after which a few friends would be invited to a small celebration. At that time, friends included a cosmopolitan set of people, including the indigenous British, Sikhs of various castes, Hindus, and Muslims. Now, weddings are attended mainly by East

African Sikhs, with only a sprinkling of non-East Africans, making them caste-orientated affairs.

The focus in the 1960s and 1970s was on the wedding day itself, and excluded all pre-marital ceremonies. The whole marriage procedure was short, and gift exchanges were restricted to presents given by friends to the couple on the wedding day. This pattern carried on well into the late 1960s until the arrival of East African Sikhs in family units containing women who had past experience of such affairs.

With the arrival of such families came the knowledge which enabled them to perform more 'professional' marriage ceremonies; there were also a sufficiently large number of Sikhs who could be gathered to have a 'proper' wedding. However, gift giving was still at a minimum, and the *daaj* consisted only of essential bridal items, a number of which were presents from friends and relations. This is quite a contrast to the post-1970s ceremonies, where the traditional patterns of giving gifts to the kin of the groom and the bride herself are generally observed in much the same strict fashion that was in existence in East Africa.

In discussing the East African marriage procedure, I shall refer to 'rituals' as compulsory *gur-riti* events which take place in the presence of the *Guru Granth Sahib*, mostly under the supervision of a *granthi*. They follow a definite pattern which applies to all Sikhs. The two obligatory rituals are the *karmai* (the engagement) and *viah* (the wedding ceremony). The rest of the events will be classified as 'ceremonies' which are both optional and more flexible. I refer here to both the modern public ones like the dinner parties and receptions and the traditional private ones like the *maiyan* and *chura* which do not involve a religious specialist. *Maiyan* and *chura* are pre-marital ceremonies. In the former, the bride and groom are rubbed with a dough of flour, oil, and turmeric, and in the latter the MB gives the bride a set of red bangles. Although these traditional ceremonies are customs borrowed from the Hindus which should not be performed by 'pure Sikhs', they have nonetheless been added to the wedding festivities.

In Chapter 4, I discussed the backgrounds of East African Sikh families who arrived in Britain in those early days, and are now amongst the oldest Sikh residents in Southall. The first two weddings that most of them remember having attended were those of the daughter and daughter-in-law of the prosperous businessman, the only two weddings remembered as having a format vaguely resembling the East African Sikh marriage procedure, despite a considerable number of modifications to it. The rest of the 1960s marriages followed the much more simplified pattern described above. The reason for the scarcity of weddings during that time in Britain is that most Sikh men went back to East Africa to marry, according to the wishes of their family. The Sikh population was neither large enough for them to choose spouses here, nor was there a great deal of contact within it. A number of them married British women, and not according to Sikh rites. For these reasons, my informants could remember having only been to a couple of Sikh weddings during the 1960s, unlike the situation in the recent past, when they have been invited to anything between five and fifteen weddings per year.

The reason for this increase in marriages in the 1970s is that even though in the late 1960s some families contained marriageable young people on arrival in this country, the process of finding spouses for them and of arranging their marriages was delayed. This was due to the difficulties of the early settlement period. Also, contact with other East Africans on a large scale was minimal. However, during the 1970s, communication links with other East Africans were established, facilitated by the development of the main Sikh institutions. Thus, by the early 1970s, marriages had changed because the process of elaboration was already under way.

Since most of the 1960s marriages in my sample took place in East Africa, there is obviously little information about the British Sikh marriages of that period. Except for the two within my sample, I did not meet any other couples who had married here during this period, although I talked to a number of the early East African arrivals about the marriages that they had attended at this time.

The two weddings in my sample took place in 1962 and 1968. In both the weddings, the pre-marital ceremonies of *maiyan* and *chura* did not take place.

In relation to the collection of *daaj* items, my female informants remembered the difficulties they had encountered in trying to get the bride's *daajs* together, even though large parts of them had been prepared in East Africa before migration. Indian shops which stock *daaj* items were not then in existence, so the women had to make do with whatever could be obtained from local European shops, unlike the present day, when all the bride's accessories and clothes can be readily bought, at competitive prices.

Neither of these 1960s weddings was conducted by regular temple *gianis*, but by close Sikh friends of the brides' families. The total number of guests in both cases did not exceed seventy individuals. At present, a wedding with two hundred guests is considered to be a small affair. In most average weddings in my sample there were at least four hundred guests, though it was quite common to find anything up to eight hundred guests at the larger ones.

The reason it is possible for East African Sikhs to arrange these ostentatious social functions with ease is that all the services and goods needed to perform the marriage ritual are provided by other East Africans in London. These are people with whom they have often had contact in East Africa. For example, they employ professional caterers (*halwais*) they have already known in the past, since the very same people who had such businesses in East Africa have now set up their own shops in Britain. Similarly, the goldsmiths from whom sets are obtained are those who had designed the ornaments the families had previously provided for the brides who were married during their stay in Africa. The same *gianis* have often performed the marriage ceremonies for different generations of brides within particular sets of families for the past twenty years in East Africa and the UK. The *giani* of the Southall Association had performed the marriage ceremonies of all the brides of an extended family within my wedding sample since the 1960s. One daughter was married in 1964 in Nakuru; her FBD was married in 1966 in Nairobi; and the third and fourth FBDs were both married in London during my fieldwork by the same *giani*. Thus, East African Sikhs do not have to move outside their immediate circle to hire services or buy the traditional *daajs* gifts, since 'ethnic services' are at present provided by other East Africans, some of whom are non-Sikhs, e.g. the *Suniars* (goldsmiths), and the *Darzis* (tailors). The strong communications network helps people to tap these services when the occasion arises, because old ties can be activated.

Fieldwork marriages

Having compared the 1960s marriages with present-day ones, I shall in the following describe the more sophisticated weddings I attended during fieldwork.

It seems that East African marriages have remained much the same since the mid-1970s and have acquired charactersitics similar to those that took place in East Africa, though the whole procedure has been concentrated into a shorter period. All the ceremonies which were earlier done away with in the UK have been re-introduced.

The East African Sikh marriage procedure is similar to that described by Vatuk (1972) for the white-collar workers of North India, by Lewis (1965) for North Indian villagers, and by C. Ballard (1978) for Leeds Sikhs. My primary purpose in discussing the marriage process is less to present some idea of the ways in which London marriages are conducted but rather to focus on the points of elaboration within them. I shall not delve into *all* the ceremonies that were observed around the time of marriage, but will concentrate on the most important ones.

As can be seen from *Table 10*, in India and in East Africa, receptions and registry marriages were not in existence. Similarly, the early British marriages had neither the modern nor the traditional cere-monials. However, the 1970 marriages followed a more elaborate procedure with an increase in the ceremonies surrounding the two main compulsory rituals. Although the latter are fixed in content, they are at present being conducted on a grander scale than previously. However, my reference to the elaborations of the East African marriage procedure concerns primarily the increase in ceremonial activity.

The first ceremony in the marriage procedure is the *rokna*, the 'stopping' of the groom, when the bride's male kin literally 'reserve' him. Henceforth, offers from other bride givers should not be considered by his family. This is supposed to be a private affair, though I was consistently told that it has acquired the character of engagement proper (the *karmai*), which is a much larger event. In East Africa, a small amount of sweets were taken to the groom's house at *rokna* by the bride's kinsmen, unlike the present day when a number of trays (*thaals*) of *ladoos* (sweetmeats), and dried and fresh fruit are presented to the grooms' families. The grooms themselves received £11 to £21 and some *ladoo* to eat, whereas in East Africa they were given 11 to 21 shillings. I was never able to attend any *rokna* because

Table 10   *Events within the marriage procedure within India, East Africa, and the UK to show elaborations*

events	India	East Africa	early UK	1970 UK marriages
1. *Rokna*	×*	×*		×
2. *Karmai* (ritual) (compulsory)	×*	×*		×
3. Reception after *Karmai*				×
4. *Chuni*	×	×		×
5. Registry marriage			×	×
6. Reception after registry marriage				×
7. *Maiyan*	×	×		×
8. *Chura/Nanki Shak*	×	×		×
9. *Gaun*	×	×		×
10. Women's *satsang*		×		×
11. *Viah* (ritual) (compulsory)	×	×	×	×
12. Reception at groom's after *viah*				×
13. *Muklawa*	×	×		×

*On a much smaller scale in East Africa and India

of their male exclusivity. In fact, one does not hear of a *rokna* till well after the event because of all the delicate discussions. At this stage, a potential alliance can be broken if a flaw or scandal is discovered amongst the families concerned. Within my sample, the *rokna* took place anything from six months to two years before the marriage, though most couples married within a year.

The *karmai*, which is an event almost as large as the wedding, followed the *rokna*, often a couple of weeks before the wedding, and both took place at the groom's home. On this occasion the bride's kin brought boxes of fruit and sweets for the groom's people (on a larger scale than for the *rokna*), along with a gold ring, a standardized sum of £11 to £21, a turban for the groom, and turbans and £1 for his male kinsmen. The groom was given a dried date to eat by the bride's father, which was considered to be the *sagan*, a sign that the groom and his kin had firmly accepted the alliance.

The *chuni* ceremony, concerning the bride, took place either on the engagement day or on the following one, when she was sent a sari or suit, a gold ring or *ticka*, and a heavily-embroidered *dupatta* by her future mother-in-law. This was often an exclusive women's event during which there was further feasting.

The registry marriage took place after the engagement, again within the couple of weeks before the wedding. The typical procedure followed by most couples in my sample was that the engagement took place on a Saturday, the *chuni* ceremony on the Sunday, the registry marriage on the following Wednesday, with the *gaun* (singing and dancing) on the same evening, when the *daaj* was displayed. The *miayan* and *chura* all took place a day before the marriage on Friday. The wedding proper was on Saturday.

The marriage ritual (*viah*) itself is obviously the most expensive event of the marriage procedure. Nearly all East African Sikh marriages followed the same pattern. The day started with the reception of the *barat* (groom's people) at the temple. The first meal provided was breakfast after the reception, during which there were *milnis* between all the important male kin of the bride and groom. These involve the exchange of garlands from both sides, though the gifts of turbans and cash (£1 attached to every turban) were given by the bride's kin to those of the groom.

The marriage ritual itself lasted for two to four hours. The groom was already seated in front of the *Guru Granth Sahib* before the bride joined him, along with a troop of young women; young cousins, sisters, Zs-in-laws, etc. An older married woman, a Z or Z-in-law always assisted the bride at the beginning of each of the four *laama*, the circumambulations around the *Guru Granth Sahib*, with the groom leading in each case. On the fourth *laam*, flower petals or confetti were showered onto the couple, though this was not allowed in some temples because of the mess that was left behind.

In all the weddings I attended, there was always a sermon (*Sikhiya*) presented by an older member of the bride's party, advising the couple on the meaning of the 'Sikh way of life' and the marriage ceremony itself. A number of couples found this advice irrelevant and only thought of it as a way of prolonging the marriage ceremony unnecessarily. In the final part of the marriage ceremony the bride's mother gave the groom around £5 and some sweetmeat as a sign of her acceptance of him into her household.

In only eight of the twenty-three weddings were the *barats* allowed to have lunch first on properly-laid out tables, before the bride giver's guests. When this was the case, there were traditional seating arrangements allowing the *barat* to finish their lunch before the second seating of the general guests, when the décor was not nearly as elaborate. In the rest of the cases, there were buffet lunches which do away with distinctions between the bride givers and the bride takers. The pattern of making seating arrangements for the *barat* was the norm in East Africa, since buffet lunches were only provided by a handful of avant-garde families. In Britain, it was far more common suggesting, that the difference in respect accorded to the two sides is not nearly as clear-cut as in East Africa and India.

After lunch at the temple, the core of the *barat* always went back to the bride's home for tea and the *doli* ceremony, when the bride was sent off to the groom's home. During this time, the *daaj* gifts were packed either into vans hired for the purpose, or given into the care of the groom's kinsmen.[2] At East African Sikh weddings, big cars were always conspicuous, especially Mercedes-Benz.

In another eight of the twenty-three cases, there was a reception given by the groom's people, often in hired halls after the *doli*. All these were in London since the grooms themselves lived locally, making it possible for the main kinsmen of the bride to also attend these functions. In all these cases, the couple had a wedding cake to cut. Music groups who specialize in Indian film music were hired to provide entertainment. The cost of hiring these groups is around £100 to £400 and they are becoming a common feature of East African Sikh marriages, both at the wedding lunches and the receptions. An average reception had anything up to four hundred guests since all the groom's friends and relations who did not accompany them to the *barats* were invited.

The final ceremony in the marriage procedure was the *muklawa*, which took place a day after the wedding when the groom's kin returned to the bride's home for lunch. Theoretically, the marriage is supposed to be consummated after this ceremony, but this did not seem to apply to couples in the UK, just as they did not stay at the bride's home for three days after the *muklawa* as in East Africa, before returning more permanently to the groom's home. Most of the couples went off for their honeymoons within a couple of days of their marriage ceremonies. This modification was not in existence in East Africa since the few couples who went for a honeymoon did so a couple of weeks after the wedding when all the post-marital ceremonies were complete. In my sample, the majority of couples had their honeymoon within the UK, i.e. ten out of twenty-three, another seven going to areas such as the Caribbean, the Mediterranean, and the USA.

In the above, I have described the general procedure of East African marriages in the UK. To illustrate the elaborations within it, I shall detail one example which has characteristics common to most East African marriages. There were thirteen events taking place in the two weeks before marriage excluding the first *rokna* ceremony that had taken place two years before this period.

The first ritual was the *karmai* at the temple followed by tea. The second function on the same day was a dinner party held at the groom's home, mainly for the groom's people and some important kinsmen of the bride.[3] The following day, the *chuni* ceremony took place at the bride's home, after which there was another dinner party. The fourth function was the registry marriage, followed by lunch at the bride's home. The fifth was the exclusively female *satsang* at the temple at which all the female kin of both the bride and groom, including their friends, were invited (about two hundred in total), after which there was a huge tea party. The sixth was the *gaun* (singing session) at the bride's home, during which time the *daaj* was displayed. The seventh was the *maiyan*, followed by lunch. The eighth was the *chura*, followed by dinner at the bride's home. An equivalent celebration also took place at the groom's home after his *maiyan*. The ninth was the wedding itself. The tenth was the reception at the groom's house on the same day in the evening, to which three hundred guests were invited. The eleventh was the *muklawa*, a day after the wedding. The twelfth and thirteenth were two dinner parties held at the bride's FB's and MB's homes with about eighty guests, after which the couple went off on their honeymoon.

This extreme shows the elaboration of the East African marriage procedure, and reflects a form of conspicuous consumption that is also present in other facets of the East African lifestyle. The gifts presented at marriage and the ostentatious festivities are examples of the overt consumption patterns that have been emerging in the past decade. Some of the elaborations are due to the re-establishment of the older ceremonies that were in existence in East Africa, while the rest have been adopted in the UK. Marriages that took place in East Africa had neither the registry marriage along with the accompanying celebrations, nor the receptions at the groom's house, nor the dinner parties. It seems that hospitality was rarely accepted from the bride takers by the bride givers, suggesting that the boundaries between the two groups were adhered to more rigidly. The level of consumption at the East African occasions was certainly not anything near that of the present British festivities.

This is especially clear from an event like the registry marriage, which reflects East African traditionalism particularly well, because it is a development in the UK that has been translated into a cultural idiom, i.e. it has been ceremonialized. In some cases, it has almost assumed the status of a mini-marriage, because at it the bride givers and bride takers meet for the first time, requiring that gifts should flow from the former to the latter. For example, at one of the registry marriages in my sample, the bride's people entertained a hundred guests. To do this, they had hired a hall and a music band, though they had made the evening meal themselves. All the female kinswomen of the groom were given a suit with turban and £1 for their husbands if they were married. This was considered to be unnecessary, though it is just one example of the elaboration within the marriage procedure. Gifts were not given to the affines at all registry marriages but they were all invited for a meal at the brides' houses. The most common affinal gifts were £5 and a turban for the father-in-law, a suit for the mother-in-law, and £1 and a handkerchief for all the guests (i.e. anything from fifty to one hundred individuals). These were more sensible gifts in comparison with the more expensive suits given to all the women. However, this increase in affinal gifts is not nearly as apparent as the expansion of the social functions around the time of the marriage.[4] For example, gifts were only presented to the affines at the registry marriage in seven cases out of the twenty-three in my sample. Hence, the increase in affinal gifts is not as universal as the elaboration of both the *daaj* itself, which reflects bridal wealth, and the social functions, which are products of parental wealth.

To summarize: I have referred to the main rituals and ceremonies that take place around the time of marriage, focusing in particular on the elaborations that have occurred in Britain. The simplicity of the marriages that took place in the UK in the 1960s, observing the bare minimum of *gur-riti* rituals and gift exchanges, was replaced in the 1970s by more ostentatious Hinduized marriages which resemble the more 'fully-fledged' affairs that used to take place in East Africa, though there have been certain British additions in the past decade. These developments are the products of an established community in the UK which is translating its wealth into patterns that are at the same time 'modern' and 'traditional'.

Reasons for the elaborations

Women's earning powers

The strong orientation of East African women towards working out-side their homes has been discussed in Chapter 4, for example, eighteen out of the twenty-three brides in my wedding sample were involved in full-time employment, mostly in administrative work.[5] The earning capacity of East African women is one of the most important factors related to the escalation of the dowry system in Britain. The previous chapter has referred to the differences in the levels of *daajs* of the brides who have worked and those who have not, all the former helping to make their *daajs*.

As can be seen from *Table 11*, eleven of the twenty-three brides had

Table 11   *Number of years brides had worked before marriage*

years the brides worked	0	under one year	2–3	4–5	6+
number of brides	5	3	11	3	1

worked for two to three years before marriage, three had worked for under a year, and four had worked over four years. Of the five brides who had not worked, two had migrated directly from India. The three non-earning East African brides had been married off soon after completing their courses. All of them were around the age of nineteen years at marriage, which makes them the younger brides in my sample. The brides who had worked the longest, between five and nine years, were obviously amongst the oldest brides, married around the age of twenty-five to twenty-eight. I have described the *daajs* of these brides in the previous chapter in greater detail. For example, one of them contained more expensive personal items such as designer garments, exclusive handbags and shoes, although it was, in terms of quantity, a twenty-one-itemed *daaj*.

Even if the bride had worked for a shorter period, she had still helped with the *daaj*. For example, one of the brides in my sample had worked for only three-and-a-half months as a civil service clerk after completing her HND in business studies. She had bought most of her personal accessories and seven of her twenty-one *daaj* outfits out of her own earnings. Her *daaj* was lacking in the more prestigious consumer items present in the *daajs* of longer-working brides, which also contained higher-quality garments such as Benarsi silk saris. The only bride who had not worked and who was given an ostentatious *daaj* in the 1970s was the wealthy travel agent's daughter. The rest of the good-quality and larger *daajs* all belonged to working brides.

C. Ballard (1978: 190) states:

'It has, however, become usual for a bride who has been working to save her wages and take her bank book as part of the dowry. Parents take pride in ensuring that there are no withdrawals recorded in the book for the months preceding the marriage, so that the daughter's husband's family can see that she has not been asked to play any part in financing it herself.'

This was not the case amongst either the East African working brides, whose earnings were not referred to; nor was there any sign of an account of the bride's salaries being presented along with the *daaj*. In fact, all the brides who had worked would openly tell me of the articles in the *daaj* that they had bought for themselves if I specifically questioned them about their contributions. Certainly I did not hear of any case in which the groom's parents had ever asked to see the bride's previous pay packets, though nearly all of them had accounts with banks and building societies.[6]

The fact that the brides pay for parts of the *daaj* did not in their parents' eyes contradict the North Indian ideology of the pure gift

(*Kanyadaan*) in which daughters and dowries are presented to the bride takers without any expectation of a return. The reasons the parents are able to justify their attitude towards this is that they themselves are not accepting anything from their daughters for their own use, since a gift cannot be accepted from a daughter by a parent or any senior member of her family. The daughters take with them in their *daajs* whatever they have bought for themselves from their salaries. This is also in accordance with the North Indian ideology that daughters must be constant recipients of gifts both before their marriages and for a long time afterwards. One of my oldest informants explained that she could never be a recipient of a gift from a daughter whether married or not because she believed that if she ever did so, this action would 'taint or spoil' her own wealth. Merit is gained from giving to daughters and not accepting; the acceptance of gifts from a daughter can potentially harm or diminish parental wealth.[7] The only people that a daughter, married or not, can give gifts to, are her younger siblings. For this reason, an older sister would sometimes give pocket money and birthday presents to younger members of her family.

Related to this theme, daughters do not, on the whole, help towards general household expenses during their years as earning members of their families, making them almost totally dependent on their parents for their basic requirements.[8] None of them ever lived away from home on their own, so that their salaries were not taxed by having to pay rent and bills. Although young girls go away to university or college, the majority of them return to their parents' homes to find jobs locally. Unlike young men, on the whole they do not invest in their own flats or houses, which means that they can keep their salaries for themselves. However, this is not to say that daughters do not ever pay towards household expenses: their contribution towards their upkeep is indirect.

The girls, by becoming earning members of their families are automatically made 'self-sufficient' economically in the following ways. They bear all their own personal expenses; they buy their own clothes, shoes, and records, and some run their own separate cars. They decorate their rooms. They share household expenses by buying occasional gifts of foodstuffs, fruits, and smaller household items. These are not obvious expenses because there is no tangible product at the end of it. They certainly never pay household bills. However, they would buy small items for the house because they could quite easily afford to do so. Hence, although the girls are not expected to pay towards household expenses, they nonetheless look after themselves in all other respects because they have the economic power to do so. This did not apply to the brides who were married in Africa or the East African young women of the 1960s in general. They were entirely dependent on their parents for all their needs until they were married. British Sikh girls, on the other hand, are totally independent in this respect, which reduces the parental burden of looking after their older children considerably, especially during their late teens.

The consequence of working girls in Britain not contributing towards the household budget is that they are free to put their salaries to their own personal use. Thus they have an enormous amount of control over their earning power. This is not to say that they do not save with building societies, and banks, but they also have a considerable amount of capital at hand with which to build their *daajs*. This is a situation that applied to all the working East African brides in my sample and others that I talked to generally.[9] Also, there is no pressure to show their savings or account books to their affines, which further releases the brides' salaries to invest in whatever items they like.

Having stated previously that the working brides' contributions are most apparent in the clothes and household goods sphere, I shall in the following refer to some examples of their precise contributions.

In the previous chapter, I described the basic twenty-one-itemed *daaj* universally given to East African Sikh brides. This amount of *daaj*, consisting of the three spheres, is fixed and presented obligatorily, whether the bride has worked or not. A *daaj* smaller than this level is only given to brides who marry grooms who have migrated directly from India.

The changes in the quality and quantity of *daajs* of brides who have worked are most clear from gifts that are exclusively for their own use and which they buy from their own salaries. To illustrate, the *daaj* of the beautician bride who had worked for two-and-a-half years was generally considered to be of particularly good quality. Of the twenty-one items in it, there were eleven silk saris.[10] Her *muklawa* consisted of eleven items, of which five were silk saris. This bride had bought fifteen of her *daaj* outfits and most of her accessories (shoes, handbags, shawls, etc.) from her own earnings. On top of this, her *daaj* contained a large range of prestigious household items. She had herself paid for the Royal Doulton china sets, the silver cutlery set, the washing machine, and a number of other smaller items like the kettle, percolator, etc. though she had been bought the fridge, the bedroom suite, stereo, etc. by her parents and kinsmen.

Another example, the clerical bride who had worked for over two years, had thirty-one items in her *daaj* and eleven in her *muklawa*: she had bought a total of seventeen outfits, along with six nighties, seven handbags, seven pairs of shoes, three coats, etc. all from her own income. Amongst her household goods she had paid for the television, the tape recorder, the stereo music centre, and the large Wedgewood china set plus a whole range of smaller household items. In her case, the washing machine, household linen, bedroom suite, the fridge, the Kenwood Chef, five bedspreads, etc. were all parental gifts, along with the thirty-one *tolas* of gold. She is an only daughter which accounts for the particularly large range of household goods and gold that she received from her parents.

The *daajs* described above are large both in terms of quantity and also for containing more expensive luxury items. I have gone into the content of these two *daajs* in particular to show that the bride's earning capacity affects the type of *daaj* she received. Even if the *daajs* are not as exclusive as the ones just described, it should be stressed that if the bride has worked, the *daaj* always expanded to a level much higher than that which could have been reached by the parents if they had had to rely solely on their own capital. In the previous chapter, I referred to *daajs* provided exclusively from the parent's incomes, in the cases of non-earning brides. These contained only the basic twenty-one items, none of the luxury goods, and only a minimum of the bridal accessories.[11]

To illustrate the ways in which the *daajs* have changed in the UK in relation to those presented in India and East Africa over the past thirty years because of the bride's earning capacity, I shall refer to *daajs* of six sisters whose family background, has already been described.

One of them was married in India in 1947, four were married in East Africa in 1957, 1960, 1962, and 1964 respectively, and the fifth, the only one to have worked, as a clerk/secretary, was married in 1973 in the UK after their father's death.[12]

Just focusing on the clothing items that were presented in the *daajs* of five of the sisters married in India and East Africa, two received eleven items and three received thirteen items, most of which were useful clothes to be worn every day. All of them received two pieces of gold jewellery each (two to three *tolas*), five *bistras*, a sewing machine, the basic household items, and furniture. The bride's personal accessories were not considered important at the time, though all of them had a couple of pairs of shoes and sandals.

The sixth sister had worked for almost two years before her marriage in London. Her *daaj* consisted of twenty-one clothing items, including eight silk saris, all the basic household goods, a washing machine, a Kenwood Chef, a sewing machine, a tape recorder, a gold set of twelve *tolas*, all the personal accessories of the bride, and £500 for buying the furniture after the wedding. In this case, she had bought all the household goods mentioned above plus ten of her outfits from her own earnings. Her *daaj* was not a particularly exclusive one in comparison with the other East African ones. However, the level of clothing items had gone up from the eleven to thirteen items which had been given to her five sisters in East Africa and India, to twenty-one items in her own *daaj*.[13]

The interesting point related to this case is that, in the traditional set-up, this *daaj* would have been smaller than that presented to the five sisters, because the bride's father had died seven years before the marriage. As a result, the wedding expenses had to be borne by her brothers, but because she was a working bride she received a larger *daaj* than that presented to her sisters who had not worked. Since she was the youngest child, she was given a gold set and £500 by her brothers, neither of which had been presented to the older sisters. The *daaj* of the sixth sister was typical of the earning powers of working girls being channelled into the *daaj* to make it more elaborate. This was also made possible by the prosperity of her siblings, who were all resident in London and who had arranged her marriage. Thus, there were two factors at work here: the bride's brothers were both earning in Britain which meant that they were able to present her with household goods on top of the basic ones, and the bride herself was able to boost her *daaj* with her own capital in a way that was not open to any of her sisters when they had married in India and East Africa.

Since I have already referred to the differences in the levels of *daajs* of brides who have worked and those who have not in the previous chapter, in the above I have detailed only a few cases, concentrating on the components of the *daaj* into which the brides themselves inject their capital. *Daajs* have not been referred to individually because the contributions of the earning brides are always restricted to the same spheres.

However, it is difficult to judge the precise contribution of a bride's earning to the *daaj* since they seem to spend on different objects. The factors that are clear are that they are certainly improving both the quality of the *daaj* and expanding the number of items presented. It is also obvious that none of them spends any money on wedding entertainment or on gold or affinal goods. For this reason, the bridal spheres of the *daaj* have shown the biggest increases. Even though East African *daajs* superficially seem to contain the same quantity of items, there are, nonetheless, differences in both the quality and quantity of *daajs* of brides who have worked and who have been able to boost a basic *daaj* presented by parents and those who have not.

Lack of overt differences in *daajs*

The standardization of East African Sikh *daajs* is related to the lack of status differences among them, because a particular category of them have migrated to Britain.[14]

In Chapter 4, the occupations of the fathers of UK brides in my sample have been described. Of my total sample (i.e. wedding and core samples) seven household heads worked for government concerns, seven were involved in technical work for the private sector, nine were skilled craftsmen, and eight had their own businesses. Although in Britain East Africans have diversified into a bigger range of occupations, with an increasing tendency to set up businesses, this is not obvious from the levels of *daajs* presented if seen in relation to parental occupations. For example, regardless of the occupational status of the fathers, the majority of brides received twenty-one-itemed *daajs*.

To illustrate with examples, the clerical bride and the optician bride both had thirty-one-itemed *daajs*. Yet, the optician's father was a machine operator and the clerk's father was an office worker. Similarly, of the 'good' twenty-one-itemed *daajs*, the pharmacist's father was a civil servant (a clerical officer), the beautician's father was a mechanic, and the accountant bride's father was a businessman. None of these *daajs* showed dramatic changes according to differences in the fathers' occupations. I have, in the previous chapter, detailed the three *daajs* to show that there were only small differences between them. The accountant had a slightly larger amount of gold, the beautician had a greater range of household goods, but neither had quite the same type of exclusive clothes as the pharmacist. Nevertheless, all these *daajs* were considered to be good-quality generous East African *daajs*.

It is not surprising that the levels of *daaj* neither reflect clearly the differences of wealth of the East Africans nor the occupational status of the fathers, because the British East African Sikh community shares many characteristics of wealth, occupation, family background, etc. On top of this, the superficial uniformity of the *daajs* is further perpetuated by their insularity as a community, since their models of emulation and status measurement lie within the British East African Sikh community. This is in contrast to direct migrants for reasons discussed earlier. In this respect, a twenty-one-itemed *daaj* is symbolic of the state of affairs in existence in East African society, as seen from the angle of the gift exchanges that take place at marriage. Since these factors are almost universally applicable to East Africans in general, and since a basic twenty-one-itemed *daaj* is presented to almost all East African brides, my suggestion that the improvement in quality, and increases in the volume of certain components of the British *daajs*, are linked to the earning powers of the brides themselves, should be further strengthened.

The relationship between the level of *daaj* and groom's occupation and prestige is not clear either. The generous twenty-one and thirty-one-itemed *daajs* belonged to brides who were married to both university graduates/professionals, and to non-graduates. For example, the clerical bride who married a non-graduate received a large thirty-one-itemed *daaj* including all the prestigious items. On the other hand, two basic twenty-one-itemed *daajs* containing a bare minimum of household goods belonged to non-earning brides who both married university graduate grooms (engineers). Similarly, the larger *daajs* of my pre-fieldwork 1970s marriages belonged to the radiographer who received sixty-one items, and the travel agent's daughter, who received thirty-one items. Both married non-graduates. These are grooms less prestigious than professional graduates in relation to spouse selection, though the ones referred to above were considered to be suited to the brides concerned, in relation to personal attributes, occupational status, etc.

This is not to say that the level of *daaj* never decreases according to the groom's status because Indian-imported grooms tend to marry brides who are given smaller *daajs*. An important factor that increases the volume and quality of *daaj* within the standard East African ones is the bride's own earning capacity. In making this statement, I have excluded factors explored in the previous chapter relating to family composition, which determines the position of the bride within it and which further influences the level of *daaj*. For example, an only daughter nearly always has a larger *daaj*, in comparison with a bride belonging to a large family or a number of sisters. I have also excluded rarer cases of brides with large *daajs* who are daughters of wealthy businessmen because, clearly in these cases, *daajs* are elaborated automatically by the father's wealth, without the help of the bride's earnings. These are exceptional cases; and, being aware of all these factors, it is still apparent in general that the fathers' occupations are not obviously reflected in the increases in levels of East African Sikh *daajs*, nor are the *daajs* increased or decreased according to the grooms' qualifications.

Further to the above theme, I have mentioned in the previous chapter that the money payments or the use of cash in dowries and gift exchanges is always restricted to men in North India. It is they and not women who negotiate bridegroom price (Vatuk 1972; Van der Veen 1972; Pocock 1972). Similarly, in the case of East Africans, the *Vadaigi*, the largest cash payment in the *daaj* (which does not exceed £101 in Britain) is presented by the bride's father to that of the groom: it is a masculine transaction. Money payments are a small part of the East African *daaj* since it consists predominantly of material gifts, of which clothing is an important part, and not cash items. These are mainly feminine transactions indicating that the elaboration of the *daaj* does not entirely link with the bride's father's wealth since the gift transactions are so female-orientated.

Hence, the acquisition of economic power and wealth by Sikh women has been channelled into areas that they themselves have greatest control over and knowledge of (especially in the case of older women) and they benefit the most from them. This is precisely the reasoning that is being reflected in the attitudes of the brides who are now themselves making a strong impact on their *daajs* through their earning powers.

Indirect reasons for elaborations

Having discussed the ability of brides to pay for their *daajs*, I will now describe other factors which have indirectly contributed to the elaboration of the marriage ritual and the escalation of the dowry system. These are a combination of the traditionalist attitudes of East African Sikhs and the developments that have occurred within the community since migration. The latter have been discussed in earlier chapters, and include the financial advantages that they had previously, and which they have been able to maintain in this country, e.g. their past East African savings and state pensions. All these, including the women's earning capacities have further added to their prosperity.

In Chapters 3 and 4, I have stated that in Britain, there are a greater number of individuals per household who have independent sources of income because they start to earn at quite an early age. For example, one household in my sample had four unmarried earning young people (two sons and two daughters) over the age of eighteen. Even though young women do not contribute towards the household budget, they still look after a number of their own interests, just as sons help out with family finances. Similarly, around the time of marriage, sons are expected to pay towards the wedding costs. Thus, there is a general increase in the amount of capital within the families. This situation does not exist in every family, but it seems to be more common here than it was in East Africa and the Punjab, where household heads had to support their children till quite a late stage in their lives.

Another factor is the influence of state benefits on households. For example, school fees and expenses for the education of young people no longer have to be borne by the parents as they were in Africa. I exclude here the children of some professional and wealthy parents who are at private schools: there were four cases of these in my core sample. Related to this is that young people who have graduated from British universities or who have acquired other forms of skills have done so not with the help of financial backing from their parents but through government grants. The interesting aspect of this, related to dowry giving, is that it is no longer possible for the groom's parents to ask for a dowry from the bride givers as compensation for having paid for the son's education.[15] As I have explained in the previous chapter, this is not to say that in the past and at present bride takers do not have implicit expectations of a dowry, but that it would be considered degrading if they were ever to make such a demand. Everyone, especially young people, and including brides themselves, who are quite outspoken despite the emphasis in the literature and media on the passivity of Asian women, is quite aware of the fact, that on the whole, grooms and brides have not been educated from parental income.

The point discussed above also gives greater bargaining power to sons to set up their own households soon after marriage (i.e. if they do not already own their separate houses at marriage) because obligations towards parents and younger siblings have loosened in the UK in comparison with East Africa and India. The picture that was painted by the men who had in the past been educated by their parents in East Africa, was that they felt a great moral pressure to repay the past expenditure by their families on their training and education. Since this situation does not apply to the grooms at present and since the brides anticipate the possibility of setting up their separate households within a couple of years of marriage, away from the control of the mother-in-law, this gives them further and greater incentive to build up parts of their *daajs*.

Just as the children's education does not have to be paid for, nor have the grandparents to be provided for in quite the same ways as in East Africa and India, where they were dependent on their earning sons in their old age. I refer here to the pensions and other benefits that old people receive in Britain. Similarly, medical expenses no longer have to be paid either except for people making use of private medical facilities. In East Africa, the lack of such state facilities taxed family budgets.[16] Having said this, I should qualify it by stating that, although the parents have in the UK been freed of certain expenses which they had to bear in East Africa, they have, on the other hand, acquired a new set of responsibilities such as mortgage costs, and other expenses involved in having to rebuild their homes from scratch after migration, etc. However, these have been reduced gradually over time as the community has settled, and as initial expenditure has been counterbalanced by the earning capacities of women, young men, and the influence of state benefits.

Conclusion

This chapter has discussed the marriage procedure, focusing in particular on the changes that have taken place since migration. The few marriages that took place in the UK in the 1960s were simple, since the knowledge and facilities required to handle such events 'properly' was not in existence. However, with the arrival of East African Sikhs in family units in the late 1960s, came both the experience needed to establish 'ethnic services' and also increased knowledge of social customs. With the development of the community infrastructure it was possible in the 1970s to organize 'proper East African-style' marriages. Early marriages observed only the compulsory *gur-riti* rituals which apply to *all* Sikhs, i.e. if the marriage is conducted according to Sikh rites. Present-day marriages are characterized by the re-establishment not only of Hinduized ceremonials that had been abandoned in the 1960s, but also by new additions such as western-style dinner parties and receptions. Thus, there has been a duplication of events combining the 'traditional' with the 'modern', which has led to the elaboration of the whole process. This is typified by the registry marriage which is a British event that has been included in the Sikh cultural idiom.

The observance of both traditional and western-style events reflects the increased confidence of the community as it becomes better-established in Britain, though this is also related to the greater consciousness of their East Africanness since migration to the UK. One feature which further stressed their exclusivity, is the elaboration of their marriage procedure through the reinstatement of traditional marriage customs. The re-definition of the East Africa Sikh community has some interesting implications. Although East Africans are considered to be orthodox Sikhs, being extremely *Gurdwara*-orientated (apart from their shared past background) their Ramgarhianess and East Africanness are paradoxically a combination of two opposing forces: their religiosity and their adherence to ceremonials that are basically Hindu in content.[17]

In previous chapters, it has been stated that their East African background is perpetuated through a number of features such as separate caste associations, their communications net, and marriage circles. Similarly, the elaboration of the marriage procedure, both through the rituals themselves and, predominantly, through ceremonial expansion, is another expression of exclusivity, emphasizing their distinct East African and Ramgarhia identity as being different from that of Indian Sikhs.

The increase in ritual and ceremonial activity and the expansion of the gift exchange system is also connected with the earning powers of Sikh women, especially the brides themselves who are able to boost their *daajs* through their personal earnings. Precise areas of the *daaj* into which the brides channel their earnings have been discussed, to show that the biggest expansion in it has been in bridal spheres, i.e. clothing items, personal accessories, and household goods. Although brides do not contribute towards wedding entertainment costs, the fact that they help to provide parts of their *daaj* further frees parental capital to be expended on ceremonial activity. Thus, two channels of capital are responsible for the elaborations: parental wealth is reflected in their ability to sustain the entertainment costs arising from increased ceremonial activity, whereas the injection of bridal wealth has been responsible for the escalation of the dowry system.

Furthermore, the lack of an initial 'a myth of return', and its related implications in structuring attitudes of East Africans; the influence of state benefits; the lack of dependants abroad draining family income; past financial assets, plus the present earning capacity of women, all combine to make a strong formula for prosperity and a certain degree of wealth, as compared with other migrants and settlers. These are precisely the factors that influence the marriage system of the East African Sikhs, leading to an escalation in both the volumes of dowries presented and to an increase in the wide range of ceremonial activities involving overt expenditure. It is the latter characteristic that especially gives their weddings the distinct East African flavour. There is, there-fore, a conflict between Sikh ideals of egalitarianism and simplified (*saadhi*) marriage, and the actual practice by East African Sikhs of rather ostentatious Hinduized marriage patterns.

EIGHT
Discussion and conclusion

The ethnography of a settler, twice migrant community and developments that have emerged among them should have some relevance to
changes that may have occurred among other South Asian minorities
in Britain. The process of migration to Britain in the case of East
African Sikhs has not led to the abolition of some of the most
traditional cultural values but to simultaneous culture 'conservatism'
and 'progressiveness'. In fact, such features as an increasing length of
residence in Britain without reinforcement from a home country, and
on orientation towards staying here permanently right from the point
of entry, have not diminished East African Sikhs' interest in perpetuating their traditions and ethnic identity. Indeed, certain facets have
been reinforced in the changed circumstances in Britain. They are
as much products of reactive pride in relation to racism from the
majority community as of the values of a community settled in Africa
during which time it developed a cohesive ethnic identity.

All this is particularly well illustrated by marriage patterns showing
a high degree of conformity to those of the high-caste Hindus of North
India, with the same underlying ideology and functions, despite
migration from India to East Africa and from there to the UK (see
Chapters 5 and 6). In fact, social and economic changes in the UK
which have affected the internal structure of the community have led
to the accentuation of certain features, such as the elaboration of the
marriage procedure through the increase in optional ceremonial
activity, and the expansion of the dowry system through the earning
powers of brides. Also, general prosperity brought about by the two
phases of migration combined with their conservatism, has contributed to the translation of East Africa Sikhs' wealth into a cultural
idiom that has always been in existence. This is happening despite

changes in domestic roles and family structure in UK. Thus, in a way, I have described the persistence of traditional patterns in an otherwise progressive community, taking into account changes that have arisen as a result of migration.

In Britain, East Africa Sikhs have rapidly developed strong communication links based on relationships formed in the past. They have established a separate community which has become much more conscious of its caste status, its 'Ramgarhianess', and its previous background, its 'East Africanness', because of both contact with migrants from the sub-continent and interaction with the indigenous British. In relation to the internal organization of the community where in East Africa they formed the majority Sikh community, they find that the situation has been reversed for them in the UK. They have now become part of much larger Sikh, mainly Jat Sikh community, and also part of the wider South Asian one, both of which were in existence prior to their arrival, and from which they are different through their caste status, occupations, previous urban experiences, and developed community sense; further in relation to other Sikhs, through their more fastidious view of Sikhism. Thus, their East African identity as 'mainline Sikhs' was seen initially as being swamped by the presence of an Indian Sikh population and also of a much larger one of direct migrants from the sub-continent.

A consequence of their minority position within this larger South Asian population in Britain has led to a greater consciousness on their Ramgarhianess and East Africanness. The latter is positively projected through their general sophistication, their middle-class and their status prosperity, in response to racism from the white British community. Their religious orthodoxy, stringent observance of external Sikh symbols, and the elaboration of their marriage customs all define their separate identity as East Africans. This is obvious from their exclusive caste associations, their shared symbols, their separate settlements, and their communications network, further widened by frequent temple activities.[1]

Their traditionalism, which defines their intra-ethnic identity is further propagated by their arranging of marriages almost exclusively within East African Ramgarhia Sikh communities resident in the UK, the USA, Canada, and East Africa. Their desire to restrict marriage circles, thus perpetuating their East Africanness, has led in the UK to the conversion of some of the previously compulsory rules of marriage arrangement into less rigid preferences. This flexibility has loosened the marriage system both in response to the perceived needs of Sikh youth in Britain, and to accommodate slightly deviant marriages. However, despite these modifications, East African Sikhs have otherwise remained orthodox in observing classical procedures of marriage arrangement, giving many of the same explanations as that of North Indians to justify their adherence to such customs. It is not much of a problem for them to arrange 'correct' marriages because not only do the majority of them belong to one caste, but they also share similar past experiences, resulting in a society in which status differences are not at present clear. Hence, there is a large pool of people from which spouses can be selected, a task which is greatly eased by the communications network and the balanced age profile of the community.

A development in the UK concerning spouse selection, which will potentially change the structure of the community making it 'couple-orientated' as opposed to 'kinship group-orientated', is the increasing attention that is being placed at present on the personal preferences and assets of the spouses themselves, e.g. the ownership of a house in the case of the groom, the qualifications of both spouses, etc. Thus, marriage is seen not so much as an alliance between families as a union between two people: an adoption of the indigenous British society's focus on the individuals. This feature, combined with others such as the increased earning powers and independence of the women, the predominance of nuclear households which tend to loosen kinship obligations, and modifications of traditional criteria of spouse selection, are all indicative of developing 'individualism' which may in future go against the perpetuation of the boundaries of the community and their East Africanness.

Changes in the values of the East African Sikh community have also influenced the structure of the marriage *daaj* itself, making it much more 'bridal' property than it has ever been. Since the 1970s, the dowry system has expanded, resulting in an increase in those components of the *daaj* that the bride herself controls such as expensive clothing items and household goods, the latter now including luxury consumer items. The emphasis on bridal gifts is partly related to themes discussed above, though the most powerful impact on the *daaj* has been that of the earning capacity of the brides themselves. They are now converting their personal wealth into a traditional framework which has not altered as a result of their dramatic entry into the labour market in Britain.

A consequence of this is that since the brides contribute towards making their *daajs*, they also expect to control them. Dowries in the UK are therefore much closer to ideal notions portrayed in the classical legal treaties (*Dharmashastras*), concerning exclusive female property (*stridhanam*). However, the big difference is that in the UK, this particular pattern has emerged due to different conditions, ones relating to the changed economic and domestic roles of women. The control exercised by the brides on the *daajs* has been further accentuated by the clear separation of affinal gifts from those of the bride. This is a process that has been in progress since the post-1950s, gradually eroding any power that may have been exerted by the mother-in-law and the groom's kin group on the *daaj* itself. Furthermore, the expectation of brides in the UK of setting up neolocal residence immediately after marriage, especially if the grooms own their houses, has given them greater incentive to build up their *daajs*, thus making them into exclusive female property under the women's own control. All this relates to the 'couple-orientation' mentioned previously, because there has been in the UK, a shift in the balance of power in favour of the bride herself and her husband, a situation quite different from that in existence in the pre-1950s and 1960s in East Africa and India.

A final point concerning the *daaj* is that the elaborations that have taken place within it have been restricted to the three traditional components which have remained constant over time. The *daaj* has not been replaced by a major cash gift, nor by the deposit on a house for the couple to set up immediate residence, though there have been internal changes in the type of household goods presented. Items that are considered to be suitable *daaj* gifts (i.e. gold sets, silk saris, etc.) have all remained extremely orthodox. Thus, the general conservatism of the East Africans which is obvious from many other spheres of their life, makes them and their women translate their wealth in a manner that neither differs markedly from that of high-status Hindus nor has shown radical change over the past seventy years.

The practice of ostentatious Hinduized marriages in the UK is contrary to the traditional Sikh ideals which recommend observing simplicity in marriage forms, and counsel against presenting dowries, Sikhism being a reform movement of the fifteenth century aimed ideally at abolishing both the caste system and Hindu customs. Yet, not only is caste endogamy obvious in Sikh marriages in the UK, but so also is the increase in ceremonials (*maiyan, chura,* etc.) which are derived mainly from the Hindus (although there have also been some non-Hindu UK additions, such as dinner parties and the translation into the cultural idiom of a British development, the registry office marriage). Paradoxically, despite the staunch beliefs of the East Africans in 'Sikhism' and their stringent adherence to external Sikh symbols, their 'exclusivity' demonstrated through their traditionalism is, in fact, a combination of two opposing forces: the 'Sikh' on the one hand and the 'Hindu' values and ceremonials on the other.

The 'traditionalism' and 'religiosity' of the East African Sikhs is all the more surprising because they are committed to staying in the UK. They were not initially monitored by an audience in a 'home country' enforcing traditional modes of behaviour, unlike other South Asian minorities in the UK during the early stages of settlement (Ballard and Ballard 1977; Watson 1975, 1977; Saifullah Khan 1977; Dahya 1973). For example, Ballard and Ballard (1977: 40–1) reporting on work carried out in the early 1970s, state that 'the myth can be used to explain and justify the settler's commitment to saving', and 'to legitimize continued adherence to values of their own homeland and to condemn the assimilation of English cultural values as irrelevant and destructive'. Such an attitude is reaffirmed by more recent publications (Ghuman 1980; Robinson 1981, 1984). The East Africans seem to present a reverse situation at present because their cultural values have been preserved and reinforced, despite the absence of roots in a homeland.

In fact, a consequence of a lack of 'home' orientation is that they are able to retain all their resources and wealth in this country, since they have never been through a phase of austere living in the UK in order to invest in properties at 'home'. On top of this, they have arrived in complete family units including old grandparents, saving them the need to remit money abroad to support dependants. All these features, combined with their previously-acquired financial assets, the increased earning powers of women, especially brides, etc. have released wealth to be consumed in this country. Thus, East African Sikhs indulge in conspicuous consumption also obvious from other facets of their lives such as elaborations of their marriage and dowry patterns, involving overt expenditure. It is this that may tend to get them labelled 'materialistic show-offs' by direct migrants, who have in the past indulged in this activity much less in Britain though much more in India, in comparison with East African Sikhs. Furthermore, the general conservatism and sense of identity of the latter encourages their prosperity to emerge through traditional channels, upholding traditional institutions. Parental wealth emerges publicly through increased ritual and ceremonial activity, whereas the injection of bridal wealth has led to the expansion and reinforcement of certain aspects of the dowry system.

A point which relates to features discussed above and to those that have been considered in Chapter 4, describing the internal organiz-ation of the community, suggests that there is variation in the conditions of life, occupations, housing, and settlement patterns, amongst East African Ramgarhia Sikhs in the UK. Internal complexity and increasing diversification of occupations, the moving away from an original concentration on white-collar and public-sector employ-ment, makes it difficult to categorize East African Sikhs as a group, as an 'under-class'. This would suggest that they were one of the 'minorities systematically at a disadvantage compared with working-class whites', and that they have become 'in effect a separate under-privileged class' (Rex and Tomlinson 1979: 275). This applies to some East African Sikhs but many others do not conform to it. The diversity of the East African Sikh community and South Asian com-munities in general, will increase in future through such features as occupational mobility, as young people brought up here emerge from British educational institutions and the increasing focus in matchmak-ing on the personal assets and qualifications of spouses through the arrangements of marriages of equally educated spouses, etc. Such trends will no doubt gain prominence in future, among South Asians in general, and Sikhs in particular, since the latter are such entre-preneurial people. British cultural values will not necessarily be widely adopted even though knowledge of these is already increasing dramatically. The cultural identity of minorities will, it seems, persist while incorporating selective elements of British culture.

Hence, the salience of class as a powerful force of organization should be an important pointer to change. In a way, the consciousness East Africans have of their East Africanness in Britain, as projected by them through their command over mainstream skills in comparison with direct migrants, is a class phenomenon as well as an important marker of their ethnicity formulated in Africa and further perpetuated in Britain. It is also, however, a reaction to stereotypical assumptions from the indigenous British, wrongly classifying them as 'Pakis', not making distinctions between them and direct migrants, many of whom have rural origins and from whom East Africans both maintain a distance and consider themselves to be different. Their perceptions are in many ways well founded, since they *are* different, in relation to both caste and class, and have entered the British system as relatively prosperous middle-class settlers with differing experiences of migration from those directly migrant, the majority of whom are working-class. In a way, the homogeneity of East African Sikhs projected through their East Africanness in Britain (Chapter 3), is a response to both the hetereogeneity of the South Asian population here and also to the presence of the dominant indigenous community. Ways of distinguishing themselves from the majority of direct migrants are through emphasis on the commonality of their East African experiences, and their establishment of separate community institutions.

The latter process is obvious from the rapid development of caste associations making it as important an organizational feature as British class divisions, especially in relation to interaction with direct migrants of the same ethnic group. Caste differences will persist in the internal organization of South Asian communities (Michaelson 1979: 352) because they are perpetuated through endogamous marriages, the establishment of separate caste institutions resulting in the further intensification of interaction between individuals of the same caste background. However, inter-caste and inter-community marriages of East Africans and direct migrants will increase as spouses brought up in Britain emerge, who share common British experiences. For them in particular, class will become a more definitive feature of interaction. However, upward mobility and shifts in class position among them, especially among those with direct migrant parents, may not necessarily result in the assumption of current British cultural values, if East African Sikhs are typical. Their situation as traditionalist middle-class settlers may be repeated amongst the directly migrant, who may also perpetuate their culture values despite increased command of mainstream skills. This process is already obvious from the demands made by minorities that their mother tongue be taught as part of the school curriculum, and also from the flourishing multicultural education industry.[2] Clues to potential developments amongst other minorities that can be gathered from the settlement patterns of East African Sikhs militate against their absorption into the majority community through assimilation.

In fact, the maintenance of Asian cultural values will be aided in future by the establishment of an infrastructure of settled communities with developed ethnic services. These in turn will help to produce 'British Asian' patterns of interaction which will amalgamate both the 'traditional' and the 'modern', being products of cultures developed independently of a home base, and without the monitoring of a kinship group in a 'home' country. Middle-class South Asians, especially, a category which is rapidly expanding, will both have command over British market credentials and the ability to assert their cultural identity in a more overt fashion than ever before. They, in particular, will be influential in determining potential developments and also modes of behaviour amongst working-class settlers, partly because of their strengthening positions as opinion makers, and partly because of their general social skills. All these features will be – indeed already are – products of a settler culture like that of the East African Sikhs, not that of a direct migrant one. Henceforth, increasing reference should be made to British Asians as opposed to South Asian migrants, because even though an orientation to 'home' *may* persist for some time to come amongst some directly migrant groups, the likelihood of their return to their countries of origin is remote.

A trend which is already emerging but which will become more important despite increasing internal divisions in the South Asian community through class and caste distinctions, will be the forging of a common 'British Asian' and 'Black' identity, cross-cutting internal differences, and directed towards political action. This will be the result of the growing political sophistication of different minorities, and the emergence of leaders from within settler communities who are, if not British-born, at least raised here. They will form over-arching identities as strategies for effective lobbying on issues of direct concern to minorities; they will develop pressure groups fighting for recognition, and establish presences in key decision-making institutions. This process is already under way amongst the young, for whom community identities are assuming decreasing importance in response to specific political issues. For example, in the case of the East African Sikh young, their East Africanness will in such instances become irrelevant as a defining marker. Just as caste divisions will definitely increase in relation to the internal organization of minorities, as is already obvious from the establishment in Britain of separate caste-based organizations, so will class differences, due to the emergence of individuals educated in a British schooling system which encourages such categories to develop. However, greater political awareness and the acquisition of mainstream skills will also lead to more united action through the formation of strategic Black and Asian identities. The class position of these minorities will be crucial in this because it will determine the position they adopt to negotiate their rights, as well as the stance they take in the political arena. A pointer for the future development of minorities is that the diversity which is incipient at present in relation to occupations and political organization, will gain prominence with length of stay.

This will also apply to their desire by minorities to maintain some traditional cultural values and perpetuate a separate ethnicity, despite upward class mobility and weakening links with a 'home' country. East African Sikhs' distance from India, their two migrations and their settler orientations have not resulted in the loss of their traditional identity; it has been renegotiated in Britain, as it was in East Africa.

A point related to the maintenance of cultural values is that of the assumed pathology of Asian and Black families from an ethnocentric perspective which classifies them as 'problems'.[3] The 'conflict problem'-orientated approach ignores the responsiveness of cultural patterns, assuming that they remain static and unchanging. On the contrary, in Chapter 5 I have demonstrated that in response to settlement in Britain, modifications in procedures of marriage arrangement and domestic organization have been brought about to make spouse selection more relevant to the changing attitudes of the young towards marriage. The marriage system of East African Sikhs accommodates change, making the system much more fluid than it may actually seem.

At present, there is remarkable fit between the expectations of the East African Sikh parental generation and that of the youth, a fit brought about by making internal changes in the system. Yet a large amount of media attention focuses on conflicts between the old and young, on the 'between and betwixt' nature of lifestyles, and the resulting tensions; and on the stereotype of arranged marriages being forced, and performed against the wishes of the young[4] (Rex 1982: Pryce 1979; Taylor 1976, 1981; Anwar 1976; Kalra 1980). The implication in such material is that 'Asian' cultural values are imposed on the young without their consent, leaving them no room for personal choice, or the expression of individual opinions. What is forgotten is that young people may actually *choose* to accept the cultural values of the societies to which they belong precisely because they make eminent sense for those involved in them. The East African Sikh material presented should have demonstrated that 'arranged marriage' itself involves complex procedures, which work because not only do they change with time and adjust to the process of migration, but also are acceptable to the young as well as an older generation having more knowledge of their underlying rules and preferences. It is this responsiveness of the system that allows it to survive in Britain, because it has neither remained static, nor unconscious of changing attitudes amongst the younger generation. Internal cultural values have evolved among East African Sikhs in response to external forces, and potential conflict has been reduced and cohesion increased not the reverse as cited in both earlier and current literature, which focuses too heavily on areas of breakdown. Also, the emerging individualistic values of young Asians are not as strained as suggested by Rex (1982: 61):

'Firstly it should be noted the family culture and values are under threat from two sources. On the one hand, the individualist middle-class culture is not fully in harmony with it as it can be interpreted to mean the denial of family obligations . . . Thus being a good Indian and being a successful middle-class student at the same time are by no means easy goals to attain. There is *bound* to be breakdown.' (my emphasis)

Clearly the situation cannot be understood in as simple a manner as portrayed by this author. By focusing on areas of breakdown, and by generalizing from particular incidents to suggest that the same applies to the fabric of all minority communities, misunderstandings of cultural constructs and their functioning, from the perspectives of minorities themselves, can result. Cultural patterns of South Asians *do* accommodate the growing individualism of the youth, since they are not rigid structures. They change by synthesizing British procedures of operation, in which the community, especially the young have the freedom to develop new combinations of local and traditional values. A mode of analysis which makes frequent references to such terms as 'persistent conflict', 'endless pressure', or 'betwixt and between' fails to take account of the flexibilities of a system which is sensitively formulating British Asian values which are neither ossified nor oppressive. This is another pertinent pointer to potential change among minorities, and should be indicative of the fluidity of the system, even though patterns that emerge in Britain may be more traditional in interpretation than those that existed in the past. Nonetheless, they are patterns that have emerged as a result of change brought about by migration.

However, this is not to suggest that there are no cases of severe breakdown in the system, and that arranged marriages for example, do not have oppressive elements in them, but that the pattern is much more responsive to forces that have emerged in Britain than is generally thought. They are also acceptable to a cross-section of the community precisely because of their place within a cultural context which can best be understood from a non-ethnocentric perspective, one which acknowledges that there *is* room for individual manoeuvring, and one which does not portray the young as rebellious, unthinking rejectors of their cultural values, and the older generation as unbending, rigid imposers. Traditional values survive, including the dowry system which I have outlined and which has become prominent in Britain precisely because it is a facet of cultural patterns which have been acceptable, for a long time and which are as much part of a settler culture in Britain as they were of a migrant one in Africa and a traditional one in India.

It is the responsiveness of the system alongside the maintenance and, in certain cases, traditionalization of cultural traits that should be a pointer to processes of change. The fact that East African Sikhs are progressive in certain spheres, e.g., as successful settlers, yet remain culturally conservative, while lacking a 'myth of return', suggest that there is no clear-cut path to 'Anglicization' and 'westernization' among British Asian minorities, but the existence of complex responses to a variety of 'settler' and 'migrant' situations. Change is controlled as much by external forces operative on minorities in Britain, such as racism, stereotypical categorization as part of racist assumptions, etc., as by their previous experiences of migration and settlement. Having said this, it should also be emphasized that their British experiences may lead to some commonality of outcome, because a number of negative forces that minorities are subject to are shared ones. Hence, there could be some similarity in processes of change among minorities, though these will depend on the stages of settlement in relation to their point of entry into Britain and previously acquired expertise in the use of British institutions.

A further point to be emphasized here, is that the term 'South Asian' is in a way defunct because it does not take into account such features as caste, class, previous background and experiences. I myself am guilty of using it throughout this book, though justifying it by the fact that it is a current general usage. A lesson to be learnt from the East African Sikh case is the need for sharper focus on these factors. Similarly, the force of racism and minorities' values as seen through their own eyes, and defined by themselves, are all potent in determining ways in which they may develop. This is important, because perceptions of their group boundaries are often finely defined: e.g. 'I am a Tamil-speaking Brahman', 'I am Jat Sikh from Jullunder', 'I am Gujerati Jain from East Africa', and so on. These categories are crucial determinants of intra-ethnic interaction, though almost irrelevant for operation within the indigenous community. If categories used to define 'Asians' are understood from the British majority perspective in a limited way, then there is a danger that change and development in future amongst them may be gauged within an equally narrow framework. Processes of change will in future reflect the diversity in existence among South Asians. Ignorance of these complexities by the assumption of a static and homogeneous 'South Asian' culture is likely to lead to badly-judged policy decisions and, most crucially, to potentially harmful developments between them. Similarly, failure to take account of the perceptions of minorities themselves is likely to lead to insensitivity to internal changes within the communities. So generalized categories need to be carefully examined for sensitive decision making otherwise they will mistakenly help to perpetuate stereotypical and ethnocentric assumptions.

To summarize lessons that can perhaps be learnt from the East African Sikh case are as follows: first, there should be far greater awareness of diversity among minorities, not assuming a homogeneous 'South Asian' community. Second, class differences should be noted, being as much products of previous experiences of migration as of position occupied within the hierarchy in the country of origin as by increasing residence in the UK, and the force of the British class system. Since the latter is hierarchically arranged, elements of it are to be found amongst minority communities even though the majority of people within them are working class. Third, generalizations should not be made despite the existence of common underlying cultural values that apply to most people of South Asian origin. Fourthly, it should be borne in mind that the situation and cultural patterns of minorities are much more fluid and complex than normally assumed by an ethnocentric perspective.

Finally, in many respects, one has to deal with the universality of cultural traits. The problems of minorities are not exclusive to them e.g. the generation gap, truancy among school children and marriage breakdown, all exist as much among the majority indigenous British community as they do amongst minorities. This is not to suggest that the situation is not exacerbated in the latter case in their still relatively early stages of settlement in Britain, but that there is large shared ground of common values and dilemmas existing among majority and minority alike.

Notes

Chapter 1

1. I feel that my concern for presenting a detailed description of both the community and its marriage and dowry system is justified especially at the present stage in the development of ethnic minority studies in the UK, in which most material that has been published is still in anthropological terms generalized, and lacking in rich ethnography. This is a point emphasized by Pnina Werbner (1980: 576) who states that most authors writing about minority communities make 'broad statements about general processes and yet their basic evidence is so selectively presented, so free of "*thick description*" that there is virtually no way this evidence can be evaluated or cross-checked in the light of other case studies' (my emphasis). Also, their arguments lack force 'in the absence of data on specific classroom situations or peer groups and families'.

2. I have used the word 'community' loosely throughout the book to refer to a group of Asians of Sikh origin who have migrated from East Africa. They share a set of features common to other East African Asian groups from their experiences as 'middlemen' in the plural setting in East Africa, where they formed settled communities with developed community institutions, cross-cutting kinship links, and close neighbourhood and work ties. Therefore my usage of the term East African community does not refer to a bounded geographical group resident in one area in the UK and from a particular region of the subcontinent but to a population that has shared past experiences and has a strong East African identity which has been reproduced in the UK. During their considerable stay in Africa, the East African Sikhs consolidated to form an 'in-marrying' group which is perpetuated in the UK.

3. East African Sikhs belong predominantly to the Ramgarhia caste group (Macleod 1974: 84; Bharati 1967: 34–8) consisting of three artisan

groups, *Lohars* (blacksmiths), *Tarkhans* (carpenters), and *Raj* (brick-layers). This caste ranks above the scheduled castes but below the *Jats* (landowners) and *Khatris* (the mercantile group) in the traditional caste hierarchy. Their move to East Africa consolidated this group much more so than on the Indian scene.

4. In the 1960s, East Africans moved to the UK especially from Kenya which had the largest number of wage earners of the three East African countries. There was a preponderance of employees working for the public sector, which was especially highly developed in Kenya since Nairobi, its capital, had the headquarters of all the government and major private concerns. These included the Railway and Harbours, Posts and Telecommunications, and Public Works departments, and the banks. Commercial enterprise was not as developed among Kenyan Asians as it was among the Ugandan and Tanzanian communities. Ghai (1965: 96), commenting on the occupational distribution of Asian employees in the three-tier system of East African countries, states that 36 per cent of Asian workers performed executive, administrative, and managerial functions; about 25 per cent were involved in skilled manual jobs; another 20 per cent in secretarial and clerical jobs; and 15 per cent in professional and technical occupations. As in previous decades, Asians provided the 'middle level' manpower, though by the late 1950s and early 1960s a number was obtaining higher-level executive positions, thus denting the three-tier system.

5. The most recent figures obtained from the Labour Force Survey of 1983 conducted by the Office of Population, Censuses and Surveys, reveals a total Asian population from the New Commonwealth of approximately 760,000, of which the Pakistani and Bangladeshi group constitutes 264,000 and the Indian, 505,000. The latter group includes 163,000 East African-born Asians, of which 159,000 are Indians and 4,000 Pakistanis.

   Of the total East African Asian group of 163,000, women constitute 75,814 and men 87,186. Whereas the Labour Force Survey figures are from a sample survey which focuses on the East African-born, the larger figure of the 1982 Census (181,321) includes household size and British-born children of East African parents.

6. Brooks and Singh (1978–9) say 'we accept obviously that East African Asians come from a number of ethnic groups. Nevertheless, it is apparent *to us that the East African experience is so important that it cuts across ethnic divisions* and, for the purposes of our argument, it is appropriate to group East African Asians together . . . whilst recognizing their ethnic identity' (my and authors' emphasis).

7. Paul Ghuman (1980: 315) describes a similar process for the Bhattra
    Sikhs who he suggests have remained 'ultra conservative and traditional'
    because of their lower caste position. He states 'that the Bhattras want
    to adhere rigidly to their religious and social way of life to compensate
    for their low status; they pride themselves on being pukka Sikhs and
    consider themselves the custodians of the Khalsa traditions'.

8. The Mandla versus Lee case was sparked off by the refusal of the
    headmaster of a private Catholic school Mr Dowell-Lee, to allow an East
    African Sikh boy, Gurinder Mandla, the permission to wear a turban as
    part of his school uniform. The main Sikh actors involved in the case, the
    boy himself, his solicitor father, and the main prosecuting barrister are
    all East African Sikhs. Similarly, Sikh religious leaders who gave it
    impetus, and the community organizations which initiated the demon-
    strations that ensued (especially after the Denning ruling, which refused
    to classify the Sikhs as a 'race' but which was later overturned by the
    House of Lords) were all largely East African Sikh in origin.

    This case demonstrates particularly well not only the organizational
    abilities and strong community ties of the East African Sikhs, but also,
    their religiosity and staunch adherence to external Sikh symbols, despite
    clear external opposition to their maintenance. The complex proce-
    dures involved in the case and their ability to succeed, albeit with the
    expertise and resources of the Commission for Racial Equality, also
    reflects their urban skills and familiarity with British institutions which
    they were able to mobilize effectively.

9. My fieldwork experiences, the joys and difficulties of working as a young
    Sikh woman within my own community in urban Britain and also within
    a geographically dispersed minority, have been described in greater
    detail in a forthcoming article, 'The Resocialization of an Anthropologist:
    Fieldwork within One's Own Community'.

Chapter 2

1. My material has been drawn from the existing ethnographic information
    on the South Asian community settled in East Africa, on the assumption
    that it had characteristics in common with the East African Sikh
    community, since the latter was part of the same set-up in Africa.

2. The Indians as a whole were called 'coolies', but in a strict sense a 'coolie'
    was an unskilled labourer. This label also seemed to apply to the more
    skilled and educated surveyors, clerks, masons, carpenters, etc., i.e. the
    Ramgarhia section of the labourers.

3. Within the Sikh society in East Africa, there was no intermarriage between the Ramgarhias and Jats (Bharati 1967: 316). From the marriages in my sample, regional endogamy was also more intact than it is in Britain at present.

4. These included Railway and Harbours, Posts and Telecommunications, and Public Works departments, and the banks.

5. I shall develop the theme of women's work in relation to the marriage customs in later chapters, since their salaries are in the United Kingdom responsible for certain elaborations in their dowries. At the moment, it should be stressed that the development of the women's earning capacity was in its incipient stages in the early 1960s in East Africa, to be further intensified in the United Kingdom with increased employment opportunities.

6. I shall develop this point later in relation to spouse selection since in Britain educational and professional skills are most highly valued by East African Sikhs in 'potential grooms'.

Chapter 3

1. The higher rate of entry into the labour market by East African Asian women is borne out by statistical surveys. For example, the Unit of Manpower Study (DOE 1976) demonstrated that, in comparison with indigenous women born in the UK, a larger percentage of full-time female workers are migrant women born overseas: 81 per cent of those born in the New Commonwealth (of which East African Asian women are a part) as compared with 62 per cent of UK-born women (quoted in Allen 1980: 333). When the category of South Asian women is examined separately, East African women constitute 52 per cent in full-time employment, in comparison with 40 per cent Indian women and 17 per cent Pakistani ones. In the South-east of Britain, which has a higher rate of female employment than any other region, there is hardly any difference in the employment percentages of South Asian women and indigenous British ones (CRC 1975: 8).

2. Chrishna (1975: 34) in discussing Asian girls in Britain states that 'young working women appear to fall into two categories: those working in factories with older Asian women and those working in offices where older women are not so much in evidence.' This occupational profile also applies to East African Sikh women, in common with the other Asian groups.

3. This trend of house-ownership among migrants has been emphasized by Dahya (1974: 83) and Mayer (1959: 25).

4. Recent statistical evidence presented in Brown (1985) reveals the relatively prosperous position of East African Asians. They now rank as one of the highest earning minorities in Britain, which shows a rapid improvement in their financial position. From being among the poorest, they have risen to the wealthiest groups, all within the past decade. The survey also shows that a higher proportion of them are to be found in prestigious positions within employment sectors in comparison with both the indigenous British and other South Asian and Afro-Caribbean groups (Brown 1984: 57, 181).

5. The balanced age and sex structure of the East African Sikhs also applies to other East African Asian communities (Robinson 1982), giving them enormous advantages of settlement abroad as communities with a sufficiently large pool of people who can marry endogamously. It also makes them unique in relation to the international migration of minority groups which tend to have younger age profile and a more restricted range of people within them.

6. This can be inferred from Roger Ballard's work (1973: 17; and C. Ballard 1977: 37).

Chapter 4

1. My sample has been described in the introductory chapter. As mentioned there, the total sample consists of thirteen core families on whom I concentrated more intensely during fieldwork, and of another eighteen wedding families with whom I had more contact during the marriage season.

2. Chapters 5 and 6 discuss these points in greater detail.

3. This involves continuous reading of the *Guru Granth Sahib* for forty-eight hours, during which time meals are served all the time for the guests.

4. The importance of networks in finding employment has been emphasized by Saifullah Khan (1979b: 127) who states that 'Women seeking work have access to the contacts of core members of their network and to their own and their husband's contacts. The successful mobilization of these contacts provides access to information from those who may be several links removed from the job seeker.' In the East African case, women often have direct contact with other women already in employment, who will in turn help them find work in their own organizations.

Chapter 5

1. Although the Sikh religion tried to establish a casteless society (Macleod 1968: 86) taking into its fold persons belonging to different castes and giving them equal status, this has not worked in practice. 'Sikh villages are divided in much the same way as Hindu villages' (I. P. Singh 1956: 241–46). The Jats are at the top of the caste hierarchy, forming 66 per cent of the Sikh population in India. They are agriculturalists for whom land is still the major criterion for determining status. Ramgarhias, considered traditionally to be 'low-born' are next on the rung, with a total of 6 per cent of the Sikh population. They are mainly craftsmen, and are also primarily urban-based as opposed to the rural Jats. Macleod (1976: 103) states that there are two general hierarchies to be discerned in Punjabi society: a small but distinct urban one with Khatris and Aroras (traders) forming 4.5 per cent of the Sikh population, and occupying a superior rank, followed by the Ramgarhias; and, secondly, the rural Jat one which is less clear in terms of order. Below these two major groups, the caste hierarchy follows much the same pattern as the Hindu one with Nais, Darzis, and the two outcaste groups of Chamars and Shudras who are to be found both in rural and urban areas (Izmerlian 1964: 23).

    The aspect of the caste system that I particularly want to stress, since it relates to the subjects of marriage and dowry, is that all the Sikh castes are strictly endogamous. This topic has been touched upon by some authors writing about the Sikhs. Khushwant Singh (1953: 45) states that 'Sikhism did not succeed in breaking the caste system.' If inter-marriage is considered to be the test of equality, there was very little of it between Sikhs converted from different Hindu castes. The untouchable who converted to Sikhism remained an outcaste for the purposes of matrimonial alliances.

    Thus, marriages have always been arranged along conventional lines. The Jats married the Jats, the Khatris married the Khatris, just as the gurus had themselves done, and the Ramgarhias married the Ramgarhias. On the one hand, there are egalitarian traditions inherited from the teachings of the gurus and, on the other, the insistent regard for some caste restrictions.

2. Morris (1967: 276) states that 'the need for caste exclusiveness was so strong that in spite of an environment almost wholly unfavourable to it, caste exclusiveness was one of the most important structural principles in organizing Indian social life in East Africa.'

    Also A. Bharati (1967: 184) states that 'endogamy is so complete and its workings so unchanged from those in the Indian sister communities in South Asia that it remains the *only* criterion for caste among East African Asians.'

3. The *gotra* is a group of people claiming descent from the same ancestor. The Brahman ideal forbids marriage between members of such a group. One should distinguish between the word *gotra* used over large parts of India as a descent-based clan which refers to exogamous sections of the sub-caste, and Brahmanic *gotras*, which are ultimately supposed to be traceable to one of the great *rishis* or holy men. Madan (1962: 59) opposes the view that gotras are often translated as clans. He suggests that they are mainly important at the time of marriage, as they tell an individual who his agnates are to prevent an unwitting breach of the prohibition of marriages within the required limit. Thus, according to him, they have no unity and are based neither on kinship nor on descent. This is a view that is similar to that of the Ramgarhias.

4. Hypergamy is defined by Ibbetson (1881: 356) as 'the law of superior marriage, I mean the rule which compels a man to wed his daughter with a member of a tribe which shall be actually superior in rank to one's own'. Dumont (1966: 159) clarifies the terminology. He states that 'a slight status difference, a slight inferiority of the wife's family in relation to the husband's is considered normal and does not in the least affect the offspring's status'. Since North Indian society has a pronounced patrilineality, it is the man's status which determines that of the children. As marriages are caste endogamous, the descendants acquire the social status of the father. For this reason, in the hypergamous system, women must have sexual relations with men of superior or equal status so that they may perpetuate the purity of the caste by producing legitimate children to become members of the caste. The status of the group is therefore defined by proper birth whereby the blood is kept unadulterated. All this follows the classical model of *anuloma* marriage which harmonizes with hypergamy because it 'flows with the hair' and is considered desirable; whereas a *pratiloma* marriage works in oppositon to the ideology prevalent in North India as it goes 'against the hair'. Hypergamy may also be defined as marriage with someone of a higher status. The term also implies that there is 'a strong recommendation for the girl's parents to find her a superior partner' (Dumont 1966: 159). In such a situation, there is an emphasis on the higher status of the wife takers and the inferior status of the wife givers. The core of the hypergamous pattern is precisely the difference in status of the wife givers and wife takers. My reference to 'formal' and 'informal' hyper-

gamy relates to the differences between the two types. Formal hypergamy applies to marriages in which there are actual differences of
standing between wife givers and wife takers, e.g. Bathelas and Desais
among Anavil Brahmans (Van der Veen 1972) and Patider marriage
circles (*ekada*) (Pocock 1957a, 1972) which are internally differentiated
into wife giving and wife taking villages. On the other hand, 'implicit'
hypergamy concerns marriages which from the outside seem isoga-
mous, since a woman may marry into a family roughly of equal status to
her own, but in which, at the time of marriage, the ideal of the inferiority
of the wife givers to the superiority of the wife takers is observed. The
important point is that there is no obligation to marry into a higher-status
family in such a case. Despite this, all marriages in this pattern are
hypergamous by definition, because of the inequality of the status of first,
the bride and groom, and second, of the two groups to which they
belong. This is precisely the type of hypergamy that is in existence
among the East African Sikh community.

5. The superiority of people from the Majha region, with Amritsar as its
    centre (a major trading and religious focus in West Punjab) and the
    inferiority of the Malwans in East Punjab could be related to the North
    Indian marriage network in which women go from East to West, in a way,
    from the inferior to the superior areas (Rowe 1960: 299–311; Gould
    1960: 476–91).

6. Endogamy is defined by Schusky (1972: 91) as 'A rule of marriage that
    requires a person to take a spouse from within the local kin, status or
    other group to which the person belongs.' I have used it here to refer to
    caste groups and regions (e.g. marriage restricted to the Jat caste or
    Ramgarhia caste) or to the specific regions of Doaba, Malwa, and Majha
    (that is those areas from which most migrants and settlers come).

7. I should state here that when I refer to the engagement, I mean the first
    ceremony of *rokna* which literally means booking or blocking the
    groom so that no other wife givers will be considered by his people.
    In general terms, this is said to be the engagement although the
    ritual proper, a big affair, mostly takes place a week or so before the
    wedding.

8. I have already described one of these families (the Ys) in the previous
    section, because one of the older deceased members was the first East
    African to be educated in the UK.

9. The concern behind this higher degree of purity expected of the woman

is related to the views posited by Yalman (1963: 54). He states that 'wherever we find the caste phenomenon, we may expect to find pre-occupation with "dangers" to pure women'. This concern is focused on the profound 'danger situation', i.e. the appearance of female sexuality. It is for this reason that the female rites are performed in such a public and formal manner. Dumont (1966: 13) states that the *tali* rites of the Nayar make a public recognition of paternity because the 'primary marriage' is always, according to the *shastras*, rigorously caste endogamous. The public nature of such a marriage is an attempt to reaffirm the ideal state of affairs in the community and also to demonstrate the correctness of status of the marriage partners. There is a close connection between the anxiety concerning female purity and the related puberty rites and caste as a 'bilateral structural principle'. That is, although the status of a legitimate child is fixed in the caste hierarchy by both parents, the pure status of the woman is of critical importance, as she cannot deny the bond between her and her child. This is one of the reasons the sexuality of men receives *carte blanche*, as they can never be internally polluted through sex relations with lower-status women. Women, on the other hand, especially in the hypergamous system and in accordance with the ideal *anuloma* marriages, must have sexual relations only with men of superior or equal status so that they may perpetuate the purity of the caste by producing legitimate children to become members of the caste. The status of the group is therefore defined by proper birth keeping the blood unadulterated. The honour of the men is preserved through their women.

10. Ballard and Ballard (1977: 47) have also referred to this, stating that 'a growing number of young Sikhs are readopting the turban, and its abandonment is becoming increasingly rare. This is partly the result of growing pressure towards orthodoxy and conformity from within the ethnic colony, but it is also a reassertion of ethnic pride in the face of white rejection.'

11. In general, information about the very early stages of matchmaking is difficult to obtain because of the delicate nature of the discussions. The whole procedure is handled secretively, in case the proposition falls through. Often even the close relatives are not aware of such activities until it is almost certain that the match will be fixed, at which time there are intense consultations among relatives to check the background of the family members with the help of the wider kinship network before making the final decision. It is only after the *rokna* that people first find out about the match.

Chapter 6

1. Although I have referred to the 'North Indian marriage pattern', I am well aware that there are castes other than the Brahmans in North India and that this pattern may not hold for them. It should be made clear that my reference in particular concerns higher castes and not lower ones.

2   Karve (1953: 132) states that 'All over India there is a custom of giving brideprice among the poorer castes and of receiving dowry among the higher castes.' Similarly Madan (1965: 114), describing the marriages of Kashmiri Pandits, states that 'There are three type of marriages among the Pandits. The ideal is represented by marriage with a "dowry" (ornaments and clothes for the bride, domestic utensils and other gifts in cash and kind for her relatives-in-law). The Pandits say that such a marriage is unsullied by any elements of bargaining on either side.'

3. There is, for example, a free association between women and cows, the supreme symbols of purity which produce all the effective cleaning agents e.g. clarified buttermilk and curd (Yalman 1963: 54). The symbolic identity between cows and pure women is particularly important here, as the 'gift of a virgin' accompanied by material goods is associated with the most sacred and pure prestation, 'the gift of a cow'. Such a gift symbolizes the substantive basis of the group, just as dowry giving is connected with its economic and interactive aspects. Thus, only the purity of the *kanya* can reflect the equally pure status of the group she belongs to.

4. Mauss (1954: 72) states that the person 'who gives magnifies himself in the eyes of others, but the individual who receives is diminished in importance. To give is to show one's superiority . . . to accept without returning or repaying more is to face subordination, to become a client and subservient.'

5. There are deviations from this norm because the dowry of the daughter-in-law may be used by the husband's parents to dower their own daughters. Although this aspect is not brought out in Tambiah's work, it is clear from both Madan's (1973) and Vatuk's (1973) data that this is not the case and that a woman's dowry may be used by her affines rather than exclusively by herself. Vatuk points out that there are a large number of gifts which accompany the bride and can seem like her property but are in fact designed to become the family's joint property. 'The wedding gifts with the exception of those items explicitly designed for the bride's personal use or for that of her husband-to-be become the

property of the groom's joint household and their disposal is, in effect, in the hands of his parents, or of the household head and his wife.' This includes cash, household goods, and clothing, i.e. all the items that Tambiah classifies as *stridhanam*. Similarly Madan (1965: 158) mentions that 'parents-in-law show immense interest in her *stridhan*, and may take away the best of her personal possessions to give to their own daughters'.

6. After the engagement ceremony at the groom's house, while the groom's kin feast, the bride's kin leave without eating 'for they may not eat while in the groom's village' (Lewis 1958: 69). Similarly, the gift giving role of the bride givers does not end at the marriage ceremony but continues throughout the lifetime of the daughter (Madan 1965: 138–40). Similarly, among the Desais (Van der Veen 1972: 77) the father continues to pay for the clothes of the daughter after her marriage, thus reducing any burden the affines may have in the daily upkeep of the daughter-in-law. This duty is further carried on by the bride's brother, ending ultimately in the presentation of the *mamera* (Mayer 1960: 219, 229) or MB's gifts to the sister's children at their marriages. It is precisely the ideology of unilaterality between wife givers and wife takers in North India that allows the latter the legitimate authority to be constant recipients of gifts without any obligation to reciprocate.

7. The general literature on the Sikhs suggests that Sikhism is the 'outcome of a conflict between Islam and Hinduism' (Khushwant Singh 1953: 21) or that it is a reform movement that arose during the period of Muslim domination in the fifteenth century, aimed at preventing the masses from being converted to Islam which was achieving a large number of converts from the lower castes (I. P. Singh 1956: 243; John 1969: 17; Beetham 1970: 9). However, according to Macleod (1976: 5) this was not so, because Sikhism was the most highly-articulated expression of *nirguna sampradaya*, the *sant* tradition which had been around for a long time. The emphasis in this tradition was on a total rejection of all such external elements as idols, rituals, temples, pilgrimages, and, most important, castes. Thus, a developed hierarchy of priests, the inferior position of women, the Hindu caste system, etc. were all abolished by Guru Nanak, the first Sikh guru, who was able to bring together a number of schools of thought existing during his time to formulate the basis of Sikhism.

8. Sikhism emphasizes that simplicity (*saadhi*) should permeate the whole of the wedding procedure and that rituals should be reduced to a minimum. The *Rehat Maryada* which represent the 'codes of discipline'

i.e. what is deemed to be correct behaviour for the Sikhs, denounce Hindu customs. These rules are part of the Sikh holy book (*Adi Granth*) and summarized the Guru's teachings. Sikhism is a reform movement of the fifteenth century (Khushwant Singh 1953: 21, 41–2; Macleod 1976: 86) which attempted to establish a casteless society by abolishing Brahman ideals. Yet, the premisses on which the Sikh marriage pattern rests is very Hindu. Thus, there is a conflict between the egalitarian ideology of Sikhism which is publicly advocated, and actual practices such as presenting dowries, and elaborate marriages.

9. 1 *tola*=11.66 gm
    1 oz=31 gms
    1 oz=2¼ *tolas*

    Price of one *tola* at present is between £90 and £100 though it fluctuates with the value of the pound.

10. It is commonly recognized even now that an only daughter amongst a set of brothers always receives a higher *daaj* than most other women. This is true of three such cases within my wedding sample.

11. As East Africa developed it came to be known as the 'America of the Hindus' (Mangat 1969: 61), hence the high status of 'Africa-returned' grooms.

Chapter 7

1. An example of the amateurish way used to arrange these functions was provided by three brothers who used to perform these ceremonies in the 1960s in London. One of them could read the *Guru Granth Sahib*, another could play the *tabla* (the Indian drums), while the third could sing and play the harmonium for the *kirtan*. None of them had had any training in doing these, unlike the *gianis* who know the proper procedure.

2. The older women would tell me that in India and East Africa, the *daaj* was always looked at by the neighbourhood in general, and often by the bride's and groom's male kin. The latter were shown the *daaj*, when it was displayed in a large open space like a courtyard (laid out either on large tables or on the floor on bed sheets) when the *barat* had finished their midday meal. The father-in-law of the bride used to fold over the *pullah*, i.e. the end of a sari or *dupatta* if the *daaj* was to his satisfaction. Hence, it seems that the views of the men were given a considerable amount of importance since they were allowed to look at the *daaj*.

From the situation that I witnessed in London, the men's opinions as to the quality or quantity of *daajs* seemed quite irrelevant, whereas the women were extremely knowledgeable about such matters. All this indicates that, since it is predominantly the women who are in charge of making the *daaj*, and it is only they who inspect other brides' *daajs*, the system has become more women-orientated in the UK than it has been previously.

3.   Dinner parties and receptions nearly always have alcohol provided.

4.   See previous chapter for a similar theme.

5.   See Chapter 4 for further details of the types of work the women in my sample were involved in.

6.   However, my female informants would occasionally tell me of brides who had been asked about their previous earnings by their husbands, always grooms who had migrated directly from India. I was never able to follow up these cases because my informants had themselves got this information secondhand. Nonetheless, it confirmed their views, which correlate with general East African opinion, of the futility of marrying grooms from India who had, according to them, 'money-grabbing' attitudes. These were supposed to be absent amongst East African youngsters because they would never question each other about their earning capacities in the past.

7.   This particular aspect was sometimes discussed by the younger women especially on events like Mother's and Father's Day, birthdays, etc. because parents, especially the mothers, would often refuse the daughter's presents though not the son's gifts.

8.   The only exception to this was one case in my sample of a girl who had not spent her salary on her *daaj* but had helped her mother with the household expenses. She belonged to a poorer family without a household head. She was married to an Indian Sikh and received a smaller *daaj*. See previous chapter for details.

9.   After marriage, the brides did help their husbands to buy houses and paid for them jointly.

10.   One silk sari costs anything from £30 to £300. An ordinary sari can be bought for £10 to £30, and a chiffon one, depending on the embroidery, costs £30 to £90.

11.   See *daajs* of three sisters married in the 1970s in the United Kingdom, neither of whom had worked.

12.   I have referred to the *daajs* of them all in the previous chapter according to the phase in which they were presented.

13..   I should explain that the *daajs* of the sisters were smaller than those presented to brides of an equivalent age and status at that time in East Africa because the father was not wealthy and his 'responsibilities were heavy' as Punjabis put it, since he had a large number of daughters to marry off.

14.   See Chapter 5 for a similar theme, the relative ease with which they find marriage partners for their children from within the UK community, ruling out the need to import fiancés from India.

15.   The situation in Sri Lanka, Burma (Tambiah 1975: 63, 151), and North India is that the more highly-qualified the groom, the larger the level of dowry that is asked for him from the bride's people, to recoup the money spent on his education. This is a reason that is often cited as an explanation for the elaboration of the dowry system in 'modern' and 'progressive' circles. This is in complete contradiction to the East African situation in the UK, where dowries have become inflated despite the absence of such demands. I have explored other factors that have kept the dowry system intact.

16.   Railways' and some other government employees could have free medical treatment.

17.   This is related to topics discussed in previous chapters concerning the similarity of Sikh explanations behind the presentation of dowries and the observation of the traditional criteria for spouse selection, with that of the high-caste Hindus of North India.

Chapter 8

1.   A similar position has been documented by Cohen (1968: 361–76) for the Hausa Muslims of Sabo. After Independence in the 1950s, their identity and monopoly over trade was threatened through the loss of both their territorial exclusivity and the spread of Islam to the surrounding Yoruba. As a result, the Hausa, who were the original Muslims in the area were being 'rapidly swallowed by the masses of Yoruba Muslims and they were no longer distinct as Muslims' (p. 365). As an expression of their 'ethnic distinctiveness', they initiated an Islamic mystical sect called the Tijaniyya. Since membership of this required involvement in frequent collectivized rituals, 'a distinct ritual community' emerged, resulting in the restriction

of social interaction almost entirely to Hausa Muslims. Just as the Hausa expressed their ethnic separateness from the Yoruba by adhering to the Tijaniyya, in a similar fashion, the Ramgarhias seem to be making a symbolic statement of their differences from the Jats by focusing on traditional activities and symbols. Of the latter, East African exclusivity is symbolized especially well by one facet of their social organization: the dowry system which has gained prominence since settlement in the UK.

2. For example, it is clear from the mushrooming of the multi-cultural industry in the 1970s and 1980s, that this has been a response by decision makers of both interest shown by minorities in perpetuating their cultural values, making the educational curriculum more relevant to their lives, and of creating more awareness of minority cultures amongst the majority. That is, it is a response to the heterogeneity of the British population and also a recognition of it. These aspects will become even more important in future, as British-born Asians go through the schooling system and as parents realize that a concerted effort will have to be made to inculcate their cultural values into their offspring, who are living in this more heterogeneous environment.

3. This issue has been discussed in detail by Lawrence (1982: 95–142) and by Parmar (1982: 236–75).

4. 'Girls are required to accept considerable limitations on their freedom of movement and above all, to *accept* arranged marriages. Boys may be *required* to give their wages to their fathers and also to accept arranged marriages' (Rex 1982: 60–1) (my emphasis).

References

Alavi, Hamza (1972) Kinship in West Punjab Villages. *Contributions to Indian Sociology* (NS) 6: 1–27.

Allen, S. (1980) Perhaps a Seventh Person. *Women's Studies International Quarterly* 3: 325–38.

Anwar, M. (1976) *Between Two Cultures: A Study of Relationships Between Generations in the Asian Community in Britain*. London: Community Relations Commission.

— (1979) *The Myth of Return: Pakistanis in Britain*. London: Heinemann.

Aurora, Gurdip Singh (1967) *The New Frontiersmen*. Bombay: Popular Prakashan.

Baden-Powell, B. H. (1872) *Handbook of Manufacturers and Arts of the Punjab*. Lahore: Punjab Printing Co.

Ballard, C. (1976) Culture Conflict and Young Asians in Britain. Paper presented to the International Congress on Transcultural Psychiatry, Bradford, England.

— (1978) Arranged Marriages in the British Context. *New Community* 6: 181–96.

Ballard, R. (1973) Family Organization among the Sikhs in Britain. *New Community* 2: 12–24.

— (1983) Migration in a Wider Context: Jullunder and Mirpur Compared. *New Community* 11 (1/2).

Ballard, R. and Ballard, C. (1977) The Sikhs: the Development of South Asian Settlements in Britain. In J. L. Watson (ed.) *Between Two Cultures: Migrants and Minorities in Britain*. Oxford: Basil Blackwell.

Bannerjee, G. (1895) *The Hindu Law of Marriage and Stridhaman* (2nd edn). Calcutta: Lahiri.

Barber, B. (1957) *Social Stratification: A Comparative Analysis of Structure and Process*. New York: Harcourt Brace and World.

Beetham, D. (1970) *Transport and Turbans: A Comparative Study in Local Politics*. London: Oxford University Press for the Institute of Race Relations.

Benedict, B. (1961) *Indians in a Plural Society*. London: HMSO.

Berreman, G. D. (1962) Village Exogamy in Northernmost India. *Southwestern Journal of Anthropology* 18: 55–9.

Bhachu, P. K. (1981) Marriage and Dowry among Selected East African Sikh Families in the UK. Unpublished PhD thesis, University of London.

— (1984a) East African Sikhs in Britain: Experienced Settlers with Traditionalistic Values. *Immigrants and Minorities* 3 (3): 276–95.

— (1984b) Multicultural Education: Parental Views. *New Community*, XII (Winter 1984/85): 1.

— (forthcoming) Work, Dowry and Marriage among East African Sikh Women in the United Kingdom. In C. B. Brettell and R. Simon (eds) *International Immigration: The Female Experience*. Totowa, NJ: Rowman and Allenhead.

— (forthcoming) The Resocialization of an Anthropologist: Fieldwork within One's Own Community. In Scarlett Epstein (ed.) *Female Ethnographer: Researchers Working in their own Communities*. Delhi: Hindustan Publishing Corporation.

Bharati, A. (1965) A Social Survey. In D. P. Ghai (ed.) *Portrait of a Minority: Asians in East Africa*. Nairobi: Oxford University Press.

— (1967) Ideology and Content of Caste among the Indians in East Africa. In B. M. Schwartz (ed.) *Caste in Overseas Indian Communities*. San Francisco: Chandler Publishing Company.

— (1972) *The Asians in East Africa: Jayhind and Uhuru*. Chicago: Nelson-Hall Co.

Blunt, E. A. H. (1931) *The Caste System of Northern India with Special Reference to the United Provinces of Agra and Oudh*. London: Oxford University Press.

Brooks, D. (1975a) *Race and Labour in London Transport*. London: Oxford University Press for the Institute of Race Relations.

— (1975b) *Black Employment in the Black Country: A Study of Walsall*. London: Runnymede Trust.

— and Singh K. (1978–79) Ethnic Commitment Versus Structural Reality: South Asian Immigrant Workers in Britain. *New Community* VII (1).

Brown, C. (1984) *Black and White Britain: The Third PSI Survey*. London: Policy Studies Institute and Heinemann.

Cashmore, E., and Troyna, B. (eds) (1982) *Black Youth in Crisis*. London: Allen and Unwin.

Castles, C., Booth, H., and Wallace, T. (1984). *Here for Good: Western Europe's New Ethnic Minorities*. Pluto Press: London and Sydney.

Castles, S. and Kosack, G. (1973) *Immigrant Workers and the Class Structure*. London: Oxford University Press for the Institute of Race Relations.

CCCS (Centre for Contemporary Cultural Studies) (1982) *The Empire Strikes Back: Race and Racism in 70's Britain*. London: Hutchinson.

Chabra, G. S. (1960) *The Advanced Study in History of the Punjab*. Vol. 1, Jullunder: Sharanjit; Vol. 2, Ludhiana: Parkash Brothers.

Chaudri, J. J. M., (1971) The Emigration of Sikh Jats from Punjab to England. In A. C. Mayer (ed.) *Social Science Research Council Report*, Project HR 331–1.

Chrishna, S. (1975) *Girls of Asian Origin in Britain*. London: YMCA of Great Britain.

Cohen, A. (1968) The Politics of Mysticism in some Local Communities in Newly-Independent African States. In M. J. Swartz (ed.) *Local Level Politics*. Chicago: Aldine.

Comaroff, J. L. (ed.) (1980) *The Meaning of Marriage Payments*. Chicago: Academic Press.

Community Relations Commission (1975) *Who Minds: A Study of Working Mothers and Child Minding in Ethnic Minority Communities*. Community Relations Commission (now Commission For Racial Equality).

Dahya, B. (1973) Pakistanis in Britain, Transients or Settlers? *Race* 14: 246–77.

— (1974) The Nature of Pakistani Ethnicity in Industrial Cities in Britain. In A. Cohen (ed.) *Urban Ethnicity*. London: Tavistock.

Darling, M. L. (1925) *The Punjab Peasant in Prosperity and Debt*. London: Oxford University Press.

Delf, G. (1963) *Asians in East Africa*. London: Oxford University Press for the Institute of Race Relations.

Derrett, J. D. M. (1962) The History of the Juridical Framework of the Joint Hindu Family. *Contributions to Indian Sociology* 6: 17–47.

— (1963) *Introduction to Modern Hindu Law*. Bombay: Oxford University Press.

Desai, R. (1963) *Indian Immigrants in Britain*. London: Oxford University Press for the Institute of Race Relations.

DOE (1976) The Role of Immigrants in the Labour Market. Unit of Manpower Study. Dept of Employment, London.

Dube, S. C. (1954) The Early Brahmanical System of *gotra* and *parvana*. *Man* (NS) 54: 64–5.

— (1955) *Indian Village*. London: Routledge and Kegan Paul.

Dumont, L. (1966) Marriage in India: the Present State of the Question. *Contributions to Indian Sociology* 9: 90–114.

— (1972) *Homo Hierarchicus*. London: Paladin.

Eglar, Z. (1960) *A Punjabi Village in Pakistan*. New York: Columbia University Press.

Fernando, T. (1979) East African Asians in Western Canada: The Ismaili Community. *New Community* 7 (3).

Foster, G. M. (1961) The Dyadic Contract: a Model for the Social Structure of a Mexican Peasant Village. *American Anthropologist* (NS) 63: 1173–193.

Friedl, E. (1963) Some Aspects of Dowry and Inheritance in Boeotia. In J. A. Pitt-Rivers (ed.) *Mediterranean Countrymen*. Paris: Mouton.

Ghai, D. P. (1965) *Portrait of a Minority: Asians in East Africa*. Nairobi: Oxford University Press.

— (1970) *Portrait of a Minority in East Africa*. Nairobi: Oxford University Press.

Ghuman, P. (1980) Bhattra Sikhs in Cardiff: Family and Kinship Organization. *New Community* 8 (3).

Goode, W. J. (1963) *World Revolution and Family Patterns*. New York: The Free Press.

Goody, J. (1975) Bridewealth and Dowry in Africa and Eurasia. In J. Goody and S. J. Tambiah, *Bridewealth and Dowry*. Cambridge: Cambridge University Press.

— (1976) *Production and Reproduction*. Cambridge: Cambridge University Press.

Gough, K. (1955) Female Initiation Rites on the Malabar Coast. *Journal of the Royal Anthropological Institute* 85 (2).

Gould, H. A. (1960) The Micro-demography of Marriage in a North Indian Area. *Southwestern Journal of Anthropology* 16: 476–91.

— (1961) A Further Note on Village Exogamy in North India. *Southwestern Journal of Anthropology* 17: 297–300.

— (1968) Time Dimension and Structural Change in an Indian Kinship System: a Problem of Conceptual Refinement. In M. Singer and B. S. Cohn (eds) *Structure and Change in Indian Society*. Chicago: Aldine.

Gregory, R. G. (1971) *India and East Africa. A History of Race Relations Within the British Empire 1890–1939*. Oxford: Clarendon Press.

Hazelhurst, L. W. (1966) *Entrepreneurship and the Merchant Castes in a Punjabi City*. North Carolina, USA: Duke University Program in Comparative Studies on Southern Asia, Monograph 1.

Helweg, A. W. (1979) *Sikhs in England: The Development of a Migrant Community*. Delhi: Oxford University Press.

— (1983) Emigrant Remittances: Their Nature and Impact on a Punjabi Village. *New Community* 10 (3).

Hershman, P. (1974) Hair, Sex and Dirt. *Man* (NS) 9: 274–98.

Hollingsworth, L. W. (1960) *The Asians in East Africa*. London: Macmillan.

Humphrey, D. and Ward, M. (1974) *Passports and Politics*. Britain: Penguin Books.

Ibbetson, D. C. J. (1881) *Report on the Census of the Punjab*. Lahore: Punjab Government Press.

— (1916) *Punjab Castes.* Lahore: Punjab Government Press.

Inden, R. B. (1976) *Marriage and Rank in Bengali Culture. A History of Caste and Clan in Middle Period Bengal.* New Delhi: Vikas Publishing House, PVT Ltd.

Izmerlian, H. J. (1964) *Caste, Kin and Politics in a Punjabi Village.* Unpublished PhD thesis in Anthropology, University of California, Berkeley.

James, A. (1974) *Sikh Children in Britain.* London: Oxford University Press for the Institute of Race Relations.

Jeffrey, P. (1976) *Migrants and Refugees: Muslim and Christian Pakistani Families in Bristol.* Cambridge: Cambridge University Press.

John, DeWitt (1969) *Indian Workers Associations in Great Britain.* London: Oxford University Press for the Institute of Race Relations.

Kalra, S. S. (1980). *Daughters of Traditions, Adolescent Sikh Girls and their Accommodation to Life in British Society.* Birmingham: Diane Balbir Publications.

Kane, P. V. (1941) *History of Dharmashastra.* Vol. III. Poona: Government Oriental Series.

Kapadia, K. M. (1966) *Marriage and Family in India* (3rd edn). Bombay: Oxford University Press.

Kapur, P. (1970) *Marriage and the Working Woman in India.* Delhi: Vikas Publications.

Karve, I. (1953) *Kinship Organization in India.* Poona: Deccan College Monograph Series, II.

Kessinger, T. (1975) *Vilayatpur, 1848–1968: Social and Economic Change in a North Indian Village.* Berkeley, Calif.: University of California Press.

Kolenda, P. (1968) Region, Caste, and Family Structure: a Comparative Study of the Indian 'Joint Family'. In M. Singer and B. S. Cohn (eds) *Structure and Change in Indian Society.* Chicago: Aldine.

Kuepper, W. G., Lackey, G. L., and Swinerton, E. N. (1975) *Ugandan Asians in Britain: Forced Migration and Social Absorption.* London: Croom Helm.

Kuper, H. (1960) *Indian People in Natal.* Natal: Natal University Press.

Lawrence, E. (1982) Just Plain Common Sense: the Roots of Racism. Centre for Contemporary Cultural Studies, *The Empire Strikes Back: Race and Racism in '70s Britain.* London: Hutchinson.

Leach, E. R. (1961) Asymmetric Marriage Rules, Status Difference, and Direct Reciprocity. *Southwestern Journal of Anthropology* 17: 343–51.

Leaf, M. (1974) *Information and Behaviour in a Sikh Village.* Berkeley and Los Angeles, Calif.: University of California Press.

Levi-Strauss, C. (1969) *The Elementary Structures of Kinship.* Boston, Mass.: Beacon Press.

Levy, H. L. (1963) Inheritance and Dowry in Classical Athens. In J. A. Pitt-Rivers (ed.) *Mediterranean Countrymen*. Paris: Mouton.

Lewis, C. (1958) *Village Life in Northern India: Studies in a Delhi Village.* Urbana, Ill.: University of Illinois Press.

— (1965) *Village Life in Northern India.* New York: Random House.

Macleod, W. H. (1968) *Guru Nanak and the Sikh Religion.* Oxford: Clarendon Press.

— (1974) *Ahluwalias and Ramgarhias: Two Sikh Castes. South Asia* 4: 78–90.

— (1976) *The Evolution of the Sikh Community.* Oxford: Clarendon Press.

Madan, T. N. (1962) Is the Brahmanic *Gotra* a Grouping of Kin? *Southwestern Journal of Anthropology* 18: 59–77.

— (1965) *Family and Kinship: a Study of the Pandits of Rural Kashmir.* Bombay: Asia Publishing House.

— (1973) Structural Implications of Marriage in North India: Wife Givers and Wife Takers among the Pandits of Kashmir. *Contributions to Indian Sociology* (NS) 9: 217–43.

Mangat, J. S. (1969) *A History of the Asians in East Africa, 1886 to 1945.* Oxford: Clarendon Press.

Mauss, M. (1954) *The Gift.* London: Cohen and West.

Mayer, A. C. (1959) *A Report on the East Indian Community in Vancouver.* Unpublished working paper for the Institute of Social and Economic Research, University of British Columbia.

— (1960) *Caste and Kinship in Central India.* Berkeley and Los Angeles, Calif.: University of California Press.

— (1961) *Peasants in the Pacific.* Berkeley and Los Angeles, Calif.: University of California Press.

— (1963) *Indians in Fiji.* London: Oxford University Press for the Institute of Race Relations.

Michaelson, M. (1979) The Relevance of Caste among East African Gujeratis in Britain. *New Community* 7 (3).

Morris, H. S. (1967) Caste among the Indians in Uganda. In B. M. Schwartz (ed.) *Caste in Overseas Indian Communities.* San Francisco, Calif.: Chandler Publishing Company.

— (1968) *Indians in Uganda.* London: Weidenfeld and Nicolson.

Naik, T. B. (1947) Joking Relationships. *Man in India.* 27: 250–66.

Newell, W. H. (1955) The Brahmans and Caste Isogamy in North India. *Journal of the Royal Anthropological Institute* 85: 101–10.

Parmar, P. (1982) Gender, Race, and Class: Asian Women in Resistance. Centre for Contemporary Cultural Studies. *The Empire Strikes Back: Race and Racism in the '70s Britain.* London: Hutchinson.

Pettigrew, J. (1972) Some Notes on the Social System of the Sikh Jats. *New Community* 1 (5): 354–63.

— (1975) *Robber Noblemen. A Study of the Political System of the Sikh Jats.* London and Boston: Routledge and Kegan Paul.

Phizacklea, A. and Miles, R. (1980) *Labour and Racism.* London: Routledge and Kegan Paul.

Plender, R. (1972) The Expulsion of the Asians from Uganda; Legal Aspects. *New Community* 1 (5).

Pocock, D. F. (1954) The Hypergamy of the Patiders. In K. M. Kapadia (ed.) *Professor Ghurye Felicitation Volume.* Bombay: Popular Book Depot.

— (1957a) Inclusion and Exclusion: a Process in the Caste System of Gujerat. *Southwestern Journal of Anthropology* 13: 19–31.

— (1957b) Difference in East Africa: a Study of Caste and Religion in Modern Indian Society. *Southwestern Journal of Anthropology* 13: 289–300.

— (1972) *Kanbi and Patidar: a Study of the Patidar Community of Gujerat.* Oxford: Clarendon Press.

Pryce, K. (1979) *Endless Pressure.* London: Penguin.

Rattansi, P. M. and Abdulla, N. (1965) An Educational Survey. In D. P. Ghai (ed.) *Portrait of a Minority: Asians in East Africa.* Nairobi: Oxford University Press.

Rattigan, W. H. (1929) *A Digest of Civil Law for the Punjab* (11th edn). Lahore: The Civil and Military Gazette Press.

Rehat Maryada: A Guide to the Sikh Way of Life (1971) Translated by Kanwaljit Kaur and Inderjeet Singh. London: The Sikh Cultural Society.

Rex, J. (1982) West Indian and Asian Youth. In B. Troyna and E. Cashmore (eds) *Black Youth in Crisis.* London: Allen and Unwin.

Rex, J. and Tomlinson, S. (1979) *Colonial Immigrants in a British City: a Class Analysis.* London: Routledge and Kegan Paul.

Robinson, V. (1981) The Development of South Asian Settlement in Britain and the Myth of Return. In C. Peach, V. Robinson, and S. Smith (eds) *Ethnic Segregation in Cities.* London: Croom Helm.

— (1982) The Assimilation of South and East African Asian Immigrants in Britain. In D. A. Coleman (ed.) *Demography of Immigrants and Minorities in the United Kingdom.* London: Academic Press.

— (1984) Asians in Britain: a Study in Encapsulation and Marginality. In C. Clarke, D. Ley, and C. Peach (eds) *Geography and Ethnic Pluralism.* London: Allen and Unwin.

Rose, A. A. (1919) *A Glossary of the Tribes and Castes of the Punjab and North-West Frontier Province.* Lahore: Government publication.

Rose, E. J. B. (1969) *Colour and Citizenship, a Report on British Race*

Relations. London: Oxford University Press for the Institute of Race Relations.

Rowe, W. (1960) The Marriage Network and Structural Change in a North Indian Community. *Southwestern Journal of Anthropology* 16: 299–311.

Saberwal, S. (1972) Status, Mobility, and Networks in a Punjabi Industrial Town. In S. Saberwal (ed.) *Beyond the Village: Sociological Explorations.* Simla: Indian Institute of Advanced Studies.

— (1976) *Mobile Men: Limits to Social Change in Urban Punjab.* New Delhi: Vikas Publishing House, PVT Ltd.

Sahlins, M. D. (1965) On the Sociology of Primitive Exchange. In M. Banton (ed.) *The Relevance of Models in Social Anthropology.* London: Tavistock.

— (1972) *Stone Age Economics.* London: Tavistock.

Saifullah Khan, V. (1976) *Perceptions of a Population: Pakistanis in Britain. New Community* 5: 222–29.

— (1977) The Pakistanis: Mirpuri Villages at Home in Bradford. In J. L. Watson (ed.) *Between Two Cultures: Migrants and Minorities in Britain.* Oxford: Basil Blackwell.

— (ed.) (1979a) *Minority Families in Britain: Support and Stress.* London: Macmillan Press.

— (1979b) Work and Network: South Asian Women in South London. In S. Wallman (ed.) *Ethnicity at Work.* London: Macmillan.

Sangroor, L. S. (1946) *Sikh Kanoon* (5th edn). Amritsar: Gurmat Press.

Schusky, E. L. (1972) *Manual for Kinship Analysis.* New York: Holt, Rinehart and Winston.

Shah, S. (1979) Who Are the Jains? *New Community* 7 (3).

Singh, G. S. (ed.) (1962) *Early European Accounts of the Sikhs.* Calcutta: Indian Studies: Past and Present.

Singh, Harbans (1964) *The Heritage of the Sikhs.* Bombay: Asia Publishing House.

— (1969) *Guru Nanak and the Origins of the Sikh Faith.* Bombay: Asia Publishing House.

Singh, I. P. (1956) Dynamics and Change in a Sikh village. In A. Aiyappan and L. K. Bala Ratnam (eds) *Society in India.* Madras: Social Science Association.

— (1967) Caste in a Sikh Village. In *Sikhism in Indian Society.* Transactions of the Indian Institute of Advanced Studies, Vol. 4. Simla.

Singh, Khushwant (1953) *The Sikhs.* London: Allen and Unwin.

— (1966) *A History of the Sikhs 1839–1964.* 2 Volumes. Princeton, NJ: Princeton University Press.

Singh, Teja (1939) *Sikhism: its Ideals and Institutions.* Calcutta: Longmans Green and Co.

Sjoberg, G. (1960) *The Pre-Industrial City: Past and Present.* New York: Free Press.

Smelser, N. J. (1965) *The Sociology of Economic Life.* London: Prentice-Hall.

Smith, M. W. (1948) Synthesis and Other Processes in Sikhism. *American Anthropologist* 40: 457–62.

Srinivas, M. N. (1952) *Religion and Society Among the Coorgs in South India.* Oxford: Clarendon Press.

—— (1966) *Social Change in Modern India.* Berkeley and Los Angeles, Calif.: University of California Press.

Tambiah, S. J. (1975) Dowry and Bridewealth and the Property Rights of Women in South Asia. In J. Goody and S. J. Tambiah (eds) *Bridewealth and Dowry.* Cambridge: Cambridge University Press.

Tambs-Lyche, H. (1980) *London Patiders: a Case in Urban Ethnicity.* London: Routledge and Kegan Paul.

Taylor, J. H. (1976) *The Half-way Generation: A Study of Asian Youths in Newcastle-upon-Tyne.* Slough: NFER.

Taylor, M. (1981) *Caught Between: a Review of Research into the Education of Pupils of West Indian Origin.* Slough: NFER.

Thompson, M. (1970) A Study of Generation Differences in Immigrant Groups, with Particular Reference to the Sikhs. Unpublished MPhil thesis, University of London.

—— (1974) The Second Generation – Punjabi or English? *New Community* 3: 242–48.

Thurnwald, R. C. (1935) *Black and White in East Africa: The Fabric of a New Civilization.* London: Routledge.

Thurston, E. (1909) *Castes and Tribes in Southern India.* 7 Vols. Madras: Government Press.

Tiemann, G. (1970) The Four-*got* rule among the Jats of Haryana in Northern India. *Anthropos* 65: 166–77.

Uberoi, J. S. (1967) On Being Unshorn. *Transactions of the Indian Institute of Advanced Studies* 4: 87–100. Simla.

Van den Dungen, P. H. M. (1968) Changes in Status and Occupation in Nineteenth Century Punjab. In D. A. Low (ed.) *Soundings in Modern South Asian History.* London: Weidenfeld and Nicolson.

Van der Veen, K. (1972) *I Give Thee My Daughter: a Study of Marriage and Hierarchy among the Anavil Brahmans of South Gujerat.* Assen: Van Gorcum and Company.

Vatuk, S. (1972) *Kinship and Urbanization: White Collar Migrants in North India.* Berkeley and Los Angeles, Calif.: University of California Press.

—— (1973) *Gifts and Affines in North India.* Contributions to Indian Sociology (NS) 9: 155–96.

Wallman, S. (ed.) (1979) *Ethnicity at Work*. London: Macmillan.

Watson, J. L. (1975) *Emigration and the Chinese Lineage: the Mans in Hong Kong and London*. Berkeley, Calif.: University of California Press.

— (1977) The Chinese: Hong Kong Villagers in the British Catering Trade. In J. L. Watson (ed.) *Between Two Cultures: Migrants and Minorities in Britain*. Oxford: Basil Blackwell.

Werbner, P. (1979) Avoiding the Ghetto: Pakistani Migrants and Settlement Shifts in Manchester. *New Community* 7 (3).

— (1980a) Book Review of V. Saifullah Khan (ed.) *Minority Families in Britain: Support and Stress. Man* 15 (3): 570–71.

— (1980b) From Rags to Riches: Manchester Pakistanis in the Textile Trade. *New Community* 8 (1/2).

Yalman, N. (1963) On the Purity of Women in the Castes of Ceylon and Malabar. *Journal of the Royal Anthropological Institute* (NS) 93: 25–58.

Name index

Subject index

Amin, General Idi 6
Amritsar 15
Asians in East Africa: and
  Africanization 27–9; and export of
  capital 28; employment of women
  27; from 1940s to mid-1960s 23–6;
  population figures for 176n5; up to
  1940s 21–9

Bahu families 82
bank book 149
Bhattras 177n7
British, tendency to lump South
  Asians together 11

Canada 28, 48, 163
capital 24, 28; possession of 9
caste 50–3, 180; and social class
  13–16; and marriage 78–9; and
  purity of women 182–83n9; caste
  associations 168; endogamy 74–5;
  exogamy 75–7; in East Africa 25–6;
  in UK 52; intermarriage 178n3;
  minority caste status 14
clothing 105, 110
communications network 8, 66–8;
  and funerals 43; and marriage
  43–4, 85–90; strength of 40–5
'community', definition of 175
community, UK: characteristics of
  30–55; and myth of return 45–9;
  communications network 40–45;
  community expertise 53; cultural

conservatism of 50–53; dispersed
  nature of 8; family units and 37–40;
  financial advantages of 36–7; not
  homogeneous 173–74;
  occupational skills of 33–5; pattern
  of settlement 31–3; relations with
  kinsmen 31–2; views on India 10
community consolidation in Africa
  12–13
community expertise 6–7, 53–4
community structure, changing
  nature of 167
conspicuous consumption 167
'coolies' 177n2
cows 184n3
cultural conservatism 4–5, 8–9,
  10–11, 48, 50–3, 162; and family
  unit 38; and marriage patterns 162;
  and minority status 163;
  responsiveness to change 16–18,
  170–73

daughters: and gifts to parents 150;
  and household expenses 150;
  control over earning power 151;
  financial independence of 65,
  150–51
direct migrants compared with East
  Africans 2–3
dowry/dowries 97–8, 101–37, 139,
  140–41, 185–86n5, 188; pre-1930s
  110–13; post-1930s 113; post-
  1940s 113–16; post-1950s 116–19;